THE PLATE SPINNER

MARIK PUBLISHING, 1995

Praise for *The Plate Spinner*

"Challenges evenhandedly the big bang theory, creationism, Darwinian theory of evolution and Ross Perot."

—Herb Margolis

"Better than sex."

—Todd the elder Margolis

"Funniest writer since Sartre."

—Todd the younger Margolis

"One of the great writers of our time—timely and timeless."

—Sam Margolis

"A slam dunk of resounding authority."

—Janet Margolis

"Music to my ears—Margolis for President."

—Jule Margolis

"Amazing, should be a blockbuster. (I wonder if I'm in his will?)"

—Brad Margolis

"Moves to the forefront of 20th century literature."

—Nicole Margolis

"Palette of amazing proportions."

—Amy Margolis

"Combines the sensitivity of a lake poet with the no nonsense approach of a Sam Donaldson."

—Sid Margolis

"A conceptual tour de force."

—Mark Margolis

"May be the last word on the subject, perhaps all subjects."

—Michelle Margolis

"Could outsell the Bible."

—Annette Margolis

"Takes your breath away."

—Diana Margolis

"Two Thumbs up, way way up."

—Gene and Roger Margolis

Selected Paragraphs
For the Discerning Browser

I cannot say enough about the opportunities that learning a musical instrument will create for you—both on and off the playing field. At the risk of sounding like an old Charles Atlas ad promising musculared popularity and less sand in your lunch, or suggesting that drinking Miller's brew will somehow brighten your sex life, I've got major, I'm talking Major benefits for those of you who sign on for this journey. Try some of these on for permanent size: life-long friendships, growth in cultural and artistic awareness, contributing to world peace and, of course, immortality.

Honest expressions of our selves are not easily come by. So much of our inner life is lived in secrecy and benign neglect that we spend most of our time not expressing (thank God) our real feelings, our most profound responses to the world around us. Although this risks losing vital connections to those we would be close to, it does allow the delicate clockwork of society to self-wind, our neighbors to carry on with a minimum of fuss.

But for this very reason, it is critical that we have some artistic outlet, some way to mine and articulate our special contribution to the social fabric. There is no shortage of media ores for this mining operation. You can find a wonderful release for your unique qualities through the exploration and manipulation of color, of sound, of forms, of movement.

Between the number of these plates propelled into their varying states of (e)motion and the distance this spin commander had to travel, the objects of his affection would sooner or later arrive to what must be their last revolution, poised to plummet to certain shardom, their spinning beauty but a memory. But our reliable hero, always sensitive to the plight of his charges, would arrive at the dramatically correct moment with the precise energy for driving each plate to a more balanced version of its wavering reality.

And what can be more nurturing than to feel accepted, respected and honored for one's mode of expression, one's methods for solving problems, one's individual style. What more emotionally sustaining experience can one imagine than to have one's inner feelings and expressions affirmed as valid, as significant, as worthy of being heard. In what other experience of life is one as likely to acquire a lasting confidence, a fullness of self, the energy to persevere as when one is fully affirmed for what one shares from within.

THE PLATE SPINNER

SPINNER

PLAYING WITH TIME

VICTOR MARGOLIS, PH.D.

Marik Publishing
10622 North Blaney Ave.
Cupertino, California 95014-6039

Printed in the United States of America

First Edition

Publisher's Cataloging in Publication
Margolis, Victor.
  The plate spinner: playing with time / Victor Margolis
  p. cm.
  Includes bibliographical references and index.
  ISBN 0-9642973-8-8

  1. Creative ability. 2. Piano--Performance--Psychological aspects. I. title

BF411.M37 1995   153.35
                               QB194-2029

Table of Contents (slightly annotated)

When you learn how to play the notes correctly, you have accomplished the lesser half and must now bring warmth and the uniqueness of your person into the picture. This is the emotional side of the picture and is, by the way, "how things really work."

This chapter and the next three are really all one but I had to separate them into four parts so that you wouldn't be put off with its length. It decries the awful experience that almost everyone has when playing in public, particularly in the classical music field, and contains some suggestions as to how things could be different. It is not essential to the primary purpose of this book but was good for my mental health and will be entertaining for some of you.

Summarizes the "findings" herein and shows how the principles throughout, customized for music play, can be adapted in the pursuit of other art forms, and, if I may be so bold, to living one's life expressively and joyously.

This book is dedicated to....

I know this is where the author traditionally pays special tribute to some person or persons to whom he feels gratitude and love, particularly when those persons have had a salutary effect on the genesis of the work, itself. For those purposes, however, this page would prove entirely inadequate.

Therefore, I have done the job more to my liking in a part of this book where the boundaries are broader and where the subject of my affection is more naturally integrated into the flow of the "story." If you can wait until pages 320-322, you will happen upon this loving expression and know it for the true dedication that it is.

Preface: The Last Words

This present work was written in the long glorious shadow of another with much the same purpose: to inspire anyone wishing to play a musical instrument to follow his or her dreams, and to provide specific guidelines for that wondrous journey. The imposing prior effort was Charles Cooke's *Playing the Piano for Pleasure* and following in its path must certainly be like attempting a remake of *Casablanca.** Written over 50 years ago, or about the time that Sam's forbidden play of "As Time Goes By" got Humphrey's attention, *Playing the Piano for Pleasure* is still the most often recommended book for (literate) adult beginners. It was composed with passion, beauty and a sure feeling for the language, and has transformed countless persons into active participants in the music community.

Yet I ached to tell you about this platespinner fellow. I was sure that his approach to life and art could add something to your music making efforts, your plans for putting paint on canvas, in fact, your expressions of self in whatever medium you might choose. For although he, too, is concerned with the learning of a musical instrument, *The Platespinner* approaches madness in wanting you to find yourself through any means of artistic expression.

So that we can more quickly satisfy his wishes, I shall mention, here, only two other differences: the first concerns the significance of a teacher, his or her proper role in this relationship, and how to find one right for you. Whereas Cooke suggests that there is little to worry about on this score, the decision of who to trust as your artistic guide is critical to your musical health and must be faced with great care early in the game, and ever after. The second concerns the building of a reasonably large and readily accessible repertoire. The fact that the typical amateur can, at any moment, play precious few compositions is a subject rarely dealt with in books of this general purpose. Although Cooke discusses the issue in some detail, frankly I found his suggestions

---

* Foolhardy, at best. Fortunately, his venerated but rather slender work now costs $45., is nearly impossible to find, and while it is worth every penny, its price and availability could make my efforts more inviting.

in need of some complement. In fact, I suspect it is in this area of helping the amateur to acquire a sizable and active repertoire, that I may (finally) have made my mark.

Oh, oh, I've just noticed something

In my constant revision of the words that occupy the pages of this book, I have made a startling discovery: the preface has already been written! So absorbed in this task, I did not recognize I had previously fulfilled the requirements of such a piece—the reasons for the undertaking of this work, the method of research used, the personal acknowledgments—when I assigned the chapter with that information to the other end of this book. However, under the unlikely title of "Sculpture," it seems content in that place, and besides, a better finish seems beyond me. But, with this discovery, what am I to do?

I have it. Let us quit this section soon. If the stylists from the Chicago manual have you convinced that you need these facts to make a proper start, read "Sculpture" first. If done in a light-hearted way, skimming over obscurities, absorbing what you can, it won't matter all that much. Actually, I had such fun with those words that I would be pleased with an early visit, and the book may seem more sensible when viewed in this way. But I will not insist. I am grateful to be in your hands and you may have your way with me.

Which is one of my better segues. While all of the chapters were created with equal love, they will not be equally rewarding or meaningful for everyone. And I would be delighted if you choose those areas that make most sense to you at the time of each reading. While the chapters do have some cumulative intentions, each, for the most part, stands on its own. There are a couple of exceptions, the chapters on practicing somewhat dependent on their being treated as a team, and likewise the four acts of the "Performance" caper. Otherwise, picking those areas that beckon you at any particular moment may be the way to begin the finding process.

And a finding process it is. And so, enjoy the search. Enjoy the book. Enjoy this time in your life. Enjoy some manner of artistic expression. I did it. So can you. In fact, anything I can do, you can do better...which is how I intended to start things all along.

V.M.

Anything I Can Do, You Can Do Better

I'm sure you can do it. I know I'm getting there. Anything I can do, you really can do better.* Come on, trust me on this one. It is as close to my soul as you are going to get. I am 62 and every week, yes, *every* week, I improve on the fifty-seven piano pieces that I practice. Once upon a time I shall be giving recitals (not all fairy tales take place long ago in a far off land, and besides, this is no fairy tale). In the finest tradition of self-help books and leaving nothing to chance, I have carefully plotted the steps needed, and have made the goal a rock-ribbed certainty for both of us.

For me, it has already started. No question. Here, I'll show you: starting at a reasonably advanced age for such things, I became the best pianist in our home (also, the only one), then our block, then our side of the street. You see, it is clearly a matter of geography.

Perhaps you will hear me when I am seventy or seventy-five and have eclipsed much of Wyoming. Musically I have had a dreadful distance to travel, but I'm a decent player now. By the time you and I get together, I shall play like an angel.

When I started I could not read a note, play a lick, carry a tune, hear (musically) worth a damn, or, even, keep time. Further, I had not had the important experiences of listening to good music—classical or jazz or folk or, really, any kind. I'm sure for those who heard me then, my becoming a decent player was out of the question. But, decent is what I am. Artist is what I shall be. And....so can you.

This book is for *any* who want to express themselves musically, but think that they do not have the right stuff—the talent, for God's sake—to make it happen; that even if they might have at one time, that time has long since passed them by.

---

* With apologies to Cole Porter for his wonderful but not so encouraging song from Annie Get Your Gun, "Anything You Can Do, I Can Do Better, I Can Do Anything Better Than You." However, if you know the melody please substitute these above amended lyrics. They are the right ones for this story.

From my biased perch, this feels like most of you out there. Benjamin Bloom, in his book *Developing Talent in Young People*, concurs:

> After forty years of intensive research on...learning in the United States as well as abroad, my major conclusion is that what any person in the world can learn (excepting 2% to 3% of individuals who have severe emotional and physical difficulties), almost all persons can learn if provided with appropriate prior and current conditions of learning. There are, to be sure, approximately 2% who are exceptionally quick learners, but the middle 95% become very similar in terms of their measured achievement, learning ability, rate of learning, and motivation for further learning when provided with favorable learning conditions.[3]

The vehicle for this journey to artistic fulfillment will be learning to play the piano but the choice is arbitrary. I happen to play this damnably wondrous instrument and it is simply what I know most about. It does, to its credit, offer many advantages to the player, not the least of which is the seemingly endless solo repertoire from which to choose music close to your heart. However, all of the principles and arguments presented concerning memory, practice, repertoire, and performance, to name some of the topics under siege, will be as relevant (or questionable) to the piccolo player or jazz whistler, as to the keyboardist. And although this may be reaching for an audience not mine for the taking, I propose that much of what is discussed has direct application for anyone seeking artistic expression through tap dancing, an artist's canvas, decorating houses or the tops of cakes.

Although the vehicle for artistic expression in these pages will be music making, more specifically the art of the keyboard, absolutely no prior knowledge of the subject is necessary, the language chosen being easily grasped by the beginning student. Moreover, principles of learning and practice will be included that I wager many advanced and even famous performers, for reasons both good and ill, do not entertain.

This approach, highly ambitious on a number of levels, focuses on helping you, no matter your age or perceived aptitude, to achieve surprising mastery of musical materials. If you will let me have my way with you, you shall have at your finger tips masterworks of music that you will perform with skill and artistry. Moreover, this will be accomplished in an acceptable time frame and with a surprising number of pieces to call your own.

Repertoire: The Sticking Point

The development and maintenance of a collection of pieces—on call, as it were—is the most perplexing issue facing the amateur musician and one not normally addressed in books of this sort. The usual case, for even moderately advanced piano students, is to have two or three pieces that they are currently working on—translates to "can't quite play yet"—while having in their "possession" a number of pieces, once played beautifully, in varying stages of progressive decline. In this usual scenario, without the possibility of rewarding the bearer, and anyone who will listen, with the fruits of his or her labors, present *and* past, the once eager neophyte will surely turn his attention to accomplishments of a less fragile nature.

That is why the platespinner is so important. I know, I know. Many of you do not know this person. And that is why I have devoted an entire chapter to his fascinating artistry and to the implications of his complex balancing act for your musical well-being.

Whistle While You Work

It is extremely important that the means to your musical ends be one of ongoing gratification. The student should be irresistibly drawn back to the instrument by a rich variety of complementary reinforcements. It must be a gratifying experience virtually every time out, not one sustained by the promise of distant achievements. Happily, it turns out that this is not as difficult as it sounds or as tradition would have it. In the first place, with the appropriate structure in place—the proper rules of the game, so to speak—the piano can be quite user-friendly. In the second, the art of playing, and playing beautifully, while an incredibly complex accomplishment, can be organized into readily doable steps—steps that you will take to *your* drummer in quick time. If it should happen to take a little longer—perhaps you are no more gifted than I—you will so enjoy the journey you won't notice or care. I intend to convince you, even if you have never played before, that it is *Never Too Late*,* that an outlet for artistic expression is more important to your health than a golden retriever, that this is your time to "go for it," and that lack of talent, time, or previous experience (childhood variety) just isn't going to stop you.

Isn't this something that you've always wanted? What about those ways of expressing yourself that come in your package only? Wouldn't it be wonderful to share these qualities freely and be accepted and loved in the doing? It is probably presumptuous of me to want this for you, yet I do. But then, I know what it is like; I know what can happen.

For many, it can take far too long for this journey to begin—this quest for your own inner voice. Finally, however, driven by personal victories won, a stroke of good fortune, or, as sometimes happens, by events of a more desperate nature, playing a musical instrument and shaping notes and phrases to your personal vision can reveal that part of you that no one else shares in or even knows about—an inner space defining your person like none other.

I believe I have an approach, one not likely discussed anywhere else, to contribute to this journey. If you follow the principles set forth in these writings, or better still, create a set of your own, you will achieve a level of technique and artistic expression that you would have thought impossible. I will try to convey these principles, which I have found to be extraordinarily useful, in the lead-pipe certainty that anything I can do, you most certainly can do better.

The first step is to lead you towards a technical know-how that will facilitate your playing some of the most beautiful music ever written. Getting started on this moving path is not nearly as difficult as you might think. There are literally hundreds of great pieces from which to choose that, with but a modest commitment of time and enlightened energy, you will soon be able to play. An example with which most of

---

* Don't miss this book by John Holt. If I don't do a proper job of convincing you, he most certainly will.[15]

you would be familiar is the sublime first movement of Beethoven's *Moonlight Sonata* or, to name another that is yours for the early taking, Chopin's *Prelude in E Minor*. And there are many others that, with the slightest editing—a slowing down of a trill, the perfectly acceptable act of modifying a difficult passage*—can also be among your permanent possessions. The feelings of competence and satisfaction that will come from these challenges conquered are incomparable.

And, although I shall have spirited opposition from the traditional music community for holding to this view, neither will you have to slog through tedious technical exercises nor endless rounds of scales. I will defend the significance of this stand in the chapter on technique, where the argument will be made for a more practical approach for attaining a serviceable technical competency.

To anticipate, technique will not be dismissed as unworthy of the artistic temperament, a necessary evil. Not at all. Without it, the playing of an instrument is an impossibility; while with it, you may pass beyond the mere playing of the notes to exploring the infinite expressive possibilities presented by the master composers. Indeed, the quest for a solid technique will be addressed with the greatest vigor and with a logic demonstrably more reasonable and interesting. And this is essential if you are to be drawn inexorably back to the keyboard and away from those aspects of living—friends, loved ones, sex, food—you once thought important.

Further, the absorbing of each lovely piece will lead invitingly to others, the end never in view. One day, not so very far off, you will find yourself surprisingly comfortable in this now foreign endeavor. And, as you speak in your own special way, so will you play in a way that becomes you. When you convey the "story" of a master work in a way that makes most sense to you, it will be one that none can assail. Then, you will be one of us, forever addicted to the growth and real-ization of your own voice through glorious patterns of silence and sound. You will not pass a keyboard without being drawn by the lure of melody, the order of harmony, the motion of rhythm, all quite irresist-ible, all yours for the taking.

---

* At least from this corner! This is a subject of much debate and I shall give it its proper due in the chapter called "Drummer."

A word of caution. Playing a musical instrument well is a glorious experience, but the normal costs—the long-term commitment, the daily time required, the tenacity, the sacrifice—are nearly overwhelming.

Wait! I can't believe I said that! This thing *is* attainable, and by you, even if, as I have promised, you have never played a note or even thought it possible. Why do you think I am working so hard on this manuscript? It is precisely you that I have in mind. Please, let me try again.

The costs of playing a musical instrument are nearly overwhelming, the long-term commitment, the time required...the sacrifice, etc., but the experience is glorious and unquestionably worthwhile. There! Much better.*

I cannot say enough about the opportunities that learning a musical instrument will create for you—both on and off the playing field. At the risk of sounding like an old Charles Atlas ad promising musculared popularity and less sand in your lunch, or suggesting that drinking Miller's brew will somehow brighten your sex life, I've got major, I'm talking Major benefits for those of you who sign on for this journey. Try some of these on for permanent size: life-long friendships, growth in cultural and artistic awareness, contributing to world peace and, of course, immortality.

At the most elementary level, playing** a musical instrument will have you vigorously involved in the discipline of learning a fascinating and complex motor skill. This kind of mastery will give you a confidence that will spread deliciously into other aspects of your (now) expanding life style. On a higher plane, it will bring you into intimate contact with serious music in a totally new way, resulting in a very different level of understanding for great musical performance and performers. The devoted piano pedagogue, Seymour Bernstein, says it with a passionate beauty:

To mingle with the great minds of composers and to express the profundity of music with one's own hands are privileges in their

---

* "It Ain't What You Say, But the Way That You Say It"—An almost jazz standard probably performed most often in the forties.
** Playing? A curious term for this activity. It is work, wonderfully gratifying work, but work nonetheless. Playing comes later.

own right. Not only does the performer thereby perpetuate the noble art of music, but he also discovers within himself worlds of beauty that bind him to his art and to all other musicians.[2]

It is one thing to listen to great music, often for only moments at a time—so difficult is it to stay focused in the passive role of the listener—and quite another, as actor, to breathe sustained life into its "stories"; to know that how you shape this curiously ephemeral material may mean a good deal both to you and to others, calming or stirring to the depths. Additionally, understanding the aesthetics of music is not only a magnificent result of its study but the beginning of a cumulative acculturating process leading surely to a better understanding of painting, dancing, even architecture—thus, a persuasive guide to the panoply of the arts.

Perhaps the best news is proposed by the extraordinary educator, John Holt: "The better you play, the more your circle of friends will expand. You can count on this as confidently as you can count on the sun rising. Music is a powerful magnet which never fails to attract new, congenial, long-term friends."[15] Some day you will get together to play with other musicians, sowing musical seeds for valued relationships. Who knows, you might even be able to captivate the appropriate sex for yourself, bringing us full circle with Charles Atlas and the Miller brew. You can travel almost anywhere in the world and find people to "converse" with. You will join the ranks of the united brotherhood of musicians, an imaginary group that functions on a very real level. Musicians tend to be a more sensitive, peace-loving group who see the family of humankind through the prism of one language, a language that substantially reduces the barriers of misunderstanding. Again, John Holt: "Musicians who love the music they make are drawn more closely together by that work than most people are, by either their work or their pleasures. The world of music, even at an amateur level, is a fellowship of a kind we don't see much of in modern society."[15]

Breaking the Sound (Language) Barrier

When countries are trying to mend fences, this universal medium is often the first called upon for reaching across the fractured divide. Music, of course, also serves a similar function for the courting mode, traditionally the man serenading the woman through songs of love, with the music every bit as important as the poetry or lyrics which it nurtures. When attempts were made to thaw the Cold War, musicians, both classical and jazz, were among the first who joined in a hands-across-the-seas program called the Cultural Exchange.* Dizzy Gillespie was one of the earliest to make this foray, embodying so much that connects the two cultures: the universal language of music—jazz being more of a common dialect, as it were—along with his delightful showmanship. Our beloved Harpo was another. Dear Harpo, who not only "played" silence as none other, but the harp, with the enchantment of the man/child he gave to us. He was a double non-threat guy for what ailed these antagonists.

OK, So Maybe I Exaggerated a Little

I'm sure you accepted the promised benefits of learning a musical instrument with equanimity, possibly taking exception, however, to the claim for life everlasting. Let me begin a defense of this startling but most reasonable claim by introducing you to the writing of Frank Wilson: "The musician enjoys the opportunity for increasing refinement and maturation of his or her skills well beyond the age at which even the most durable football or baseball player has retired to the sidelines. Arthur Rubinstein, for example, claimed that he did not really begin to play as he wanted until he was nearly eighty."[33] Horowitz made his historic return to Russia well into his eighties where he gave an outstanding recital knocking the audience's collective socks off. And it wasn't nostalgia or nationalism that removed their noski (Russian for, oh, you know). It was incredibly fine pianism, perhaps as well as this legendary musician has ever played.

---

* Curiously, it may also have worked the other way. That is, the political maneuverings resulting from the Cold War may have been responsible for the realization of some hefty careers. The most notable example is that of the Van Cliburn victory at the Tchaikovsky competition in 1958. This may be doing Van Cliburn a disservice but there is no doubt that the political climate added to the brouhaha of his winning and to the raising his name into a household word. "He was, for a while, the highest-paid musician of his time, the hottest thing in show business."[30]

I began playing music as a way of grappling with this mortality problem that troubles the agnostics among us—and probably not a few of you other guys. It clearly was something that you could do into your old age and beyond, something that if you played your notes right could extend the "outer limits." As I see it, if you saved your musical stamps religiously and your collection just grew and grew, you would live in harmony forever after (or at least until the coda).* So far, I am living proof of this proposition. I am 62 (I know I said this before, but this time it is really important) and play basketball with men in their early twenties, occasionally being accepted, if high fives are a respectable index, as one of them. Does this not qualify? We're not talking about aerobical clean living or working out with dumbbells (nothing personal, guys), but the finely tuned anaerobic pumping of the whites and blacks.**

One of the gratifying things about playing the piano is that what begin as secondary goals—the collecting of repertoire, the increasing of competence, the learning of a new language—will take on separate lives of their own. The wait for the real thing, the performance in front of an expectant and adoring audience, which for most of us will take somewhere between a very long time and never, becomes no wait at all and, again, takes on the cast of time without end.

On the Road to...

Along with helping you get started on this artistic journey, I am going to share some unexpected and improbable adventures. If my playing never takes me to the concert stage, and I am steeling myself for that possibility, it has allowed me to live out some marvelous fantasies. Had not my hands traversed the magical landscape of the keyboard, these experiences would have remained in Walter Mitty land. With a tiny course adjustment to the life you lead, you too can play with great

---

* A concluding musical section that is formally distinct and of indeterminate length from the main structure.

** That scoundrel Frank Wilson—in his most excellent book *Tone Deaf and All Thumbs?*—had the nerve to use this expression before I thought of it independently.[33]

artistry *and* have adventures unlike those you have ever dreamed of. ♪
Anything I can do, you can do better...♪

This is, in the end, a self-help book, one that seeks to awaken and
reinforce the special person that you are through the expression of music
making—or whatever artistic path you may choose. After you are
convinced that this is something you really can do—and I intend to pull
out all stops so that there can be no mistaking this—I shall provide you
with the tools for bringing it about. As a result of this two-pronged
assault on your sensibilities, you will enter into a collaborative effort
with the great composers of our incredible musical history, recreating
their music in a way that reflects the only you around, and that no one
else can deny!

Oh, while I'm at it, be glad that you are an amateur. You can
become as great an artist as anyone—certainly there will be none like
you—without the awful burdens. You will not be practicing with
deadlines or headlines in mind, putting a whole new cast on what you
are doing and why you are doing it. You will not face unfriendly pianos,
sometimes cruelly so, with your career on the line. You will not live out
of a suitcase and lonely hotel rooms. You will not experience this art
world as an Olympic event, suffering your way through torturous
competitions. When you practice, you will know at that moment that this
is what you want to be doing more than anything in the world. And, you
have the rest of your life to find out all that you can be through this
extraordinary means.

Besides the Crackerjacks

In sum, you are going to learn what it is like to take up music late
in life—defined as older than 12, or 20, or 45, or 75—and what can
happen to you when you do, including:

(1) a presentation of the evidence and arguments that you can do it,
and do it well, no matter that you might think about your talent for
doing so. Along the way, in fact, you will learn that talent is a ter-
rifically overblown concept, that it is not part of the job description

and that virtually anyone, who really wants to, can accomplish absolutely great and artistic deeds, and by means that are pleasurable;

(2) a discussion about blooming late in life, and about some who have. Then I will begin the pressure for you to join the party;

(3) a confession about what got me to take this plunge, what people made it possible, and how you can find some of those people;

(4) suggestions about learning to play, including how to structure your sessions so that you will return to the keyboard more than you want—in this way I am serving notice that this is a course of action that must be monitored carefully, since it can easily and delightfully get out of hand—how to memorize, how to practice, how to develop a large stamp collection (a tag for repertoire), how to concentrate on what you are doing, leading gradually into how to play for others, and finally, how to wear your accomplishments gracefully. (This last claim is sheer hyperbole since I haven't a clue.)

I would like to point out that great emphasis will be placed on the structuring of the experience, particularly the practice times. This is not an approach that makes it possible to play in six easy lessons. Nor is it, on the other hand, one insisting that you must have unparalleled discipline together with mega tenacity—the no pain, no gain school, as it were. No. This is a method of helping you *arrange the conditions* of your practice sessions such that you have no choice but to make progress happily. And while you are getting better (and happier), you are accumulating great treasures literally within your reach. And so many, many of them. That—the many, many—is the avowed purpose and considerable legacy of the platespinner approach.

Oh, there's more. As I said a few pages back, and just for the fun of it (at least for me), I will tell you about some of my adventures. I will tell you these things so that you can see what happens when you take up an artistic endeavor later on in life. If me, why not you? Also, I will take the liberty of discussing (it's my book!) some vaguely related issues that I'm hoping will have passing interest for you, such as the im-

portance of the non-analytic artist, and whatever happened to performance in the classical music world that was actually a joy for both the
performer and the audience. I'm not talking about meaningful. I know
it's meaningful, but is it fun?

Finally, in order to help you make the transition from outsider to
full-fledged member of the musical community, and to get from this
chapter to and through the rest of the book, I see as part of my task the
challenging of a number of assumptions most commonly held by the
insiders' club about the playing of a musical instrument. Perhaps the
most sensible starting place is to take on that which seems to be of most
concern for the aspiring musician, talent, that much overworked and
little understood trait which supposedly separates those who can from
those who cannot. Is the possession of this illusive "substance" a
requirement to be able to play? Do I have any? How can I get some?

The answer to these questions, if I may be permitted, is that the
only talent you will need to play music with all of your heart is your
willingness to trust for these few pages that it could happen to you.
Unless you are hellbent on remaining in hiding, I am going to help you
to create whole new expressions of yourself. It *will* happen.

C'mon. Follow my lead. It's about time.

Talent, Lateblooming and You

The overriding objective is to develop fluency in a musical language and the competence to use that language to speak in a voice that would otherwise be silent - Frank Wilson

Chopin's attention was always directed to teaching correct phrasing. With reference to wrong phrasing he often repeated the apt remark, that it struck him as if someone were reciting, in a language not understood by the speaker, a speech carefully learned by rote, in the course of which the speaker not only neglected the natural quantity of the syllables, but even stopped in the middle of words. The pseudo-musician, he said, shows in a similar way, by his wrong phrasing that music is not his mother-tongue, but something foreign and incomprehensible to him, and must, like the aforesaid speaker, quite renounce the idea of making any effect upon his hearers by his delivery - Sorry, my friends, I can't find the blasted source!

Both Wilson and that other excellent musician, Chopin, seem quite matter of fact in describing the act of musical expression as a special kind of language behavior. Most languages, of course, are spoken or written and, in those forms, used for telling stories, conveying information, or expressing sentiments from one person to another. Nonetheless, I think it is useful and appropriate to consider musical expression to be analogous to the spoken language, even if not so noted by such authority as *Webster's New Collegiate.*

The lexicographers at that highly regarded word house must have missed pianist Dave Brubeck conversing musically *and* intelligibly with saxophonist Paul Desmond; pianist John Lewis of the Modern Jazz Quartet tapping out economic replies to the musical questions malleted by vibraphonist Milt (Bags) Jackson; or Dizzy, Miles and Monk cooking with the same linguistic recipes. Certainly Leon Fleisher and George Szell spoke the same language, even, perhaps, the same vernacular, on rendering their legendary reading of the Brahms first piano concerto.

Moreover, the wordsmiths at Webster's have probably never listened in on two jazz musicians singing the praise of "a cat really saying something", or remember that the critics of their day marveled at the whole new vocabularies brought shockingly into the musical mainstream by the (then) radical compositions of Schoenberg and Chopin?

Although the language of music is clearly different from the one that you and I are on speaking terms with, it is every bit as expressive and communicative. It has its own grammar, structure, sentences (phrases), even, as in a play, stage directions: forte (louder), retardando (slow things up), andante (play in a walking tempo). Musicians who "speak the same language" tend to forge lasting musical bonds, e.g., Pete Fountain and Al Hirt, keeping them together through good times and better; or the Modern Jazz Quartet, wailing in incredibly close-knit fashion with the same personnel for over a quarter of a century. It's every bit as true in the classical world; witness the longevity of many string quartets whose members' lives are bound by the prolonged sharing of common musical values.

The presence of musical conversation seems most obvious in the field of jazz. In this genre the players frequently perform on-the-spot dialogue not very different from our daily conversations. To be sure, the players, depending on their creative talents, will fall back on cliches and other expressions known to both—just as you and I, in the midst of talking with each other—but when it is going well, when musicians find themselves exploring new ideas in a mutually responsive manner, the exhilaration generated by this dynamic language can reach remarkable heights affecting not only the players but those lucky enough to be invited to the party.

The classical player, on the other hand, is more like an actor giving voice to lines already prepared, with a particular reading of the noted script giving it its life and distinction. The classical players, moreover, must voice this "dialogue" as though spontaneously cast, lest they lose their audience in the making.

In *The Great Gatsby*, F. Scott Fitzgerald has his protagonist pronounce the very rich as people very different from you and me. (It's not really a club you can join!) I think that is how most of us think about artists, generally, and musicians, especially: that they possess a mystical quality we cannot hope to approach, understand or encompass.

Two factors contribute to this unfortunate view: (1) the belief that there is an early and limited period of a person's life when this learning must take place, if it is going to happen at all, and (2) a shortsighted and "geneticized" view of the mysterious ingredient called talent. Although these tend to overlap, we shall take them up separately.

Those Damned Early Birds

In the field of psychology there has been a great deal of research on a so-called critical period hypothesis, an interval of an organism's life, a window, if you will, within which something must be learned if the opportunity to learn that something is not to be lost. The study of imprinting—a form of learning in which a very young animal fixes its attention on the first object with which it has sensory experiences—is one of the better known instances of this brief but profoundly meaningful encounter. This field of inquiry owes a good deal of its intellectual heritage to two of the founding fathers of the psychological field, William James, and the ever present, and usually wrong-minded, Sigmund Freud. Freud, consistent with his tiresome contention that your psychological self is essentially cast early on, actually had the temerity to say that "Old people are no longer educable." And James, one of the earliest and most prominent of American psychologists went further:

> Outside of their own business, the ideas gained by men before they are 25 are practically the only ideas they shall have in their lives. They cannot get anything new. Disinterested curiosity is past, the mental grooves and channels set, the power of assimilation gone. Whatever individual exceptions might be cited to these are of the sort that "prove" the rule.[16]

It now seems there are so many exceptions to this rule that they "prove" the exception. Either James made this curiously inappropriate statement before he was thirty—not being one to trust those over that suspect barrier—or he wasn't keeping a perceptive eye on his illustrious brother, Henry, at his creative best in his late 50's with such works as *The Ambassadors*, *The Wings of the Dove*, and *The Golden Bowl*.

Because of the eminence of Freud and James and their followers, this notion of the critical period of learning received a great deal of attention, affirming, unfortunately, the Western cultural bias that learning is most felicitously reserved for the young. And to add old salts to the wounded, it became axiomatic that this tendency accompanies us in our final years on a swiftly accelerating downward slope. This, sadly, has led to many self-fulfilling prophecies—daunted souls turned away from their dreams, rebuffed by the scientific "knowledge" of the day.

One theory, for example, holds that natural language acquisition can only take place in a child's life between the ages of two and ten years. This theory has had a creditable and reasonably long shelf life with much research supporting what seemed at the time to be a sensible assertion. And, as affirming evidence, there were a number of studies which investigated such things as the acquisition of appropriate songs for particular bird species.

One researcher studied variation in the timing of vocal learning during the first year of life in male song sparrows. Results showed that imitations of songs acquired early in that period were more complete than those acquired later on.[21] This would seem to support the idea that musicians are born, not made, particularly those born with feathers.

Skipping back to a somewhat less musically gifted species, there is evidence of the supposed ease with which one can shed an accent when moving into a country of a different language. Ostensibly, if you move before the ripe old age of eleven, you will have no trouble disguising yourself as a native of your new land; if you move after that, however, you will forever be heard as an alien creature.

Besides the sizable amount of evidence lending unappetizing credence to the ease of youngsters learning languages, when compared to their older and presumably wiser parents, this research is consistent with the anecdotal evidence that no pianists, or any musicians on the concert level, make it to the performance stage without having been involved in serious study in their early years. Moreover, many of our great concert artists have been so-called wunderkind, that is, prodigies far advanced over children of their own age and, indeed, over many persons of a more advanced age.

There are few exceptions, if any, to this rule depending on your definition of what a late starter is. This kind of evidence, which most people "know," has discouraged many persons taking up any form of artistic expression in their later years because they assumed that it was clearly beyond them, that it required a mysterious ingredient called talent, and that this talent must be nourished upon its earliest stirrings.

If you promise not to tell, I will share with you that I rely heavily on this fiction when I relate the age at which I began to study. I do this, of course, so that my listeners will be mightily impressed with how well I play, considering the "handicap" of not having played as a youngster. I'm not proud of the fact that I do this—I don't even like telling you—but I do love the extra credit that comes my way. Someday, when I can resist engaging in this kind of transparent aggrandizement—and I have succeeded more and more as time goes on—I will have reached a personal goal of moment. More importantly, I will be in a place where I am not continually apologizing for my playing but ready to put it up against anyone's.

That, in fact, is my goal for you. For, you see, I take it as my charge to convince you of the uniqueness of expression that resides in your soul. And, for both our sakes, I intend to succeed.

To chip away at the widely held view that it is too late if we have missed the early boat, I would like to reintroduce you to John Holt, a gifted thinker and writer in the field of education, author of such books as *How Children Learn, How Children Fail, Freedom and Beyond*. John questioned...

...the widely held idea that what happens to us in the first few years of our lives determines everything that will happen later, what we can be, what we can do. Musical people are particularly prone to talk this way. The great Japanese string teacher, Suzuki, whose work I have long admired writes that if children do not hear, almost from birth, good music (by which he means classical music), if they hear, in short, the kind of popular music that was all I heard as a child, they will grow up tone deaf...Countless other teachers say that if we don't learn to play musical instruments as children we will never be able to learn as adults.

This happens every year to tens of thousands of children, perhaps at home, more likely in school. The children are told to sing a song. Some child does not get it quite right...Before long there is a suggestion made that when the class is singing...this child sing very softly. The child gets the idea...and the story is passed on.[15]

Well, I had never heard a classical piece of music until I was 18 and, speaking of singing very softly, probably my most important musical memories concern the importance of silence in music, or at least my silence. Many of you have either shared this embarrassing and oft told tale or know someone who has. It seemed, however, unique and important at the time and that no one in the entire universe was being so pointedly humiliated. I was asked to move my lips soundlessly in our 5th grade music class lest it reduce the beauty of the program on Handel that we were tackling. Since we were to perform it for no one but ourselves, it was a particularly demeaning and powerful message as to my musical aptitude and Lord knows what else about my person.

Some years later this received confirmation when I was asked to be a part of a marching band where I would carry a trumpet, put it up to my lips and pretend to blow. This latter experience was not so bad— since I had never played the damned thing anyway, they needed to complete the letter H and I looked like an H type—except that it reminded me of my earlier silent showing. Even today, my dear wife Annie, the one whom I claim is so supportive, does not tolerate my hazarding a tune. I will say, do you know this piece? I will hum a few bars in what I think is a relatively tolerable approximation of how the thing goes, and she, with not sufficient sensitivity, asks that I not do that anymore, suggesting that it is hurting our relationship.

Despite such transgressions on my fragile self, I have become reasonably resilient and continue tunelessly on my way, positive that a person with sound hearing will get the "obvious" musical references. But Kingsbury, in an anthropological look at conservatory life, suggests that a small child is likely to have little resource, such as other battles won, or, at least, a sense of the absurd, for such mini-confrontations:

The youngster in the third-grade choir who is told to mouth the words but actually not to sing with the other children confronts a situation of relative adversity. Such a child generally has no way to combat such conditions, and almost certainly has no way of knowing what might be done to improve the singing. What is wrong with the child's singing? Too loud? Too raspy? Off pitch? Not only does the child not know the answer to such questions, she or he is likely to be unaware that such questions exist. To the child, the only thing wrong with the singing is likely to be that she or he is the one who is doing it...It is not a minor point to note that among adults who consider themselves to be untalented or unmusical, childhood experiences of this kind are a very common phenomenon indeed. Significantly, people who as children encountered such experiences are likely to report them only as evidence of their own complete nonmusicality: "I'm so bad, why, I couldn't even make the third grade glee club."[18]

And although this may sound melodramatic, the implications of this kind of interaction may be even more serious. Kingsbury has suggested that, when a child is characterized as unmusical (untalented), this is tantamount to questioning his loveability in front of his peers.[18]

John Holt believes this happens to thousands of children every year and probably subdues whatever yearning that child might have had to make music some day, their (ostensibly) having so little aptitude for the subject. Remember Frank Wilson's words, "The overriding objective is to develop fluency in a musical language, and the competence to use that language to speak in a voice that would otherwise be silent."[33]

And Dr. Wilson, who has written a splendid book on the subject of our—meaning each and every one's—natural potential for making music, continues: "The trouble with predictions of failure in music is that they normally go unchallenged. They then take a foothold in the mind, as it were, as a rationale for inertia. For most children, a diagnosis of tone deafness becomes the basis of a lifelong conviction that music is out for them. And it is a great loss."

I intend to join the optimistic parade given by the Holts, the Wilsons and the Kingsburys. If you are looking for evidence that you can play an instrument, or sing, later in life, I won't let you down. I have more evidence than you possibly have time for. This thing is doable, as you will see, but I must build the case slowly, carefully, and with a certain rhythmic persuasiveness.

Let us return to that damned bird who couldn't learn its song unless he took lessons as a fledgling. I never did like sparrows anyway, even those who could sing; maybe especially those, they never seem to be in tune. There are some birds that can learn at any time in their life. One study demonstrated the ability of male brown-headed cowbirds to learn to change the structure of their song and flight whistle, with other birds acting as tutors, well after the juvenile stage.[27] You, of course, could say that this only proves that some birds have it and others don't. Well, if this bird did it (your author), so can you.

But what about those troubling language acquisition studies? Happily, there is a raft of such work in more recent times that seriously calls into question, even refutes, the obscene conclusions by the early researchers that children have the edge. Instead of presenting you with a long list of pleasant particulars, let me suggest a concise review of the literature (1984) by P. Prakesh which does the job nicely and has, over the last decade, stood the test of time and assaults from the bad guys.[24]

And just to extend this ray of optimism towards those of you who are older than thirty-five years, or intend to head in that direction, the study by Therese Sibiga showed that in the performance of a large sample of 862 men and women who took the Canadian civil service training programmes in learning French, almost the same percentage of students over fifty obtained A or B standing as those of any other age group.

Finally, remember that study suggesting that you would have difficulty shaking an accent on emigrating after the age of eleven? Well, so what! Even if this were true, and there is good reason to be skeptical, does this mean that you cannot be a wonderful speaker in a foreign tongue, perhaps a great scientist, Einstein; statesperson, Henry Kissinger; or magnificent actor, Paul Muni, with their attractive—or in the case of Kissinger, infuriating—accents? While music may not be your native tongue, you most assuredly can become an accomplished musician, perhaps even one with a charming rhythmic accent, and, by your special presence, bring something new and wonderful to the creation of this art.

OK, OK. We see that some birds can learn the songs of their peers at any age, and that people are not handicapped in the learning of a new language simply through admission to adulthood. But what are the facts about the learning of a musical instrument later in life? That is, after all, a much more complex endeavor, particularly when one takes into consideration the psychomotor activity involved.

Instead of responding directly, let us take a detour into the lives of the late bloomer making his or her startling appearance in any of a number of fields. This has direct implications for the adult beginning musician and frames a more suitable reply for what may, in a more general sense, be possible. A late bloomer, as you might guess, is someone who comes into his or her own later than would be considered the usual time frame. In case you're interested, a second definition in the *Random House Dictionary* adds the words "glowing, as with youthful vigor and freshness." Now, that's the ticket!

Although this can describe the unusual person generally late "making it," it can also refer to most of us taking up, with a measure of success, any endeavor later in life either denied us by earlier events, or, given our perceived limitations, not one considered a reasonable possibility at an earlier stage.

Some have their education interrupted, yet finish later with high-flying colors. Others take a wrong turn in the road, settle for something not to their liking, only to blossom in a foreign endeavor for which they have an overwhelming passion. For some it is a matter of trial and error, for others, good fortune.

Whatever the reason, whatever the route, the world is teeming with these heartwarming achievements by people who wanted more from life, took a stand, rejected their own form of the status quo and went on to achieve, albeit in their time, to their drummer, the satisfying feelings derived from these kinds of victories. Could you be such a person? Do you know anyone who deserves it more?

I apologize. I was prepared for your reaction since I've asked that very same question of many persons, usually people with whom I was trying to curry favor (essentially everyone!). It didn't matter who it was, where it was, when it was, that person became my prisoner. Seized by its compelling argument, virtually everyone that you "challenge" with these words responds in the expected fashion with remarkable focus and energy. It demonstrates how most individuals, particularly when taken by surprise, will confess to their own specialness, and feel justly deserving of any good fortune that comes their way.

Well, it's true, you know, you do deserve it. And one of your inalienable rights, perhaps even obligation, as holder of this unique prize, is to share yourself in some story or idea; or by creating or re-creating music; or by the way that you move or teach or paint or write poetry; for God's sake, something!

If you resonate to these last words, if you find yourself wanting some of the truly good life, a life of expressive fulfillment, then you have come to an important juncture and would appreciate these words by Carol Colman in her reassuring book on late bloomers:

> Coming to grips with this desire by recognizing that we not only want more but are able to achieve more is the first and most critical step in the blooming process. The message of *Late Bloomers* is a simple one. There is no right or wrong time to pursue our dreams and goals. All of us develop and grow at our own pace, making changes in our lives when we feel that it's the right time for us. As long as we begin the process of becoming whoever or whatever we want to be, it doesn't matter if we are early, average, or late. Each of us will bloom in our own way, in our own time.[5]

Those Who Have Gone Before You

Let us look at some remarkable stories of some who have reached for that ring of brass, then hung on for dear life. Although late bloomers can be harvested in any heart-warming color, I have chosen, in keeping with the spiritual intentions of this book, examples primarily from the world of arts and letters.

Wouldn't you know. Just after writing these words, I heard something from the next room that I must tell you about. A television sports reporter has just announced that Tom Wargo has won the Senior Men's PGA Golf Championship for 1993. Hooray, you yawn. Well, listen up.

Tom won over a field that included some of golf's all time luminaries: Arnold Palmer, Jack Nicklaus, Gary Player, and many others. Who's Tom Wargo? At this writing Tom is a fifty year old guy who at the age of twenty-five took up golf—while holding down a full time job in the steel mills!—taught himself how to play, became the pride of Centralia, Illinois and the club golf pro there—never qualifying for the PGA tour—and exulted famously with this previous, and not inconsiderable, achievement. But the Senior Men's Golf National Championship? Hooray for Tom, indeed. He had the entire golf world cheering for him and that beats the heck out of par.

Addendum, written almost ten months later, July 22, 1994: Tom Wargo has just won the British Senior Men's Open! If this book takes much longer, Wargo is going to have quite a collection of trophies.

Another story that beggars the imagination is that of Jim Cameron, who made the dazzling ascent from blue collar worker to writer and director of *Aliens*, in 1985, in just over four years. One night after an exhausting day of driving a semi, his then chosen profession, he went to see the movie, *Alien* in 1979. He found himself wishing that this was the sort of thing he could do, and there and then decided that it was something he *would* do. Through a series of incredibly well-timed jumps, beginning with getting himself on as a know-nothing art director for film director Roger Corman; graduating to *Terminator* (as film director!)—turning a slated minor league effort into a mega hit—he so impressed the powers that be with this instant track record they gave him a shot at *Aliens*. *Aliens*, of course, was the sequel to the singular *Alien*, the same picture that turned him around just those few short years earlier. If you want the complete story, check out the Calendar Section of the *LA Times*, July 11, 1986.

As far a journey as both of these fellows traveled from their relatively modest vocational beginnings, they cannot touch the dramatic leap made by Charles Dutton, a convicted felon-homicide, who turned his life around *in jail* to become, later on, a highly lauded broadway actor. In 1985, Dutton was nominated for a Tony award! Colman: "Through acting, Charles had discovered a constructive, creative part of himself. He sought fulfillment by finally recognizing that he wanted more out of life and was entitled to it."[5] No matter what others might think, Charles had no problem with the question of "Who deserves it more?"

Going from the high drama of Charles Dutton, to one of the great dramatists, I nominate George Bernard Shaw as one of my favorite late bloomers, especially for his tenacity over the very long, and for the most part, fruitless haul of his early years. You might argue that GBS wasn't that old when success came his way. But from the vantage point of literary mileage, it was a excruciatingly long period of time. When Shaw thought about the journey traveled, the thousands of pages fashioned—forty hand-written pages a day, never an exception—only to have his carefully crafted work rejected time after time, year after year, he must have wondered, himself, how he stayed with the program.

He was, in fact, in his thirties before there was the slightest success with even one of his plays, which, it must be noted, represented a new literary direction taken by Shaw after the failure to get any of his six novels published. Six novels! Six novels completed and totally rejected; none of which saw printer's ink until he became "George Bernard Shaw" many years later. But not back then. There was nothing, not a hint of affirmation from any corner.

Who would have bet on Shaw at that point? What would allow or compel someone to start novel number four or five and most particularly six after such a spectacular lack of commercial success? Actually, Shaw only gained reasonable notoriety when he had reached his forties and while this is still not terribly old, it was, for Shaw, experientially and writing-wise several lifetimes. Clearly, something is going on here which must cast serious doubt on the usual concept of talent. But, I am anticipating a discussion whose time has not yet come.

Writing seems a particularly rich province for late bloomers. When Edith Hamilton, well into her sixties, retired as headmistress of Bryn Mawr School for Girls, she probably had little idea what lay ahead. Prodded by friends and family whom she had regaled with her stories, she turned into book form a number of these classical tales: First *The Greek Way*, then *The Roman Way*, and still others, likewise enjoying world-wide distribution.[22]

Persons charged with ending lives, as well as saving them (it might be interesting to speculate which of these was which), have ended up as members of the late blooming writing community. Cervantes spent most of his life soldiering only to write *Don Quixote* when he was nearly 60, and the world famous Wilder Penfield took enough time from his surgical duties to pen *No Other Gods* when older than that.[22]

And how about the late bloomer's Late Bloomer: Helen Hoover Santmeyer who wrote her first novel *...And Ladies of the Club* in her mid 80's, published when she was 88! It was a highly respected novel about life in a city much like her native Xenia, Ohio. And what, if I may ask, dear reader, will you be doing when you're 85?

Moving from pen to brush, most of us know the story of Grandma Moses who didn't begin painting her primitives until she was 78! But how many of you are familiar with the story of...

Clementine Hunter, a black painter, age 91, living in her birthplace, Natchitoches, Louisiana who did not put brush to canvas until she was over 60. Although a youngster compared to Grandma Moses in terms of when she began painting, Ms. Hunter's story is certainly as remarkable because of the distance she had to travel sociologically. She had no formal education; she was for years a farm hand, picking cotton, then a worker at the Melrose Plantation in the Cane River county of Louisiana. One evening according to the writer and critic Francois Mignon, who was then a guest at the Melrose Plantation, she simply appeared at his door with several tubes of used oil paints which she had discovered, and announced that she, too, could 'mark a picture.' He told her to keep them and the rest is a history that you would be well disposed to look into. Her talent is unmistakable and exciting.[22]

Besides the many wonderful stories of people coming into their own later in life, there are those fortunate souls, and it seems particularly prevalent in the arts, who find success early on and are able to manage remarkable creativity over most of their lifetime. Before we take this rather incredible roll call, with its additional implications for productivity into one's later years, let's look at some laboratory research to see if what they achieved is possible. I know that sounds absurd, but you know as well as I that citing the literature lends an air of respectability to one's argument. Also, we need to make sure that this is a land promised to everyone, not just the ones who got there first, the so-called "gifted."

An article in the *San Francisco Chronicle* May 10, 1983, titled "Some Good News About Growing Old," discussed research challenging some popular notions about growing old, including the belief that people begin to lose millions of brain cells as they advance in age, and that this loss is irreversible. In this study by Dr. Marian Diamond, a neurologist at UC San Francisco, "It was demonstrated repeatedly that senility has more to do with environment and inactivity than with age. If older rats are kept in an enriched environment and fed a steady diet of interesting challenges, not only did their cortex actually 'grow,' but they, in a series of laboratory tests, outsmarted younger and faster competitors." With the evidence that even very old brains can grow, and be useful, the slowing of mental processes associated with aging in humans may be concluded to have as much to do with unchallenging surroundings as with any inevitable chemical process. "This work affirms that it is *never too late to learn* and that with environmental stimulation, brains can stay active much longer than expected" [Emphasis added].[33]

Pablo Casals, the famous cellist, made sure that his "environment" stayed in the stimulating mode at the age of seventy by practicing with a profound sense of inquiry and found immense pleasure in seeing that he could still learn and learn very well. From the lessons learned by the venerated Casals and the many other musicians who seem to mature in their art like fine wine, we see that it is not only rats who can add these precious layers of smart cells to the cortex in their later years.

The research literature on ageing and its relationship to learning—and there are many such studies—is a source of profound affirmation for those of us who intend to grow older and to do it right. "Age as age probably does little to affect an individual's power to learn or think. These faculties have been shown to stay relatively constant throughout his lifetime." It is most reassuring to know that taking up an artistic endeavor now can mean a great deal, not only for the short run, but forever after; that life later on, when one's confidence is most often in harm's way, can be lived actively and creatively.[22]

Practitioners of the arts, professional or amateur, in their later years are wise (or fortunate) in having provided the self with an arena of unusual potentiality for maintaining zest of life and creativity. This is sometimes spectacularly seen in noted professional performers. Here is a very small list of quite famous artists coming from music, dance and writing who maintained a productive time of it into their later years possibly effecting the length of their lives. This is not to say that you will someday be accepted as a member of this group—although I can't think why not—only that at whatever level you begin to learn or create as a young to middle-aged adult, you can continue to produce for the rest of your life.

Instead of reciting the grand accomplishments of these people at ages where most persons have shut down shop—their 60's or 70's, even 80's and in some cases 90's—I'm sure browsing through this list is all that will be necessary. John Kenneth Galbraith, Handel, Goethe, Verdi, Whitehead, Balanchine, Yeats, Picasso, Toscanini, Rubinstein, Ralph Vaughan Williams, Horowitz, Shaw, Will and Ariel Durant, Thomas Mann, Agatha Christie, Wodehouse, Eubie Blake, Ellington, Martha Graham, Robert Frost.

Of course these persons, who came by their "talent" earlier in life, are certainly not late bloomers. A more appropriate term might be ever-bloomer. Like the evergreens, the ages (seasons) of life had little to do with their constant quest for expression and output, and growing old was no exception. "What the lively arts do for those who participate in them as professionals or amateurs in their later years is clearly to permit the reinvestment of the self in new adventures—where the process of self-discovery is continuous."[22]

Well, you say, you've told us a great deal about people taking on new things late in life, and you've shown how numbers of people in the arts, particularly in writing and painting, have gone on with infinite grace and dazzling productivity. But where does the performance of music fit in, particularly for the want-to-be late bloomer. What about the making of music, which not only takes learning a new language at an older age, but takes grappling with those damned psychomotor skills, a process infinitely more worrisome? And what about talent? Remember, you said you would deal with this talent thing!

Good points. We seem to be faced still with hurdles of no small consequence. Let's begin with a few latebloomers in music, first, and then, finally, to dispatching this talent thing.

Let us start with a most remarkable feat—although, because of the qualifying circumstances, you might not consider it so. It is the story of the musical accomplishments of Harold Bauer (born April 28, 1873 near London, died 1951, in Miami). Mr. Bauer had been a concert violinist—primarily self taught(!), already somewhat of a miracle—until he was nineteen when he decided that he did not have a sufficiently promising career. Miraculously he embarked on a pianistic quest, became equally proficient with this instrument—again, primarily self taught(!!)—and concertized extensively throughout the world. He even became a musical emissary of sorts, taking on the serious responsibility of introducing works by Debussy, Ravel and Franck to the U.S. audiences. Now you might say, well, what's the big deal. He obviously could read music, and he clearly was enormously talented.

I don't buy it. Even in the reading of music, the violinist is primarily concerned with single note production—primarily of a melodic nature. More importantly, the two techniques are not only dissimilar, they may be, in terms of habit strength, cruelly antagonistic. Consider in each case what is asked of the hands in the production of sound. In fact, because of something the psych boys call proactive inhibition, one could argue that Bauer became a success on the piano despite his background with the violin. What he did have, undoubtedly, was an incredible tenacity, and a great willingness to work at his craft. (If this is what you mean by talent, then I accept your argument.) Additionally, he had most certainly acquired methods of practice and a way of organizing his materials for the piano that had served him well in the learning of the violin.

I would like to surreptitiously offer myself as the next example of a musical late bloomer with, I hope, the proper degree of humility. It is not easy to cite myself under these conditions, particularly following the estimable Bauer. However, since I hold with a passion that anything I can do, you can do better, it seems important for you to know what standard I have set. Actually, there is a possibility that you will soon hear me play and can then judge for yourself. If you would like, turn to page 324, the last in this book. It's OK. There is no suspense as to how this is going to turn out—with you as artist in the making—and there you will learn there what plans I have for the two of us.

And, of course, you remember John Holt, the noted educator, who challenged the Suzuki approach. Suzuki held that a structured musical experience early in life is an absolute prerequisite to the mastering of a musical instrument—a view affirmed by too many music teachers. John's challenge amounted to more than abstract musing on the subject. He took on the cello when he was in his forties, pursued doggedly if somewhat erratically an amateur musical "career" over the next 20 years, and described the process in the wonderfully absorbing and forthright book, *Never Too Late*. John proved by his example what can be accomplished, even with a rather lengthy list of supposed liabilities. In addition to his rather late start in life, he describes a relatively impover-ished cultural environment. Actually, for my money, a far more serious handicap was his described practice methods, but that is another story. However, as inspirers go, you just can't top John Holt. Read *Never Too Late* and there will be no stopping you.

And then most of us know of individuals who have taken up music late in life and made remarkable progress. I have just been introduced, for example, to Ms. Lilli Hill of San Diego, California, who started taking piano lessons at age sixty-three for the very first time, and who is just thrilled—as am I—by what she has been able to do. I have listened to her play some luminous Debussy, one of the arabesques, and some popular standards that she has a nice feeling for, this despite the fact that in the interim (she is now seventy-three), she has reached a state of legal blindness. Perhaps, on reflection, this compares favorably with the Harold Bauer story.

John Holt was asked whether he wished his parents had made him take music lessons when he was little: "No, I don't. I think that such forced exposure would probably have turned me away from music, as it has so many others."[15] In fact, there may be a number of other advantages to waiting. In addition to setting you apart from your peers, playing a musical instrument as a youngster can take away from other experiences important to a child's development. Secondly, as an adult beginner, you will have experienced, and presumably mastered, a number of other challenging tasks outside of the musical environment which can be of immense utility in the learning of an instrument. You will, to some extent, have learned how to learn, how to organize, how to set goals, how to be philosophical when challenges don't give way over night. Finally, like the child who has grown up in a poor environ-ment driven towards an accumulation of wealth, many adult beginners develop a musically voracious appetite, a kind of making up for lost time, and, indeed, can be powerfully motivated in a way that a child often isn't.

Janos Starker, one of the world's great cellists, told John that "It's extremely difficult for someone of our age to learn to play this instrument well, because we have to develop a whole new set of muscles, and a whole new set of coordinations...On the other hand, we have an advantage. We can think up problems, and find solutions." To which Holt silently rejoiced: "With these words he strengthened my hunch, hope and faith, that old dogs can learn new tricks. Not only that, but can perhaps learn them even better than young dogs—once they get over the notion that they can't learn them. Which is what too many people, some of them music teachers, keep telling them."[15]

We shall give the final word on the supposed disadvantages of adult beginner to William Newman, famed piano pedagogue, who suggests the problem of the adult "lies not, as he [or she] supposes, in relative speed of advancement—for he usually learns at least as rapidly as the child—but in his attitude toward his progress. Too often he is impatient because his more mature tastes and interests remain far ahead of his abilities."[23]

Well, now I've cited some real pros who actively support your plans for musical expression. I've presented evidence of the ability to learn late in life (certainly later than 12). I've argued, I've pressed. But apparently you're still not sure. There is this matter of talent—and then the coordination involved, the fine muscle dexterity that you're certain is not yours. I'm sure Janos Starker's words—"It's extremely difficult for someone of our age to learn to play this instrument well, because we have to develop a whole new set of muscles, and a whole new set of coordinations"—were not lost on you.

First of all, let us put into perspective the intimidating virtuosity displayed by today's concert players. They *do* exhibit a speed and ease that seems astonishing to the casual observer—just as people who converse in a foreign tongue often seem to be speaking more quickly than could possibly be understood, even by their own linguistic family. Moreover, all too often these dazzling displays become the focus of both the player and his or her audience, eclipsing the intended meanings and aesthetic values of a serious piece of music. This business—and "business" may be right since these displays have undeniable box-office appeal—of virtuosity is a seductive phenomenon capable of misdirecting not only concert audiences' minds but the performing musicians themselves. Certainly, rousing ovations are more frequently evoked by displays of pianistic fireworks than by the fashioning of poetic statements. In fact, one could say that glitzy technique is to a musical performance as the mechanics of sex is to the experiencing of true love.

Recently I was listening to a radio broadcast of a live performance of the Gershwin *Concerto in F.* At the end of the vivacious and technically impressive first movement, the audience gave the performer a deserved and rousing cheer. At the end of the second, played, perhaps, at an even higher level of artistry but technically unassuming, the audience remained silent. What was being applauded? What effect does this have on the pianist? I'll try to answer these very important questions later on in the chapter on performance.

The effect of these experiences on the general listening audience is to come to value technique for its own sake instead of its higher function—that of allowing the artist to get to the heart of the matter. "I could never do that," while observing a believe-it-or-not performance, should, after all, be irrelevant to the spirit and value of the musical experience. One would be hard put to consider it an asset for a painter or a novelist to create rapidly except in the most mundane economic sense.

Another effect of the virtuosic display is the conclusion that this satanic wizardry could only be learned at some mysterious time in one's pre-adult life. When most of us hear and see this kind of virtuosity, we are sure we are in the presence of the unattainable; that the Gods have bestowed on this person gifts at an early age, which age we can only dimly recall.

Actually, the curious thing, and most musicians will agree, is that the simplest of pieces, in terms of sheer mechanics, are often the most difficult to play. First of all, they are, in some sense, transparent, allowing the audience to attend easily to its unfolding story. Any departure from good storytelling, then, will be easily discerned. Too, these pieces do not possess the "sleight of hand" inherent in technically difficult pieces which can so easily distract and impress the unsophisticated listener. Finally, slow moving pieces are often deeply meditative requiring the utmost in control to bring off the mood intended.

Arthur Rubinstein pointed out, for example, that in some Lizst pieces the difficulties he (Lizst) contrived were a camouflage, and he exploited them for greater effect: "Chopin was interested only in the musical idea, and the difficulties of his works are logically inherent in his thought...I can play a pyrotechnical Liszt sonata, requiring forty minutes for its performance, and get up from the piano without feeling tired, while even the shortest etudes of Chopin compel me to an intense expenditure of effort."[30] All of these reasons are, in effect, why so many pianists, particularly young ones, avoid Mozart, the "simplest" of the composers.

Well, I'm reasonably certain that virtuosity for virtuosity's sake is not what my readers want. Remember, we're talking life-nourishing self-expression here! When you and I are ready to perform, we will have our musical priorities in order. You simply don't need excessive speed to get you where you want to go artistically. Some of the most beautiful music in the literature is written at a very modest pace, and it breaks no law if you slow other pieces which the big guys play (not so beautifully) at speeds approaching the sound barrier. You need, for the grandest of joys, only to play what is meaningful and expressive of who you are. There are untold numbers of such pieces in the candy store of the musical repertoire. Just press your nose up to the glassical music counter and start your wishing ways. Someday this can all be yours, even with a hurdle that seems so intractably in our way: that of the oft misunderstood and ill-defined quality known as talent.

Is it talent, for example, that allows the virtuoso to perform from Olympian heights? Is it some mysterious power that permits Arthur Rubinstein to wring from the score of Beethoven more than is on the page? Yes, says Claude Levi-Strauss, noted social anthropologist. He rhapsodizes that the distinction between those who "secrete" music and those who do not is so profound, so obvious, and yet so mysterious that musicians are in effect like Gods.

If not talent, what is it that separates you from these other fellows so inspired, so fleet of hand, so musical? It is time to take a serious look at this quality, the possession of which is (irritatingly) considered essential to the world of the artist.

For it is the position here that talent is a concept upon which there has been an unreasoning overemphasis particularly by the "non-talented" (read non-achieving) person. "Talent" as an explanation for the other guy's accomplishment is what allows us to forgive our inability to do the same. As Kingsbury observes, "talent is a concept frequently used to explain something that couldn't be explained otherwise."[18] The conventional wisdom has it that this is something like blue eyes that you either have or not depending on the luck of the gene draw. The fact is, most of us are capable of incredible feats, not the least of which is the unique expression of our inner voices. More essential to the process, clearly, is the will, the need, the commitment, and, most importantly, the tenacity to keep one's focus on getting our story out of its usual hiding places.

Before we get to a working definition on which you and I can agree, it might interest you to know that whether someone is deemed to have talent is often very much debated by respected artists, even when they, themselves, agree on how that concept should be defined! A serious example of such a disagreement was described in the Kingsbury study of a conservatory where one of the students had been decreed, in a testing situation at year's end, to be unmusical. In these circles, you can read this as untalented and fatal! But let Kingsbury tell the story:

> The gravity of Johanna's failing her promotional was grounded in the fact that although the voice faculty agreed that she had a wonderful singing voice, they had found her to be very "unmusical." This is a serious judgment, for it is commonly held among conservatory musicians—and it was explicitly stated by several of the voice teachers—that a person either is or isn't "musical," and on such a matter there is little that can be done to change things one way or the other. The statements that Johanna was "unmusical" were parallel in their thrust with saying that she was untalented. The voice faculty's judgment of Johanna was in effect a statement of doom; drawing musical expression from an untalented or an unmusical person is taken, in the conservatory, to be about as easy as squeezing blood from a stone. However, Johanna's distress was complicated by the fact that at the previous year's promotional she had been characterized by several of these same voice teachers as very "musical" indeed; apparently the passage of time and the rush of myriad auditions had obliterated their memory of her previous promotional.[18]

The importance of this sad incident, of course, is that even the same person at different times may be considered to be in the possession of, or wanting, this precious commodity by professional musicians. One would expect professionals in this setting to exhibit some consistency on this matter. Since the person in question cannot presumably have lost her talent after a year of training at the conservatory, the subjective nature of this process is dramatically revealed. Of course these findings allow for a more damning interpretation—one that would question what happens when raw talent bumps up against tradition—but that would take a whole new chapter.

If, through the reading of these paragraphs, you are beginning to feel stirrings as to your own possibilities, your own capacities for achievement, and are ready to listen to some other encouraging findings, we are making great strides, you and I. Let's continue in the usual way, however, when trying for in-print respectability, and consult a dictionary definition or two. *The Random House Dictionary of the English Language* tells us that "talent" is "a special natural ability or aptitude: e.g., a talent for drawing." Immediately, you see, there is a problem. The difficulty here is that you can only decide that a person possesses this mysterious quality *after* he has shown the work that his or her talent has ostensibly produced. Since almost any achievement is the end product of so many elements, with talent being in many cases a minor one, it doesn't seem very useful to have a concept that "postdicts" success after the fact. Many hearing a great musician will judge this to be evidence of his or her God-given talent, a gift, if you will; but where is it taken into account the endless hours, the trial and error, the awful fears of falling short? One can so quickly assume that expressions of talent just come tumbling out from those whom the Gods have smiled upon; but how does one measure; how does one know?

The second definition reads, "a capacity for achievement or success." OK. That sounds more like it. It seems closer to my perception of reality and more inclusive of any traits leading to success, ranging from a natural inclination for certain achievements to a willingness to pay the price, whatever that may mean.

In one other definition Random House includes, as manifestations of talent, television and motion picture performers, particularly those who have achieved stardom. You would assume that such personages as Jack Nicholson, Dustin Hoffman and Gene Hackman would be eligible for membership in this titled club. Surprisingly, all three of these estimable "talents" spent many long years of hungry frustration before making it. Where was their talent then? Was it unrecognized, as some would say, or did they grow and *become* talented?

Throwing the skeptical spotlight elsewhere, did you know that Thomas Edison tried some 10,000 substances before he hit upon the right material for the incandescent bulb? Why so many trials to get this most illuminating filament? You would think that one of us mere mortals would have stumbled on the right one by the 7500th trial. Was this genius in action—the nth degree of talent? Tenacity? Or are they the same?

As suggested earlier the concept of talent can serve to mitigate one's own perceived (or real) lack of success. On a more worrisome note, it can inhibit action—action that might otherwise have led to seemingly unattainable accomplishments. This is particularly true in the field of music which, in addition to being a "foreign," or at least, second language, seems to require the skills of a sorcerer.

Wait, you complain, there are things that most persons simply cannot do, no matter the motivation, no matter the commitment, no matter the effort expended. You are unlikely, for example, to become a world class sprinter, dunk a basketball, compose like Aaron Copland, or play like Horowitz. But these achievements are certainly off the charts. It is, you will grant me, the enormous middle range of the human endeavor, and particularly in the mystical land of the artist, where the idea of talent can excuse us from the fray, or, of greater concern, place an unfortunate and misplaced damper on our spirits.

Frank Wilson, in his book, *Tone Deaf and All Thumbs?*, presents seemingly ironclad evidence for practically everyone having the innate physiologic capacity and the psychological wherewithal to make music and to make it well. Wilson shows us that music making is, first and foremost, a physical skill of which we are all more than capable, thus dispelling the myth that it is the special province of the gifted. He brings to the issue the credentials of the neurologist in academia and takes us patiently through our physical systems—audition, brain functioning, the musculature, etc.—step by step, showing us how it all works and how it will propel us into musicianhood if we but set the stage. As Wilson avows: "We all have music inside us, and can learn how to get it out, one way or another. We are natural musicians because of the special .nature of the human brain and the phenomenal muscular system to which it is attached."[33]

To prove the point in a highly personal manner, Wilson took up the piano rather late in life and was, despite a confessed case of Tone-Deaf-and-All-Thumbsness, able to achieve personal vindication, even, possibly, in the eyes of his musically accomplished children. Strengthened in his conviction, he has this to say about the talent thing: "If you are like most people, you would *like* to play an instrument, or sing, but have accepted the myth that musicians have freakish powers and you were left out. Nothing could be further from the truth." In an interesting definition that certainly eluded Webster's, he suggests that "talent has to do with the degree of success our efforts have with the public. If we please an audience, or the critics, we have talent..."[33]

Hooray

And now, the crusher. Initially, when I began my search of the psychological literature, I found practically no work of consequence which would support or refute the contention that talent is a much abused term. What looks like the fruits of a "talented" individual is usually the product of many characteristics, most particularly determination, tenacity, luck, etc. Further, these characteristics are available to virtually anyone and everyone. Naturally I had hoped to find data supporting the view that for most of us there exists, in fact, a reasonably level playing field. When I came across Benjamin Bloom's book—a collection of papers concerning a study of some 120 persons in six different fields from within art, athletics, and academia including sculptors, research mathematicians, research neurologist, Olympic swimmers and tennis champions, and twenty four concert pianists, who were judged to be at the top of their "talent" fields—I knew my luck had changed.

Of course, in such a study the kind of working definition you use can make a profound difference in the conclusions reached. I found the following definition put forward by the Bloom group to be reasonable and balanced (never mind that it agreed with my own): "By talent we mean an unusually high level of *demonstrated* ability, achievement, or skill in some special field of study or interest."[3]

Bloom's book is a thoughtful review of the evidence compiled from this research project that I did not know existed when I began considering the problem, but which conclusions I just knew in my bones to be true. Since this research has raised serious questions about the necessity of possessing special gifts and innate aptitudes for high achievement, I pass these findings on to you with joy in my heart for their glorious implications.

Concerning the musicians' segment, for example, it was observed that "although they [the twenty-four pianists] share a profession and have demonstrated similar very high levels of expertise at the keyboard, in most other ways they are as different from one another as they are different from people in general."[3] This has interesting implications for those who think that all people who make it to the rarified strata of the concert world are from some mystic place—raised in formal clothes, talent always on display, separated from the rest of us by some iron caste system—and seriously calls into question almost any stereotype one might hold of classical musicians.

But other conclusions from this study were far more exciting. They were of such moment, in fact, that they rated a headline in the *LA Times* on Sunday, Feb 17, 1985: "The Key to Success? It's Drive, Not Talent." The article read, in part: "A five-year study of 120 of the nation's top artists, athletes and scholars has concluded that drive and determination, not great natural talent, led to their extraordinary success...We expected to find tales of great natural gifts," said University of Chicago education professor Benjamin Bloom, who led the team of researchers. Instead, the researchers heard accounts of an extraordinary drive and dedication through which, for example, "a child would practice the piano many hours daily for 17 years to attain his [her] goal of becoming a concert pianist....Again, investigators originally thought that their subjects would have exhibited unusual giftedness as children and, as a result, received special attention and instruction. But it seems that the reverse occurred: the children developed their talent because of the special instruction and attention they received."[3]

Because natural talent seemed to play such a minor role in the development of these performers, Bloom was convinced that a large number of individuals could achieve at extraordinary levels if given the right encouragement and training. The research "points to the enormous human potential available in each society and the likelihood that only a very small amount of this human potential is ever fully developed."[3]

The report further speculates that it would have been difficult if not impossible to predict, for any but a very small percentage, that these youngsters were on their way to stardom. The child who "made it" was not always the one who was considered to be the most talented. Many parents described another of their children as having more "natural ability." "Only rarely were these children given their initial instruction because the parents saw in the child unusual gifts but rather because their parents placed very high value on one of the talent areas—music and the arts, sports, or intellectual activities. The parents wanted all of their children to have a good opportunity to learn in the talent area they (the parents) preferred."[3]

Holt's observation concerning children, who were involved at an early age with the Suzuki method, is consistent with this finding: "That his (Suzuki's) helpers have taught thousands upon thousands of otherwise unselected four- and five-year-old children to play the violin with astonishing skill...makes me feel very strongly that musical talent, the ability to play a difficult instrument at high levels of skill, is not rare in the general population but is very widely distributed." In other words, it was the interest of the adults and the environment provided by these adults that led to this "talent" explosion.[15]

In the Bloom study, the characteristics that distinguished the high achiever in the field from his or her siblings was a willingness to work and a desire to excel. Persistence, competitiveness, and eagerness were the traits most responsible for the success of these "talented" performers. And although we may not make it to Carnegie Hall, the path of the artist is open to us all if we but accept and embrace these truths. So armed, we need only to begin. The journey of a thousand miles *does* begin with the first step.

But, to get to the end of the line, we must be thoughtful about the nature of the journey. We must create a structure that leads us step by rewarding step to the place of our dreams. We do this by making certain that what we are doing is giving us great satisfaction, moment by moment (a play as you go, as it were). We will talk a great deal about how to organize these reinforcers, this heretofore implausible scenario, when we take up the chapter called "Structure."

Well, I believe we've just about got all of your objections out of the way. We've dispatched this critical period of learning business. And, in terms of learning principles, you are no longer thinking of music as distinct from other languages. When you have read *Tone Deaf and All Thumbs?*, you will see, unequivocally, that if you are near average, you have all of the tools necessary to make music. Perhaps you are ready to agree with Dr. Wilson about everyone's right and potential to be involved in such ventures:

> The more I thought about the transformation of my own responses, the more irritated I became at my own lifelong unquestioning acceptance of the exclusiveness of music-making...Music-making doesn't just belong to people with talent; by biologic heritage it belongs to everyone. I certainly don't expect all the musicians to agree with this thesis, but some will, and perhaps the late bloomers and non-prodigies will be taken more seriously by teaching professionals. That would help.[33]

Finally, I hope you are with me on this talent thing. With all of the evidence, argument and encouragement, surely you are raring to go. I won't even bother to ask. What? You're still holding back. Is there no end to this? Well, what is it now? No time? There just isn't time you say. There really isn't.

Well, that *is* a reasonable objection and problem, not unrelated to the mortality issue we all must face. And, that is precisely why I propose that you join me in the spinning of plates. The artful platespinner has learned that there is always room for one more well-balanced addition to his burgeoning agenda. If you will allow me to introduce you to his ways, you will understand how to play with time *and* have time to play. Onward, then! Let us, in the language of Abraham Maslow—a psychological, air freshening response to the dank, pessimistic and morbid atmospherics promulgated by Freud—begin the actualizing process. It was Maslow's contention that if we make a conscious effort to change and grow, we can achieve unimagined heights; that each of us has a vast, untapped potential; that the way to become all that we can become is to choose that which becomes us. In other words, you can do this thing, if only that is your wish. It is not a gift for playing that you need, but a readiness to play with your gifts. Mix this with Bloom's talent—

drive, tenacity and the rest of the good stuff—and, to paraphrase Erik Erickson, you will be happening to life, rather than it's happening to you.

If this becomes your goal, in a relatively short time you will be playing the music that you love, and shaping this music in a way that becomes you. You will be part of a collaborative process with partners of unimpeachable credentials, great masters who must trust you with the reins.

When you are able to complete this shaping process to your personal specifications, you will have as valid an interpretation as *anyone, anywhere*. After all, it will be uniquely yours. Only you, with the richness of your memories, experiences, and feelings could express these sounds in just this way. If this is sounding like Mr. Rogers, pontificating from the safety of his neighborhood, I will not apologize. It most unashamedly is true. While no one realizes more than I that having a degree in psychology does not confer special powers of observation on the human condition; still, if I have learned nothing else in twenty years of seeing folks in various states of repair, each person is astonishingly, even wondrously, different. Psychologists (the other guys) are always trying to crowd people into categories, thereby losing, by this insidious form of prejudice, the uniqueness of the individual. Not only is it a miracle that we exist, it is a miracle that we exist in a separate and different package from all the others. Come on. Be honest. Have you ever met anyone "Exactly Like You?" ♪

And if you own up to this uniqueness, why then, you are well on your way. Know this as a salutary sign. It means that your personal drumbeat is getting more insistent, your hearing more acute, and that you have decided to grant yourself, finally, exactly what you deserve.

And speaking of drum beats...

Drummer

If a man does not keep pace with his companions, perhaps it is because he hears a different drummer. Let him step to the music which he hears, however measured or far away -
Henry David Thoreau

One is never better served than by one's self - Claude Debussy

Beware the letter doth rise up and slay the spirit -
From the lost writings of Civ Silogram

Today's professional musician, especially one involved in the life-defying rigors of the concert soloist, is faced with a job description of daunting complexity. In the first place, to be embraced as a bona fide member of that artistic community, she must render her play with note-perfect fluency while not stinting on her expressive responsibilities. This is no mean feat. The technical requirements alone fill the hours to the brim, leaving little time for the thoughtful reflection on one's poetic impulses.

Perhaps more vexing, the performance artist must also honor the precise text the composer has provided while evidencing no more, but no less, than a modest degree of individuality. In other words, she must show unflagging fealty to the composer while somehow preserving her own person in the bargain. But how is this possible? In order to project the authentic "meaning" of the piece as envisioned by the composer, then demanded by the academic music community, she must, without exception, play at the speed, cover the dynamic range, utilize the shadings and, in general, adhere to the myriad "stage directions" woven into the fabric of the composition. Where, if reproductive craftsperson is the only accepted course for the performer, is there room for the artist's contribution.

And what has all of this to do with you? Well, at this point, probably not much. While these conflicts are disconcerting and even crazy making for the professional, you, with the advantages of your amateur standing, will resolve them with dispatch. Moreover, these are elements of practice and performance that are practically unknown to the listening public and seem, I'm sure, of little import. These difficulties for the concert artist do have an interesting history, however, and sooner or later will affect your own musical experience. Additionally, this knowledge is highly relevant when you are looking for a teacher compatible with your goals and your person. Most musical pedagogues have strong views on these issues which, undeniably, have a profound, and, usually, hidden, impact on the teaching experience. You are best served if, from the very beginning, you are well armed on the subject.

The underlying issue being examined is the degree to which a student feels bound to the dictates of musically significant others as he or she enters into the seemingly straightforward act of playing a piece of music. It is, really, a question of whose piece is this, anyway. And turning the spotlight on you, dear reader, it is a consideration of how prepared you are to heed the internal rhythms of your personal drummer.

I intend, with unashamed bias, to present both sides of this issue. The guys on the other side, the ones in the black hats and tails, maintain that the integrity of the group must be upheld, that tradition is of undeniable importance to this art form, and that to be accepted as a legitimate interpreter of the musical arts, you must go with the group flow. If, on the other hand, you wish the musical force to be with you, you must accept that your special way of looking at things has value, that your voice must be clearly and unmistakably heard, and that that really is the whole point of involving yourself in this or any medium of artistic expression.

If you are with me on this, you will see this latter as the way to becoming a happier musician/person on the road to that fabled self-actualization state about which we've all heard. Perhaps a good exercise, to stay on the right side of things, would be to invoke the following rather lengthy affirmation (with appropriate breathing exercises): *I shall work on the special listening required for being in touch with my inner voices and will resist all outside forces not in absolute harmony with these*. There, doesn't that feel better? Clearly, the piano is not all that needs tuning.

My intent is to show that your inner voices will serve you most happily and well in your emergence as a practicing musician—from your physical approach to the keyboard, to the knotty questions of musical interpretation. At this point, however, you are probably thinking that you have precious few opinions, voices, drumbeats to pay attention to. First, you protest, you will need time to absorb the wisdom of your teacher, to become informed on the various styles in music history, to learn, really, what classical music is all about.

I will try to be patient—remembering my own uncertainties—but, rather early on, you will detect opinions, feelings, tendencies of your own. The question then becomes: when is it appropriate to begin paying attention to these inner stirrings? I say, much sooner than later, and, in the pages that follow, I will try to convince you of the rightness of this position. For now, if nothing else, following your instincts, doing things your way, particularly in these early stages, will encourage your staying on the artistic path you have chosen. In fact, because of the rewarding properties of your willful participation in this process, an entire chapter, called "Structure," is given over to its development.

Let us look now at a few of the perplexing questions you will face as you begin the complex process of learning to play a musical instrument. On almost every one there are a number of competing possibilities. From the most basic elements, the manner in which one physically approaches the keyboard, to the most ethereal and subjective of questions on interpretation, there exists widely diverging views. This is true, surprisingly, even in the development of concrete technical skills, where differing viewpoints over the importance of finger exercises, the way to position the hand at the keyboard, the accentuation of slow practice—to mention just a few—fill shelves of the music libraries with their largely unproven assertions. Unfortunately, almost no controlled research of consequence has been attempted on the various strategies purporting to build technical expertise. And, as is usually the case with such matters, the less evidence available, the stronger the feelings and rhetoric each camp musters to defend its position.

To take an example, many pedagogues assert that, for highest proficiency in the manipulation of the notes, one ought to hold one's fingers in a graceful curve over the keyboard. This is probably the majority view and is touted (by the more certain) as the *correct, best and only* way to develop a satisfactory technique. Since one does see a certain number of accomplished pianists with this physical attitude, it can be tempting to accept this position; until one considers a Horowitz, he of the flattened, indeed, almost splayed, fingers approach. Oh, how he must have suffered on discovering he had not learned to play as he should.

Let us stay with the subject of hand positions since it is typical of the many and various issues that you will be dealing with in pursuit of musicianly goals. The arguments presented and conclusions reached will hold, in general tenor, for such subjects as posture at the keyboard, what fingers to use in the playing of a piece, organization of practice methods, the strategy to choose for memorizing and, of course, that most important area of self-expression, the extent to which you put your personal stamp on the pieces that you play.

As noted, in the early stages of taking piano lessons, and in authoritative books on the subject, there is normally a discussion of the correct way to hold one's fingers at the keyboard. Teachers in conservatories preach the proper attack with "shoulds" cascading all about. This may be your first opportunity for musical selfhood: I say, don't let the bastards should on you. No matter the consensus of the royal ardor of piano teachers, it is delightfully clear that in this endeavor, as in so many others requiring complex levels of coordination, there are more ways to competent playing than one dare imagine.

All one has to do is to observe the diversity of physical styles displayed by the extraordinary role models of the concert stage. Although it has been noted that well-controlled research about which physical strategies lead to best technical success are practically non-existent, one does at least have available these grand masters of the keyboard at work and at play. Certainly, these great artists must know the way. Or, is it an embarrassment of ways?

We have already talked about the miraculously splay-fingered Horowitz. Others cup their hands inwards, the fingers seeming to dart out and back from this safe harbor; or to roll these programmed digits as dominoes falling across the keyboard. Some pianists move vigorously around, others are still; some raise their hands to bring power into play, while others never leave the keyboard, no matter the demands. Leon Fleisher, when playing repertoire for left hand only, likes to get a good grip on the wooden right end of the piano. Some pianists, on depressing the keys, can be seen moving their hands and arms in a circular motion, perhaps to coax a miraculous vibrato from the instrument.* One school favors the arm drop method, another the loose wrist, still others .... and the beat goes on.

You are then thrown back on your own devices, or your teacher's, if that is your inclination, neither of whom really knows at this early juncture what will work best for you. You profess ignorance, and your teacher, in the unlikely event that he or she is a sensible person, realizes that both technical and musical problems must be incorporated into your particular physical and psychological boundaries. All that counts, of course, is what comes out, and anyway that you can accomplish a musical success story, with a minimum of stress, is most assuredly as valid as every other way.

As exemplar, Vladimir Ashkenazy—the distinguished Russian pianist, in an interview with Robert McNeill, of the McNeill-Lehrer Report—was complimented on the quietness and beauty of his hands as they traveled the horizontal reaches of the keyboard. His reply was to turn his hands over, confiding that if he played with his knuckles, like a crab on its spine, and the music came out in the manner intended, he would be every bit as pleased.

With regard to fingering, that is, which fingers to use for which keys, a subject closely related to hand positioning, such a luminary as Debussy was impressed with the importance of individualizing things for each player: "It is obvious that the same fingering cannot suit differently shaped hands. The absence of fingering (he did not finger his own compositions for other players) provides excellent practice... and proves the truth of the old saying: 'One is never better served than by one's self.'"

On the question, then, of what attitude your hands should have as you bring them to bear on the keys, the "right" answer is, any way that

---

* Experiments have validated what has been known all along by the less mystical about the physical makeup of the piano: once the key has been struck, thus, the hammer thrown, the player's influence on that note is essentially history.

you please; perhaps more accurately, any way that is pleasing to you. If you are lucky, it will be clear what works from the outset. If not, trust that it will happen, just as miraculously as, given the special way you are put together, you learned how to walk, run, hop, skip and jump. Speaking of which, is there a correct way to put one foot after another? Perhaps, but it probably is overwhelmed by individual differences of body type. Did someone teach you your singular way of getting from here to there? How long do you think it would last if they did? Rather than a self-conscious effort, this is another learning adaptation that can go on most felicitously without your awareness. And when you have it "down pat," it is as expressive of you as your manner of speaking and the style of your dress.

This leaving yourself alone, to at least a moderate degree, may be of singular importance to the smooth learning of motor skills. You may quietly observe your attempts at putting your hands "into play." In fact that will be helpful. But kibitzing*—either from your own need to manage the learning process, or from an outside intruder, even your teacher—must be kept to a minimum.

Well, that is quite enough about one's hand or digital style at the keyboard—although hopefully it is about much more than that. Once you apply the principle of self-determination to this element of your playing and multiply this expression of self by all of the choices encountered in the pursuit of musicianly goals, the compositions that you take on will increasingly become authentic representations of who you are. And, if you are ever to achieve a finer tuned self-hood through the exploration of this medium, this is the process that will take you there.

But these variations on your approach to the keyboard are just one of many questions you will face. Should each practice session, for example, include a number of finger exercises or scales and arpeggios? If so, how many and with what variation? How is one to memorize most efficiently? Should sight reading be a significant priority, or is it more important to practice without the music?

There are so many of these kinds of questions that it can be quite overwhelming. Generally, of course, the student will adopt the methods

* Kibitzer: one who watches (a card game, for example) and gives unsolicited and unwanted advice.

and philosophy of her teacher, assuming, reasonably enough, that this respected representative of the musical community would have good reasons for his or her choices. In many instances this will work just fine since a number of approaches will yield nearly equivalent results. In that sense, it is not unlike tennis or golf, where different physical styles abound. But even if you are comfortable with the questions of finger technique, of memorization, of orienting yourself to the keyboard, and the many other issues to be faced, there remains the most puzzling of issues: how does one know how this piece of music is supposed to sound. In other words, having solved all of the mechanical problems for getting the notes out there, the question of interpretation—the creative-aesthetic side of performance—remains.* And, where do you turn for this knowledge? Your teacher? Your inexperienced, thus "soft-spoken," drummer? The composer, as represented by his or her printed instructions? The musical dead sea scrolls?

In this regard, and reasonably soon after learning the basics, most teachers will impress (repress?) their students with the need for proper respect due a "master's work." If reasonably docile, these students will soon be playing only that which is duly noted on the printed stave; they will have learned that there is a right, proper and accepted answer to all musical questions; that when it comes to tradition, Tevye and the rest of that Fiddler Bunch appear as howling iconoclasts; and finally, that to remain in good standing with members of this convention-bound community, the student must, with utmost fidelity, adhere to the intentions of his or her many masters.

Most teachers will echo this party line, will preach the infallibility of the composer, will shout semper fideles ad musica. And most of us, including, I am slow to admit, your author, will be cowed into submission, bringing into this fancy new neighborhood the usual baggage of insecurity—wanting acceptance and reassurance from the members of this elite circle—and willing to join in lock step to the insistent beat(s) from without.

---

* Much as a broadway actor might encounter in the reading of a script. A host of other persons, the director, the writer, other members of the cast and even the critics, will have a number of ideas as to the right and proper reading of his or her part. Although it may sound a bit off key, the musician, even a beginner, has a like, albeit less complex, process to go through.

In the philosophic halls of the academic music community, the two extremes on this issue are often labeled (1) the objective school—top dog these days, no contest—those who follow the score with strict allegiance to the letter *and* the spirit of the composer, suffering no (foolish) deviation from this pure, and if I may say so, elitist position; and (2) the subjective school, those who feel that any particular piece of music was composed as more or less a starting place for performance, that while the notes are the composer's, the job of bringing these to life, for sounding an unique statement, belong to the performer. Condemned by the objective performers as profaners of the score, the subjectivists charge the opposite camp with a lack of imagination coupled with a slavish adherence to the tried and true.

Point and Counterpoint

Perhaps some feeling for the ebb and flow of these forces will help you wrestle with this problem. It has, in fact, helped me to resolve this issue with an ever increasing degree of comfort and bias. Let's begin with the present. As I am sure you have discerned from the strident declamations above, the overwhelming viewpoint among mainstream classical musicians is that the composer is king, all those who would make his music, his vassals, subject to his every dictate (the notes as written, no substitutions on this menu, please), subject to his moods (when I say staccato, I want to see jumping fingers), subject, even, to his occasional bad writing (I don't care what you think of this piece, my name is Brahms. Who the hell are you?). The balance of power, in terms of performance, has shifted radically from the performer, previous feted title holder of the throne, to the composer. Yesteryear's star of the concert stage has been reduced castrati-like to a mechanical figurine of the royal court, no longer even a pretender to the throne.

Does this sound like exaggeration? All of the above is the prevailing sentiment, as silly as it may sound, and as unfair as you might think my portrait. And it is true despite a series of powerful contradictions. One of these concerns the fact that many composers were less likely to regard their scores as engravings than their followers and most particularly than the musicologists and performing artists of our times.

The following will give you some idea of the intensity with which such a position can be held:[12]

And how should it be played today? Nothing shall be imposed …without notice of the alteration; nor shall conjecture be wantonly or unnecessarily indulged: The master's music is an inheritance, not a lottery prize. To tarnish it is easy: to squander it, contemptible. To link one's own name to the composer's with a hyphen is to pimp on his capital; to efface his style with one's own music falsely bearing the name of a man long dead is to mint counterfeit money.

Rather strong language, that, but not far from reflecting what most respected musicians of today feel about changing the slightest detail of so-called classical music, i.e., any music by the accepted masters.

Today's younger virtuosos have been trained to the point where they would as soon cut off their hands as knowingly change a note, a phrase, a dynamic indication. Whether or not this concentration on textual truth has led to emotional inhibition is a point that teachers throughout the world would do well to discuss. It probably has. For slavish adherence to the text can be a fine prop to support a musician without ideas of his own. Not only that, but many musicians, afraid to tamper with holy writ, end up obeying the letter but not the spirit of the music. With all the advance in scholarship, many young artists nevertheless still do not realize that the baroque, classical and many romantic composers fully expected their music to be somewhat changed by the interpreter.[30]

If you view this tradition-bound attitude only in the narrow confines of the music field itself, it is possible to consider it praiseworthy devotion to a proud heritage, as well as a necessary antidote to the excesses of the Romantic period. But, if one widens the focus to include similar deference to other sets of ideas and principles, i.e., religious, socio-political systems, theories of personality, it becomes clear that this tendency to deify the composers and to celebrate their every whim amounts to a kind of artistic fundamentalism.

I have always had difficulty with what seemed excessive tradi-
tionalism within the field of music, but it was only with my perceiving
this kinship with other expressions of fundamentalism that it came home
to me what this discomfort was about, and it has emboldened my ascent
to this soap box. Let us be clear about my bias. I am a card carrying
anti-fundamentalist in any dress. For me, fundamentalism, no matter its
variation, is to be avoided like the spirit dampening virus that it
inevitably becomes.

Many historic movements have started out with the best of humanitarian intentions only to be knocked off course by followers living by
the letter rather than the spirit. Within Christianity, where fundamentalism is best known and distressingly manifest, people have been savaged
if they did not believe in the "word" no matter how preposterous, no
matter how obviously such text went against common sense. And, I
don't mean to single out you Christian guys. Jews, Muslims and just
about every sect that has made it through the ages have their share of
world class fundamentalists. Worse, it is wider than religion, occurring
in such movements as Freudianism, Marxism, even with our own constitution. And they all drive me crazy, demanding of their followers that
the letter of the thing, whether it be religious, psychological, or, as now
seems the case, musical, shall reign supreme.

This reliance on scripts, or scripture, in the world of Christianity
can be seen, albeit in less consequential terms, in the pronouncements
of the orthodox of the music community, taking as the gospel the
"written word" (notes plus "stage directions") of the masters. If a
passage is marked forte by his eminence, Amadeus, the purist sees it as
having been writ by the moving finger. For the true believer, these
notes, both musical and textual, take on the force of the commanding
tablets admitting no exception.

Ironically, many of the great masters in music have been sanctified
in a way that would have been an anathema to them—their every note
accepted as divinely chosen—when, for example, a phrase was arbitrari-
ly and hastily penned and could just as easily have gone in other
directions. And they themselves would frequently change a note, a
tempo marking, any of the "road signs," because that is how they felt
about it *that day*.

To be sure, some composers, even prior to the current abiding emphasis on literal values, were more demanding of their prerogatives than others. Beethoven, for example, wished his dictates to be followed much more rigorously than composers before him. Moreover, in his rigorous quest for impressing his quite explicit musical intentions onto the performance of his music, Beethoven anticipated, and no doubt influenced, the mind set of some of the most important composers of the twentieth century. But even he, as we will see shortly, was not as consistent about this as the objectivist scholars would lead you to believe.

Some of those whom Beethoven influenced on this reifying score, composers like Stravinsky and Schoenberg, leave the interpreter no freedom whatever: every nuance of dynamic, tempo, phrasing, rhythm and expression is rigidly prescribed. The performer is reduced to the abject status of a pianola or a gramophone... The final step, Stravinsky argues, must be taken and the whole matter of "interpretation" thrown overboard. The idea of interpreting music is rejected out of hand, since interpretation reveals the personality of the performer rather than that of the composer. To qualify for the task of competent performance, one must, above all, transmit the composer's thoughts without ever falsifying them by personal, wilful interpretation. This progressive annihilation of the performer's share in the re-creation of a master's composition is an alarming phenomenon, one that has never occurred before in the whole history of music.[30]

Moreover, if the truth were known, many composers have not been as demanding as their vocal followers. Again, this is the hallmark of fundamentalism. More Christian than Christ. More Freudian than Freud. More Marxist than Marx. What is the point? Why so much fuss for something so elitist? Perhaps the answer is that for many this philosophical stance is psychologically reassuring. There is a right way, a textual answer to all questions of taste and conduct. One doesn't have to rely on one's own intuition or resources for the making of choices, for arriving at correct (read acceptable, even laudable) modes of behavior.

For me, then, dripping in self-righteousness, musical fundamentalism is a nasty concept, and I use it because I feel this point of view is so clearly flawed; and because I am angry at a position that so straightjackets, so narrowly defines what is acceptable behavior in this magnificent and heretofore liberating art form.

An illustration of this narrowing effect may help to clarify the dilemma for the free spirits out there. As Kingsbury observes in his study of the conservatory, "musicians consistently distinguish between playing the music and playing the notes."[18] Playing the notes in this quote really means "only" playing the notes—like an actor mouthing the words in a play—and is the height of damnation from one pro to another. Better the speaker to have attacked the player's mother, God and country than to suggest that his playing has accomplished the least important dimension of performance, that of reproducing, as would a piano roll, only the noted facts. On this side of the ledger, with an absence of risk and with little exploration of his creative juices, this performer is seen as missing the soul train, an unworthy companion on future musical journeys.

However, let this same performer unduly flex his aesthetic imagination, let him dare impose his own ideas as to tempo or dynamics (louds and softs and in betweens) or the handling of rhythm, let him swing in this personalistic direction just one degree too far, and he will be equally dishonored for failing to play what the music demands. The margin of safety between these two classical restraints, this narrow zone of acceptability so tightly bound, is the musical tight rope on which today's performer must balance or perish.

Let us consider a variation of this dilemma. Suppose the intentions of the composer for certain effects or affects do not seem, in the opinion of the concert artist, to be realized in performance. Much as a line in a play not evoking from the audience what the author intends, or a comic line falling short of its mark, the composer of yesteryear cannot be aware of how musical phrasing will "play" to a live audience of today,* particularly when that composer has been removed by time, distance, cultural context and, of course, his own demise.

Jorge Bolet, one of our finest pianists, has strong feelings about this dilemma, one in which he feels the objectivists have placed him: the performer is the one who has lived with the piece, sometimes for a life-

---

* In the theater world, as opposed to the musical one, the director is often encouraged by his peers, the public, and even his critics to put his own stamp on the text with which he has been provided. For an excellent setting out of this tradition—or lack of one—in the dramatic arts of the twentieth century by one of its great practitioners, director Elia Kazan, see his autobiography, *Kazan, A Life.*

time, playing it over and over, agonizing over how it seems best to play, what seems most expressive of his own feelings and what seems to bring forth the most affect from his audiences. Often, says Bolet, the composer, needing to meet some deadline or move on to the next project, may have simply dashed something off without a great deal of thought about all the possibilities.

One for the Good Guys

A basic and pervasive difficulty to the position of the musician/ fundamentalist is how often professional musicians disagree upon the basic data. In the field of government, it is troublesome enough for scholars of our own constitution to agree on matters of interpretation. Imagine the difficulty if there were several drafts of this document floating around or if the notation (language) was not universally accepted. Again Kingsbury: "It must be emphasized that the matter of what is and what is not in accordance with the dictates of the score, that is, what constitutes honoring the score in performance, is almost always problematic and frequently at issue among conservatory musicians."[18] Although written in black and white, incomplete editing, inconsistencies between editions, ambiguous "stage directions," and even lack of any direction at all, allow for vigorous disagreements about what the composers intentions really were.

If It's in Print, It Must Be So

How did it get this way? When did the seemingly free and flexible art form of music get taken hostage to tradition? How did musicians, as opposed to the members of virtually all other art forms, come to feel so hemmed in by this immaculate fidelity to its origins, the (usually deceased) composer and his deathless creations? Why have literalists such as Toscanini and Schnabel and Serkin—as opposed to musicians of a more liberal and romantic bent—become heros and models of the rank and file, having untold influence on their colleagues and successors?

What could possibly have happened to the performance of music to provoke this revolution by members from its conservative wing, whose ideas have been so nearly universally accepted by the musical community? It certainly was not where the musician/performers of the 19th century were headed, those freewheeling extroverts commanding the attention and adulation of their audiences.

Well, as is so often the case in history, it may have been an overreaction to these very unbridled spirits, to these "undisciplined" practitioners of self-expression. Today, those who preserve the intentions of the composer faithfully, who do not intrude their own concept of what "works" in performance, are lauded as possessing impeccable taste. But definitions and meaning have cultural and historical contexts. As Schonberg points out, "every age has its notions of taste and in the nineteenth century it was this very inclination to infuse the performance with one's own ideas, personality, style, originality and, not unimportantly, virtuosity that helped to define those musicians who possessed this prized quality of good taste."[30]

Virtuosity was significant in the age of romanticism because it allowed the artist to embellish the text—often in ways idiosyncratic to that performer—and to astonish the listener with dazzling displays of dexterity. Many of the romantic pianists had particular feats of bravado, of specialized prestidigitation, that were his and his alone. These unfettered presentations had the effect of bringing to the concert stage unique personalities, adding immeasurably to the effect of their performances and to the importance of these performers. In the musical currency of the times, the concert soloist, particularly the virtuoso performer, possessed as much prestige as the composer. Some had far more—witness the likes of Paganini and Franz Liszt—who pulled out all stops to impress and seduce their audiences. Artist as sterile conduit was being rejected. No longer, at least for this shining period in musical history, did the performer accept his role as another face in the crowd.

"This shining period," when the performer ruled, or at least shared the reins, was known as the romantic period. "Although owing much to the preceding period in music history, the so-called classical tradition, romanticism ushered in an era where…the performer's individuality gradually appears as the driving force of a personalized interpretation."

The dates given for this period are generally said to approximate the years of the 19th century. There are, however, a number of differing opinions as to the years actually covered by this powerful force in musical history. In fact, although Romanticism was itself a reaction to that which had come before—the so-called Classical period of Mozart, Haydn and others—in certain important respects it was not the abrupt change that at first seems apparent. Certain elements of the classical period were, in fact, natural progenitors of the romantic mind set. Most notably, the performer of the classical era was encouraged to elevate his own importance in the art of performance through the practice of thoughtful improvisation. This edition of The Performer was expected to compose, on the spot, and often in response to pieces written by others, musical works or variations which showed his ingenuity as he "interpreted" the original composition.*

Besides the raising of prominence for the performer, by dint of his or her ingenuity in the art of the musical ad lib, virtuosity in a more general sense was also rooted in the classical period, where the means, that is, the technical wherewithal, to make music was becoming, in some quarters, as pronounced as the music itself. Certain players became "headliners", e.g., Mozart, Hummel, of marquee proportions, for their awesome manual skills, during a period in music history when restraint in such matters had previously been the rule.

And so it becomes clear that the current period of keeping the performer under wraps contrasts not only with the romantic period of the nineteenth century but with romantic playing in general (or, I would add, musicality, spontaneity, and the freedom for improvisation) which has a much longer and, for the most part, honorable history.

True, the Romantic Period did raise the level of questionable musical and extra-musical behaviors to an unacceptable level. In the idiom of today, certain matinee idols gave new meaning to the word "excess." Of course, there have always been musicians more than willing to favor glitzy superficialities over weightier considerations and to submerge beautiful music under a welter of cheap effects. But in this era, excesses became commonplace, pandering to public taste, the rule.

---

* Not unlike the rules of the game for today's art of jazz. One doesn't go to hear music by Jerome Kern at a Miles Davis concert but to hear Miles play Kern, and many other composers, through his distinctive filter.

Debussy, a refined musician, had far greater sympathies for the composer: "The attraction of the virtuoso for the public is very much like that of the circus for the crowd. There is always hope that something dangerous may happen. M. Ysaye may play the violin with conductor Colonne on his shoulders, or M. Pugno may conclude his piece by lifting the piano with his teeth."

The temptation to pull out all stops was seductive for both audience and artist alike. Driven almost certainly by commercial considerations, a kind of musical anarchy obtained with an anything-goes-performance-spirit. Controlling the excesses of the Romantic Period, "getting back to basics," then, became the rallying cry of the generations of musicians passing into the early years of the 20th century. The primary tenet of these new guardians of the realm, one which would act as governor on the reach of the musical extrovert, was the assertion that the composer's intentions were to be respected to the exclusion of all other considerations. Indeed, the word interpretation narrowed to mean realizing the composer's will, and not in giving new meanings of one's own.

The movement took hold. Whether it was certain leaders, masters like the aforementioned Toscanini, Schnabel and Serkin, imposing by example their collective wills on the musical community—a great man theory of history in musical variation—or whether they were merely representatives of their times, is a question always difficult to answer. However, the effects were both salutary and chillingly apparent. The concert hall became respectable, serious and staid; insufferably staid, unbearably serious, puritanically respectable. No longer would the shameless show biz of a Paganini be tolerated, which, in truth, may have resembled a Las Vegas concert by Liberace. No longer would the De Pachmanns of the world amuse and astound audiences with their antics.

You've not heard of De Pachmann? Well possibly his name has been purged from most music history books by the objective revisionists. Vladimir De Pachmann was born in Odessa, Russia, in 1848. He toured Europe and the U.S., mostly playing the works of Chopin, regaling large crowds with his unique presentations. Listen to this story—perhaps you will spot some of Victor Borge's "inspired" material—and try to imagine the response of a modern day audience at one of your city's subscription concerts to this kind of display:

A good part of his fame came from his shenanigans. De Pachmann would talk, mutter, grimace and lecture his way through a recital. He denied that he did this for effect, and insisted that the speech and the platform goings-on were necessary for him to express what was surging within his artistic soul...His struggles with the ups and downs of the piano stool were legendary. One of his tricks was to raise it, lower it, fiddle around with the controls until the audience was desperate. Then he would rush into the wings and come out with a large book placing it on the seat. No good. Then he would rip out one page, put the remainder of the book on the seat, and smile beatifically at the audience. Now he was comfortable. Like as not he would stop in the middle of a piece and ask the audience what it thought of the performance. Of course there would be applause and cheers. Whereupon de Pachmann would inform the audience that it was deaf and idiotic; that he was playing terribly; that now he would play as only de Pachmann could.[30]

No. There would be no more big top at the concert hall. In fact, with the exception of Leonard Bernstein's famed children's concerts or an occasional full dress symphonic presentation accompanied and driven by an organizing text—Andre Previn and Michael Tilson Thomas have put together such programs—or concerts with a decided pop cast, such as the Boston version, the door to the fourth wall* has been unmistakably closed, the separation between audience and performer complete. Respectability was restored and, in this correct environment, the composer was able to regain his primacy. But at what price?

A major loss, for example, was the serious creative artist with the potential and the desire to contribute his or her vision to the proceedings. This (for me) idealized and idealistic performer would not be interested in relating to the broadest possible audience, nor in achieving new levels of virtuosity. No, this would be a person with creative gifts seek-

---

* The invisible fourth wall. In a typical room, you have four walls; in the theater we have an invisible fourth wall so that the audience can peer in. In the unwritten code, you must never break this illusion—so say the traditionalists of the theater. Of course, this precept has been violated by the more adventuresome: one notable, Clifford Odets in his play of social unrest, *Waiting for Lefty*, with great dramatic effect. And, of course, there was a fellow named Shakespeare.

ing to preserve the spirit and structure of a composition while expressing his unique vision in its refined expression.

Only when that rare musician comes along, whose force of personality and musical convictions are too powerful to ignore, would the community of musicians and music lovers make exception, and then most begrudgingly. Glenn Gould was such a player and by some miracle—probably owing to his eccentricities as performer and to his mega-individualism—was able to slip past the self-appointed cultural gatekeepers of the conservative music community. (And withal, he had to absorb a great deal of criticism. And then, he did not really survive.) He unquestionably possessed an acute sense of inner direction and resolve manifesting itself in his music and how he lived his life. Whether it meant wearing gloves when others would think it peculiar—how many of us are cowed by this kind of group pressure—or shocking the cognoscenti with a novel conception of the Brahms 2nd piano concerto, Gould did not shrink from defending who he was or how he expressed himself. He took this dizzying leap onto the stages of the concert world and its surround, holding fast for a short but dazzling period (almost 15 years), before being beaten back by the musical moral majority.

Gould made his dramatic entrance to the classical music world with a most original reading of the Bach Goldberg variations.* It is no accident that the vehicle was a recording of a Bach piece where the "rules of order"—the directions that the composer sets out for the performer—are less clearly delineated than those of the great composers that followed. It is hard to imagine Gould crashing the party with a like recording, in terms of his personal prism, of Mozart or Beethoven—that persuasive probably no rookie could be. But between his most compelling interpretations, his original way of being on the stage—quite extroverted, singing loudly and tunelessly as he played, conducting one hand with the other as though collaborative alter egos, slouched over with his hands seeming to hold onto the keyboard from below—and his idiosyn-

---

* This was his first recording. As the fates would have it, his last recording, made some 30 years later, was of those same variations. And as if to show consistency as the hobgoblin of a small mind, Gould played the Goldberg Variations at a startlingly slower tempo. This recording was received with equal if not greater acclaim although it was a very different recording beyond even the tempo deviations.

cracies off the stage, he became big time box-office. Since box-office success can further acceptance (at least on some level), Gould commenced a career as a throwback to other, more romantic, times, plying his trade to his own drummer in all ways, getting a mix of reviews, yet potentially opening doors for other artists of strong egocentric, creative and unselfconscious bent.

The artistic community was thrown into a quandary. Glenn Gould was definitely not playing by the rules, but the public—who knew not and cared less—demanded more and more of this original, having not seen his like since the romantic players of the 19th century. One infamous episode brought this conflict into clear relief. During a concert featuring the Brahms *D Minor Concerto* with the New York Philharmonic, Leonard Bernstein gave what seemed a personal disclaimer. For "what you are about to hear," decried the dramatic maestro, "I take no responsibility." Although Bernstein denied that this was meant as a critical disassociation from Gould, rather, as he claimed, a giving credit where due, it may well have been a natural consequence of the unnatural alliance between traditionalist and original.

How Gould had the strength to stay in touch with what was true for him, particularly in such an insular field and in these other-directed times, is beyond the ken of this author. Moreover, his pursuit of individuality was remarkably evident from his earliest days in performance.

And, Gould gave it the good fight. He lasted more years in the concert halls than seemed likely; for while he was receiving ovations from his adoring public, he continued to receive mixed reviews for his play, and unmixed and unfavorable notices for his extra musical lifestyle as it appeared on and off the stage. Wanting to be totally accepted, and certainly not in agreement that his extroverted behavior on stage should have any bearing whatsoever on his musical conceptions, Gould did not outlast his critics. Over the years the criticisms turned more shrill and, if possible, less kind. "The fact that I tend to sing a great deal while I'm playing, that I tend to conduct myself with one hand—all that sort of thing...I had never given any thought to the importance, at least to some people, of visual image. When I became aware of this, I became extremely self-conscious about everything I did. The whole secret of what I had been doing was to concentrate exclusively on realizing a conception of the music, regardless of how it was physically achieved. This new self-consciousness was very difficult."[10]

And it unquestionably drove him from the stage. By the time he had reached the latter stages of his concert career, "Gould saw himself walking into a gladiatorial arena, where the audience sat ready to give the thumbs-down signal for his death."[10] Of course this is a rather dramatic reaction, one might say overreaction, but Gould was also responding to the unnatural (to say the least) environment of the concert artist, a subject we shall cover with love and fury later on. Once, this environment had been tolerable to him, even comfortable, allowing Gould the expansive opportunity to be himself in a public forum. But ultimately his rope, too, proved finite, the pressures to conform, too powerful, even for one with his remarkable ability to ignore the externals.

Gould, of course, was an aberration of our musical times. This approach, this need to go beyond the re-creation of a masterwork to what the performer can, in a collaborative spirit, contribute to the material, was once again rejected as the inappropriate indulgences of the self-centered upstart. As a result, not only did the community of creative performing artists suffer, but the public has been cheated of risktaking and deviant (in the best sense) expressions of artistic talent. In other words, gang, we went too far.

Again, what can this all possibly have to do with you and your learning to play these masterly works of art? Well, besides the fact that this history tends to make some sense of these rather unfortunate developments, its effects may well have a profound influence on how you will come to think about the playing of a musical composition. You will be affected by those who teach you and those you play for, many of whom will have attitudes shaped by the mores of this cultural community. Are you prepared for that? I was not. I had given it little thought and would have been much more comfortable if I had known even as little as this sketch has provided, had known that what the experts, i.e., my teachers, were telling me about performance practices was a reflection of our times, not facts inherent in the art form; that how I was being shaped was, in some very real sense, arbitrary; that my adhering to these dictates had partially to do with what I knew—or, more importantly, didn't know—about music history.

What I didn't know then, but am reasonably sure of now, is that the conscientious music player must find his bearings between the two extremes of rigid objectivity and unwarranted liberality. As with many things, moderation *may* be the most satisfying course, with each player deciding where on that spectrum he or she belongs. Excessive fidelity to the score—too much bowing and scraping to the musical Gods—will certainly negate your personal contribution, thus the great satisfaction that comes from thoughtful self-expression. On the other hand, ignoring the composer's intentions in a wholesale manner will thrust you into the position of musical leperhood and, if that doesn't concern you, may violate a valid psychological precept, inherent in any artistic endeavor, of a proper balance between the familiar and the novel. In the performance of a musical composition, this kind of balance allows others to respond to your work as a true collaboration between the composer's intentions and your own.

What makes us all the same is that we are all different.
(Used in a commercial for American Airlines or some such.)

And now to the question of authority in music. Since you are going to be a musician, or artist of another stripe—I hope by now that you are used to this idea—you may find yourself, even if reasonably inner-directed, needing to turn to others for reliable musical "advice." Based on what "moral" authority, for example, will you play a piece by Mozart: from a respected teacher? from observing or listening to famous players? divine inspiration? your own Self 1? or perhaps, Self 2? (These arbitrary selves, different aspects of our being as seen by Timothy Gallwey, will be discussed later in the chapter.)

I have already noted how respected figures in the music community have resolved these questions within the context of their (our) cultural heritage. Without embarrassment and putting it off no longer, I now intend to do some pontificating of my own, championing what I consider to be a kind of philosophical rule of thumb, and which rule, in fact, makes up the internal engine of this book.

I have decided to start with the punch line. The rest (taking up many pages) will be how I got there, which you can skip if you are already persuaded of the rightness (or wrongness) of my position. Here it is then: there is no right or wrong way to play a piece of music; there is only what you come to after immersing yourself with the structure and language of that piece, only what you come to after living with it for some practiced period of time. Since you will be vulnerable to the criticism of others no matter what you do,* *there is no other course but to play this piece the way that makes the most sense to you, the way, in other words, that gives you the most pleasure.* In so doing, you will, without apology, be expressing who you are and what you stand for. If it is right for you, it is who you are. And, if it is who you are, it is right for you.

If this seems a flagrant tilting in the direction of self-indulgent liberality, it will be tempered by the process for arriving at what makes it "right for you." The short version of this argument suggests that when you have considered the options through a careful study of the materials, you will, almost by definition, do the musically right thing. For the more extended version, I'm afraid, you must read on.

How I got to that conclusion will be contained in the pages that follow. In these, hopefully, rather than the strident pronouncements of a musical rebel without a cause, there will be a thoughtful line of argument bringing us inexorably to that position. Part of that argument posits a reasonable assertion that you should always be damned skeptical of what others say—even highly respected authorities, maybe most particularly highly respected authorities—about how you choose to go about your (musical) business. And while you have on your skeptical hat, you might want to take a wary look at your present author.

In fact, if you can read the following story and continue as my trusting reader, well then, our relationship has survived an important crossroads. This is a story that illustrates the importance of not listening blindly to authority figures, even those in whom you have a great deal of faith. It happens to be one which touched my own life. It also happens that the so-called authority figure here was me.

I once aspired to be a basketball player. I practiced very hard and did well considering the personal equipment I was dealt. As in music,

---

* (great technique but no soul) (very musical but too schmaltzy) (interesting but not really Beethoven playing) (too broad {too narrow} an interpretation) (too fast) (too bangy) (too introspective) (nice for an amateur) (etc.) (etc.) (etc.)

my limitations were to cry for. I was slow of foot, had your average white man's jumping ability, took up the game late, had poor court sense, was modestly put together, and had the same stage fright that I bring to music. Not much of a package, you will admit. But with my tenacity and with well crafted systems of practice—not unlike the methods that you will hear about later for even more artistic purposes—I made it to better than average and even played on the University of Cincinnati freshman team for almost twenty minutes (it actually was longer but that's the way it seems as I go to the mail box for my social security check). At any rate, I was not only better than average, but much better at knowing the fundamentals than most, even those players who had played extensively in organized ball.

In the neighborhood where I was living at the time (circa 1949), there was a young man who was four years younger and four years behind me in school; in other words he was in his freshman year at the local high school near the University of Cincinnati. We met while shooting baskets in the neighborhood park; he was extremely pleasant, shy, and hungry to learn. He was able to make the freshman team (or junior varsity, whichever), but didn't enjoy or entirely trust the teachings of his high school coach. Thus, it happened that I became, for a brief period, his informal coaching buddy. I showed him the stuff that everybody who plays basketball should know, the so-called fundamentals, and we would practice drills together to strengthen those fundamentals.

He was coming along just fine with a potential, however, which seemed sharply limited by his smallish height and frame. But he worked diligently, had a fine intelligence, and consistently made gains. In his sophomore year he made the varsity, and, although he did not play a great deal, became ever more energized by his fantasized prospects. Sometime in the summer between his sophomore and junior years, he began tinkering with an absolutely new way of shooting a basketball. By this time he was all of five foot four or five, and, in light of this, seemed, I was sure, to be headed for an embarrassing fall with his new creation. I urged him to put this silly thing aside fully expecting that he would. He had been, heretofore, a dutiful (remember, I told you he was quite bright) student who saw the wisdom of my ways. However, something told him to continue on his errant path and so declined to listen on this one, not unimportant, issue. He still sought my support and advice in between games and we simply didn't talk about this strange procedure he was using to launch his shots.

Well, to cut to the fast break, in his senior year in high school, he averaged 39.5 points a game—this was back when (1952) a high scoring guard in high school might have averaged 9 points a game—then went on to Ohio State where, in his junior year, he led the major college scorers in the country with a scoring average of over 32 points a game. The preposterous shot that he had concocted was the now common, but still awesome, jump shot. There may have been other people in the country who were experimenting with such a shot but I, a basketball freak of a fan, had never seen or even heard of one. And his shot wasn't just jumping before shooting (this part is for you basketball aficionados out there), his jump shop was with the ball almost behind his head so that the defender could not defend the shot even though he, Robin Freeman, had grown to no more than 5 feet ten inches. He probably was, then, the first jump shooter in the dramatic style that we know it today—a true pioneer.

You see, if I had had my way, he would have been just another good ballplayer; and basketball would have had to wait for another original thinker for the audacious, graceful jump shot. Certainly, he would have been a good scorer with any shot that he practiced—he was that disciplined—but this innovation gave him a leg up on the opposition. What he did, in the best tradition of Thoreau and Emerson, was to pay strict attention to his own drummer who, unbeknownst to me at the beginning of things, was beating out an unrelentingly deviant rhythm from the rest of his playground buddies.

Where did he get the strength, the instinct, the tenacity to do what was so outlandishly different. All of us have this capacity, this internal drummer, some with a beat so faint that we must close our eyes to hear, others with a bombast drowning out all else around. But *all have that drummer.* The point is that somewhere, somehow, you must summon the strength to disregard any but your own soundings, else what does your separateness count for. You must ignore the Victor Margolises out there (those so sure they are right) and listen to the person who will always be there for you...Your Self!

But, *Which* Self?

One of our selves, however, must be regarded with great caution. This may be the harshest, most unyielding authority figure of them all. He is with us always with his unrelenting shoulds—a shadowy figure, more invasive than big brother, more inhibiting than church or state. Tim Gallwey calls him Self 1, a repository of all authority figures still weighing on your soul, skeptical of your natural ability to grow, needing conscious control of your every act. How can we possibly learn anything with this guy hanging around waiting to take over?

A typical Self 1 script in a student trying a new piano piece might go something like this: "That was a bad mistake I just made and I keep making it. I will never learn this damned piece. I am a worthless piano player. In fact, it is dawning on me that I have never accomplished a damned thing in my whole (censored) life."

Of course this may be an exaggerated scenario. Perhaps it takes more than a few mistakes to blow you away. But you take my meaning. Being subjected to unrelenting criticism from a compilation of authority figures you have tried to please since you were a child—a kind of critical mass, if you will, of corrections, shoulds, thou shalt nots, etc.— is a fact of life for most of us.

Gallwey's answer to this petty tyrant is to encourage the individual to be a neutral but highly sensitive observer of his own actions. If you can successfully adopt this role as non-judgmental observer of your actions and their consequences, then, according to Gallwey, Self 2, a throwback to more innocent times, takes over and learning occurs in a more natural and even-handed manner.

It's Gallwey's Self 2 that we start out with. It is Self 2 that we must reclaim if we are to go about our business with calm and dispatch. In the following, you will recognize Self 2 before his half brother, demon Self 1, has had a chance to mount his hostile takeover. It's a description of a baby learning to walk. You will see for yourself that Self 1 is pleasantly absent. Gallwey describes it well:[11]

Fortunately, most children learn to walk before they can be told how to by their parents. As a result, children not only learn how to walk very well, but they gain confidence in the natural learning process which operates within them. Mothers observe their children's efforts with love and interest, and if they are wise, without much interference. If we could treat our tennis games [my readers may substitute in this discussion the playing of a musical instrument] as we do a child learning to walk, we would make amazing progress. When the child loses his balance and falls, the mother doesn't condemn it for being clumsy. She doesn't even feel bad about it; she simply notices the event and perhaps gives a word or gesture of encouragement. Consequently, a child's progress in learning to walk is never hindered by the idea that he is uncoordinated. Why should not a beginning player treat his backhand as a loving mother would her child? The trick is not to identify with the backhand. If you view an erratic backhand as a reflection of who you are, you will be upset. But you are not your backhand any more than a parent is his child. If a mother identifies with every fall of her child and takes personal pride in its every success, her self-image will be as unstable as her child's balance. She finds stability when she realizes that she is not her child, and watches it with love and interest—but as a separate being. This same kind of detached interest is what is necessary to let your tennis game [music playing] develop naturally.

We will return to Gallwey in the chapter on concentration for his salutary help in such matters. above para

And now, if you will permit an apparent digression—although, to be sure, prompted by all this talk about selves—I am going to take you into a field that I have been schooled in, worked at, and, finally to my good fortune, escaped. That field is psychotherapy and it is how I earned my way for over 20 years. I have a degree in psychology from the University of Cincinnati and, after spending a short time in academia, worked this art form in private practice for the rest of my sentence.

After a number of years interacting with others who performed the same or similar services for the community, and after doing considerable research on the therapeutic effectiveness of people in our field, I became aware of a peculiar and negative—and, it must be admitted, unproven—correlation that I hadn't previously suspected: the probability of finding effective help from a therapist for most psychological problems appears to be inversely correlated to the accepted pecking order of the helping discipline. Said another way, the higher the prestige of the helping profession, the less likely it is that the help you receive will prove to be effective. The accepted top of the order is, of course, the psychoanalyst, those psychiatrists who practice the Freudian approach. At the low end, as arrived at by how much respect is given to them by professionals in the helping community, by how much money they make, and even by the community at large, are social workers providing help in various mental health agencies or in the private sector. Off the low end of the scale, since they are not professionals, and, often times, the most effective helpers of all, are friends, bartenders, barbers, and otherwise just good listeners.

As you ascend this mythical scale, which includes a number of other groups, such as psychiatric nurses, psychologists, and those psychiatrists not using Freud's number, one becomes aware of an increasing emphasis on abstract personality theory, on a medical model with its heavy reliance on diagnostics, on a philosophical position that assumes that the doctor knows best, and, finally, on a general puffery about one's own importance to the healing process. Consequently, instead of perceiving the client as a unique person—caught in complex and troubling life circumstances that might have knocked any of us off balance—and responding to that client with respect, support, warmth and empathy, the high-enders are more likely to impose their own values and prescriptions* upon the client, in effect negating the client's own unique strengths, his or her own tendencies towards self-actualization. Put in the terms of the current discussion, the higher the choice of helping professional, the more likely will the client hear the beating of distant drums in the treatment room, the drummer often being the self-appointed representative of the community, the therapist, himself. Since, as you begin this adventure, a music teacher is most likely to be your most consistent source of musical authority, your therapist for problems in music making, I intend to give you some things to think about concerning this new relationship in your life. It is where your structuring of positive reinforcements really begins; it is, in fact, the first focal point where the pursuit of music making becomes a turn-on or a chore.

* Sometimes, and all too often, these prescriptions are, in fact, really prescriptions, i.e., drugs.

For now, it would be a natural inclination on your part to seek out one of the more highly respected teachers in your community, making the quite reasonable assumption that a person of this description would serve as an apt guide for your initial efforts. An educated choice, though not necessarily the correct one, then, would be to find someone greatly accepted by his or her peers as artist and/or teacher, one, possibly, who has done some concertizing, and, finally, one who stands for the finest of musical traditions, including, whenever possible, the possession of a distinguished lineage.

> The importance of the lineage (the teaching ancestry of a particular teacher or performer) is to represent that person as the individual conservator of a distinct and distinguished musical heritage. The implicit message is that if one studies with a person who has studied with a person who has studied with a person who studied with Beethoven, that one has been taken into a *fundamentally* correct blood line and will, thereby, be considered to possess a correct pedigree.[18]

I'm sure you are way ahead of me at this point. For now I am going to suggest that the same curious relationship between competency and the psychotherapy hierarchy may have a similar expression in the field of music.* And, why not? On the face of it, what could be a more apt comparison? Functionally, both are, for the most part, experiences in which the client does the letting go, conveying expressions of his soul, exposing his vulnerability; while the professional seeks to provide help—whether of a didactic or emotionally supportive nature—that, hopefully, leads to problem solving and growth. Moreover, ascending the hierarchical ladder in most fields, and most certainly in the field of music, generally implies a rising respect for tradition, and that the proper locus of power and knowledge resides in the professional rather than the client. The inherent problem with taking on a music teacher with rave reviews from his colleagues, particularly as performer, is that this may well be a person committed to adhering to some mix of his

---

* I am, of course, speaking in broad brush terms. There are, thank goodness, a number of exceptions.

own will and that of the "scripture," and, therefore, less interested in accepting and encouraging your embryonic ideas on musical aesthetics. For the most part, this kind of teacher will be a representative of the teacher/tradition-centered school, and what I am suggesting is that, even from the beginning—perhaps most particularly at this point—the thrust of this experience, and the creativity generated, should begin to emerge from your internal wellspring. The ultimate authority for how you express yourself should reside in your own person and receive encouragement both from yourself and those around you.

Although, admittedly, this authority—your own person—is based on a musical self yet unsure of its bearings, it can relatively quickly be educated, refined, made aware. And if this sounds intimidating (and as I read it over, I'm sure that it does), let me hasten to add that further along I will describe how this process will work without a great deal of effort on your part, and how your own musical feelings will begin to develop and flourish. And then, and this is a promise not lightly proffered, given enough time and encouragement, you will become a musical presence to be reckoned with!

The following quote from *The Inner Game of Music* by Barry Green—bassist with the Cincinnati Symphony Orchestra and former teacher at the Cincinnati College Conservatory of Music—underlines this almost certain eventuality:

> When Tim Gallwey [essentially a non-musician who you will recall started this inner game business] finally suggested that I should find out for myself by paying attention to my own experience, I was almost shocked. We have come to expect that authorities and teachers will supply us with their insights and their definitive answers to everything. And yet the answer we're looking for is often right under our nose all along.[14]

The right tempo is the one the artist feels - Sibelius

And now, since I feel I may be carrying the day, I intend to use the very words of our most venerated composers as counter to the traditionalist's position. Moreover, if in their behavior—as for example, Chopin—they have shown a willingness to view their own scores as more fluid than solid, more elastic than brittle, more resilient than a dusty manuscript might promise, should we not be more skeptical of the supposed immutable tablets presented to today's aspiring players? In fact, it is difficult to see, when these facts are viewed dispassionately, how one could take the other side. Let me assure the reader that the information and stories that follow are but a small sample of the evidence, and anyone who reads the literature on these composers through biography and through books on performance practices will find many such instances.

Let us begin with Mozart. It seems a good place to throw down the gauntlet since Mozart's music has unquestionably been given less slack by the traditionalists than any other. The rules for proper Mozart playing are more clearly delineated, agreed upon, and rigidly enforced than is true for the rest of the great composers. You can mess with lots of these creative artists, my friends, perhaps they need your help, but not under any circumstances are you to modify Mighty Mo.

For openers, He (sic) composed at a time in musical history which has come to be called the classical period. Although all music likely to survive the ages is called classical, those whose business it is to classify such things have made this period—the 18th century and part of the nineteenth century—the Classical Period, a sort of creme de la creme, if you will, or, perhaps, holiest of holies. This Classical Music within classical music is characterized as being orderly and homophonic, meaning having one melody predominate, and apparently, since it was embodied by the one true God of the music spheres, Ama Deus, untouchable.

But have we missed the point of Mozart's legacy? Does his greatness mean relegating his notes to the state of an aural painting where there can be no true interpreter, where the creator's contribution is the only currency of value? Painting is indeed a great art form but an unrelievedly static one. The Blue Boy is The Blue Boy is The Blue Boy. There is no place on its canvas for a contribution by the curator. Music, on the other hand, in much the same way that our histories came down before there were books, only lives in the hands of the storyteller. Remember that music is a living and dynamic language and in this way

more closely allied to those other arts involving this form of communication—fiction, poetry, plays and movies—than the more concrete, albeit
wondrous, arts of painting, sculpture and architecture. And as long as
the storyteller gets the main outlines of the story right, as long as history
is served, the narrator/filter must reflect the times and his own predispo-
sitions, his own "reading" of the tale being told. It cannot be helped.
There is no other way with something so dynamic, so personal, so
immutably plastic as is the evanescent, almost uncapturable, beauty of
sound.

Schonberg suggests, for example, that the "piano parts of Mozart's
concerto scores sometimes are little more than a skeleton of what he
actually did on stage," that he occasionally wrote "in a kind of short-
hand, with single notes in the treble and bass" so that he, and presumably other skillful musicians, could exercise freedom and creativity in
how this blueprint would come to life. See, for example, the slow
movement of the Coronation Concerto. In fact, according to Schonberg,
"Mozart constantly improvised not only cadenzas but also embellished
the melodic line as he went along. It is a mistake to approach Mozart's
music with the attitude that the printed note is the final word. Often it
is, or should be, just the beginning."[30]

Not unlike the jazz musician of today, Mozart, whose mind was
always searching for new things to "say," rarely played the same pieces
on different occasions the same way. Indeed, we have his word for it.
In 1783 he wrote home that whenever he played his D major Concerto,
"I always play what occurs to me at the moment."[30] So that what Mozart
put on paper at any given time may have been a result of how he was
feeling the day he faced a deadline for the publisher, how he last played
it in performance, or some other equally random event, with that
version becoming the accepted one. And if you accept this line of
reasoning, it is not a stretch to consider that today's performer—with the
proper feel for the music, for the style, for the story being told—might
supply a new spin, a novel approach to phrasing, a new concept of
balance, that would delight even Mozart and other adventuresome listeners not bound and determined for another replication of the accepted
standard.

With Beethoven, the composer we shall consider next, the evidence
is frankly not as compelling, more shaded with uncertainty, yet withal,

continues to support for this writer the position of a subjective, or freer, interpretation of his music. (I did warn you, remember, that this account would include some serious bias.)

For example, by all accounts of Beethoven's playing, the performances were bombastic, possessing great swings of dynamic change, and tending towards anarchy. He is reported to having literally destroyed many a piano upon which he "played" in his attempt to subdue his audience, wanting them deeply to understand the drama that swept him along. Today's performances of his music, in adhering properly to the text, would pale before such emotional outpourings.

His performance notwithstanding, Beethoven continued to teach his students to have great respect for the composer's intentions and, as you might imagine, was very serious about the importance of the notations of his own scores. The amount of this direction by Beethoven far exceeded those of his predecessors and, as has been suggested earlier, clearly anticipates current practice. For example, his pedaling instructions are very clearly marked, and it is known that he expected these followed to the letter. Yet, it is just as clear—at least if his star pupil Czerny is to be believed—that when he played he all but ignored these markings. Certainly the overuse of pedal does seem inherent in the accounts of his playing from other sources. Do we believe, then, his own text, or the reports of his performance? Or, more pertinently, should we pay attention to either?

In the spirit of fair play I am forced to concede that Beethoven's approach to composing was less the issue of the moment than some others—especially the fecundity of a Mozart—and included a great deal of self-editing, often rejecting one draft after another. His final version often bore little resemblance to his earlier work, particularly in the well-worked development sections. The particularity of his "stage directions," therefore, had generally been arrived at only after agonizing reflection, having lived with the material for extended periods. This is not to say that I believe them sacrosanct, thus immutable (clearly against my religion), only that they perhaps need to be taken more seriously than those of some other composers with other mind sets, other priorities.

Of course, this inconsistency—between Beethoven's playing and his detailed direction—may be a case of the veteran, the experienced performer, the genius, suggesting that you do as I say, not as you see (hear) me doing. It is, I suppose, one of the perks of great accomplishment, but where is the logic; and how does it relate to the controversy over fidelity to, versus flexibility in, the interpretation of a score? When a young pianist or initiate takes liberties, it is forbidden, but when an established artist does the same, it is, depending on his or her status in the musical community, given exaggerated approval. It is even suggested by some, particularly those who do not mind traveling in circles, that this is, in fact, why he or she is considered a great artist.

Perhaps it is a case of your having to pay your dues. And although I can somewhat, if dimly, perceive the psycho-logic here, I cannot say the same for the rational logic. Certainly it is intimidating and bewildering to the neophyte who hears great artists do things that his teacher says are not acceptable practice when the student tries them on.

Brahms was asked why he seemed to play at different tempi—among other changes—from one playing to another: "Do you think I'm such a fool, he explained as to play them the same way every day?"[2]

In fact, no matter how we might try, it is quite impossible to play a composition twice in precisely the same way. Moreover, rather than staying with a "grooved" reading, time after uninvolved time, it is imperative that you be responsive to where the music is taking you. Since on a certain occasion the piano is uneven, your fingers are cold, somebody coughs, or, most importantly, you have new ideas, the piece that you are playing will go in surprising directions, and it is then that you must be most alert and receptive to all the wondrous possibilities before you.

There is a raised consciousness that you must bring to it, a willingness to be vigorously reactive to a changing reality. A note or a phrase, after all, is meaningful only in context. If you have, for whatever reason, played a passage louder than rehearsed, the measures following must take their cue from these unplanned raised voices. Perhaps it would be instructive to consider an actor remaining blindly loyal to his text no matter what others are "feeding" him. The alert performer, knowing the overall structure of the play, must take as his guide, even if falsely given, that which does occur as he scurries (improvises) to bring the sequence back on familiar ground.

And so, Chopin, on one occasion of the playing of his own *Barcarolle,* arranged to reach the climax at a pianissimo level (very soft-

ly)—as opposed to the clearly marked forte (loudly) of the score—and
as forced to modify the surrounding passages to accommodate this surprising reading. That he did so successfully can be seen by Halle's
reaction: "one remained in doubt if this new reading were not preferable
to the accustomed one."[30]

According to other observers, this was not at all unusual for Chopin
and, in fact, may have been the norm. "One of Chopin's pupils
complained that: 'his only method was to play like an angel and then
tell me to do likewise...the hopeless part of it was...each time he
played, his interpretation was entirely different.'" And again, Dart:
"those who heard (both) Liszt and Chopin play wrote in admiration of
the elegant way in which they varied their music from performance to
performance, adding new passage-work and revising the layout of the
accompanying chords."[8]

This willingness of Chopin to experiment, to edit, to search for
more interesting ways of presenting his material, must call into question
the sacrosanct inflexibility with which his scores have been represented.
All of the evidence, for this composer at least, is that had he survived
until contemporary times, he would still be modifying the score; that
change, novelty, surprise was a great deal of the charm and excitement
in his music. Although he might not have agreed with many of those
attempting to "improve" on his score, particularly if these efforts were
either excessive or lacking in creativity, he would have been even less
attracted by those who reified his efforts. And Mozart most certainly
would have agreed with the contemporary composer Walter Piston—to
a young musician on the playing of one of his works—"I don't care what
ideas you have—as long as you have ideas."

"It must be repeated once again that composers are far less finicky
about having their music edited by imaginative musicians than most
traditionalists begin to realize."[29] The key here, of course, is imagination. But it is important to note that by throwing out the contributions
of the thoughtful interpreter through narrow censoring practices, you
have deprived the cultural community of untold artistic resources. Is it
not time to swing the pendulum, if not back to extreme liberalism, then
away from excessive adherence to the norm?

*****

Listening to (Significant) Others?

To refrain from imitation is the best revenge
Marcus Aurelius

There arises a question in the process of choosing a new piece, or even in the early stages of its practice, as to whether a student should listen to how it is played by the great musicians of our time. This is, clearly, a variation on the theme of who or what is the proper authority for your interpretation of a piece of music. Of course by now, I'm sure, you feel you know my position on this topic, and essentially you would be right. However, this is not a simple question. After all, the only way that you can decide whether a piece is meaningful for you, one you want to work on (and work on and work on) is to listen to it first. In fact, it may be important that you listen several times to be certain this is music you will love in December as you did in May.

But, clearly, as soon as you are involved in the listening process, you are unavoidably receiving a number of leading signals as to how this piece is played by one of the master pianists of our day. You are acquiring a bias that is a natural consequence of your investigation. And this influence may be in competition with other sources: your teacher—if your teacher is typical—or the editor of your particular music edition— and these can be dramatically different.

As you can see, there certainly is no shortage of cooks serving up this musical broth. It's like making a movie with the writer supplying the original material, then having his or her product go through many, many other hands—the writer of the screen play, the cutter or movie editor, the director, the actor, and many more—before its final expression on the screen. Although the cast may not be quite so crowded around your project, you still must keep a wary eye on them.

As I thought about this subject—whether to listen to established artists play a piece before bringing one's own feelings into play—I was struck by the similarity to the doing of research on a book before the writing of that book. Although on a first hearing this connection may seem tenuous, intrinsic to both is the possibility of expressing yourself in a deeply personal, and potentially public, manner. And, in both cases, you have a choice from the outset on how much you will rely on others as you formulate, and gear yourself up for, that expression. Since this is something (the writing of a book) which is new for me and since I suppose I would be deemed a self-taught writer—probably the norm for most writers—I have never been sure what I was "supposed" to do to get the thing going.

I have tried writing many times in the past. Each time I would begin by dutifully reading, and taking notes on, everything even remotely related to the area of interest. In other words, before hazarding a single word onto the uninviting, cold blue screen, I would do the research "required." How else could you learn what the big guys have said on the subject? At a bare minimum, you would not write a book that has already been written. *And, you would also be in a position to use others more experienced and wiser as support for your uncertain theses.*

Well, whether this decision to spend hours in the library writing on 3 by 5 cards was an effective initiation to literary accomplishment, or a reasonably sophisticated defense against potential foolishness, it invariably had a massive inhibiting effect on my efforts. I simply had to know what everyone else knew before I would commit myself. This is, of course, a life time endeavor for any subject of consequence.

It took quite a while but I finally figured out two things, each more important than the other. The first is that using this approach had never resulted in a book being finished and *never ever would!* And second, that I was simply not trusting that I had anything original to say; further that I had to have permission for any position I was going to take, and support or evidence to back up every point on which I was in the least uncertain. It seemed important, in other words, to avoid any position of vulnerability, of being defenseless or *without authority*, on ideas bubbling up from within.

While there is no question that research has validity, that reading and consulting what others have to say can stimulate your thinking, garner rational support, and/or challenge you into effective rebuttal; it can also, if done without a governor, stifle creativity, channel thinking, even encourage the use of a vocabulary and a rhythm not in your "native tongue." If these latter sound like arguments against doing research while attempting a scholarly work, they are not. It is simply a question of order.

And speaking of order and returning to the advisability of doing "research" on pieces that you are interested in playing—listening to recordings, consulting others, making notes (pun unintended)-it is my suggestion that the best way to "find" yourself, once committed to this process of discovery, is to listen to others in a studious way *only after* you have made a considered "argument" in your own behalf.

I know! I know! How will you be able to tell if you want to live with a piece if you haven't heard it enough to know your connection to its story? I propose this compromise: listen a few times in a non-analytical, naive way. If the answer is yes, I must have this piece, I will not be denied, then, by all means, start working on its mysteries—but, without a "listener's guide." Put the recording away! When you feel reasonably comfortable regarding your interpretation—and this can take weeks, months, even years—then, and only then, unearth this original spur to your imagination and compare notes (this time it was intentional). It will be quite the experience for you to compare your level of congruity with other members of your working crew: the composer, the editor, and your teacher (if she or he has been able to practice even a modicum of self-control).

Oh, one other thing. Besides biasing your own creative potential, listening to a great artist play a piece on which you are currently working can be an incredibly intimidating experience. The technical difficulties are usually tossed off effortlessly evoking serious doubts that this is something that you could, in your wildest, ever do. Unfortunately, many great pianists play things fast simply because they can. Often as not, the same piece might get a fairer shake, even a more beautiful reading, at a more modest tempo.

But the great danger, especially if the artist is widely acclaimed, is a conclusion that what you are hearing is the correct and accepted interpretation, that this is how this piece is "supposed to" go. Trust me, in my book (and that, thank God, is where you are) there is no "supposed to." I know this is a tough concept but if you are going to go down my garden path, you must be prepared to wear some heavy mettle (sic). In other words, go it alone. Don't rely too heavily on your teacher, don't look around for permission to play it as you would like. Plow that ground yourself. You will be surprised that the more you exercise this critical function of musical self-determination, the more you will want to.

You can always listen to the master players, and solicit your teacher's point of view, *after* you have gone through this process, *after* you have made all the small and large decisions leading to how this piece will sound best in your hands. Following this approach you will arrive at a relationship with a composer and a reading of the piece that is entirely original, compelling and, yes, valid. Upon hearing others play a composition that you are on intimate terms with, you might find yourself saying without apology, "Hey, I play this piece if not better, then differently from this other fellow,"—beginning, in this gradual way, the profoundly important process of musical self-acceptance.

As a result you will begin to gain a confidence and an increased tendency to paying attention to that inner drum, to turning up the signal from the barely audible tap tapping to pounding tympanic toms. With all of the pressures bombarding us from without for all our years, most of us have naturally lazied in the external mode. Paying attention to what is for you the right and separate path takes a great deal of resolve and constant practice.

And I wouldn't be in any great hurry to do this listening to those others out there, to this unessential endpoint of the process. Personally, I take years with a piece of music, growing into it until it feels like I had a part in its creation. Each piece becomes a cherished friend. And a friendship that matters is one that has a lot of give and take, of testing of boundaries, of "talking" things out. Finally, with this kind of loving patience, you will find the right voice and, by golly, it will be your own. Only then is it time to listen to others, to take freely when they have something interesting or remarkable to say. Having gone through this process you are now in a position to know what is helpful, what is not, what is consistent with your auditory "vision," what would only detract. You have the best of both worlds: you are your own person and your very best musical friend. If I may turn Pogo on his head, I have seen my friends and they is us.

Should we put our soul into the older works according to their own soul? Not at all! Only in approaching them with our soul are old works capable of surviving. It is only our blood that makes them speak to us. The really historical performance would talk to ghosts -
Nietzsche

My sweet irreplaceable you - Line from Gershwin song, "Embraceable You"

I like you just the way you are - Mr. Rogers

Gordon Allport, a psychologist who did the seminal work on intolerance, said that all of us are in some ways like all other men [persons], like some other men [persons], like no other men [persons]. While this is demonstrably true, it is the latter, the realization of how we are like none other, which can most reinforce our feelings of self-satisfaction, of self-love, of a sense of immortality as we assess this life of ours. "He was one of a kind." "When they made this person, they threw away the mold." "They don't make them like that anymore." Statements of ineffable praise, indeed, sentiments that most of us either believe about ourselves or yearn to be true. That is what this chapter is all about, of course, with the taking on of a musical journey just one supremely gratifying alternative for finding the way.

The paths for finding your own way are everywhere. You can be like all other sales persons, some other sales persons, no other sales persons. You can dress like all other persons, some other persons, no other persons. You may need to be different in all respects—a heightened pursuit of individuality—or to find your place in the sun by some powerful and focused form of expression.

After all, music lives through interpretation. Between a musical work and the world stands the interpreter who brings the score to life by his performance. Who better than you knows how you feel about this work? Who is better qualified than yourself to express this love?

There is one last point concerning your right, even obligation, to impress your own sensibilities recognizably into the performance of a musical composition. Beyond the fact that it is critical for purposes of authentic self-expression, there is a compelling reason which relates to the learning process itself. As neurologist Frank Wilson puts it. "The musician engaged in an active process of organizing, shaping, and harmonizing sounds is by this means changing the sound-processing mechanism with which he listens to music." The person who learns in an imitative (passive*) fashion is not learning nearly enough about what (personal) music making is all about, and will not be altered sufficiently either on a physiological level nor in the confidence needed for the performing of other pieces of music to come.[33] Simply parroting what others have suggested—the composer, the editor, a teacher—is not unlike the student who transfers a lecturer's text to his notebook and then to the test booklet without mussing his brain in the process. For the learning and assimilation of a musical composition to be a truly meaningful experience, one that changes your ability to hear and to contribute, you must enter into the collaborative mode; you must bring your creative self into the relationship. It is your activity that is important. It is the imposing of *your* ideas into this now sacred arena, the effects of *your* thoughtful mediation into this music making process that will facilitate the emergence of a voice that is your own, for now and for all notes to come.

If all of the discussion about doing it your way smacks of self-indulgence, I would suggest that it is the act of reaching inside that will allow you to make contact with another in ways authentic and meaningful for both. To perform another's conception is to act the part, to realize your own is to risk before others. It is this latter, ultimately, which has the potential for a truly moving expression of your self.

In this vein Vladimir Ashkenazy discusses the experience of listening to Sviatoslav Richter:

> I think he communicated more than anyone else complete devotion and sincerity to his art. When I look back, this is what attracted me most to him then, and continues to do so today. *I now understand that the strongest element in his magnetic appeal to audiences is his conviction that what he does is absolutely right at that particular moment.* It comes from the fact that he has created his own inner world, absolutely complete in his mind, and if you argue with him about anything it's almost no use. He might say "Yes, perhaps you

---

* If you have been a passenger in a car trip which has a number of twists and turns, you know how much more difficult it is to remember the route as passenger than if you were the driver and the getting there depended on your actually making the decisions (left at this street, right after the 7/11, etc.) along the way.

are right, but I just don't feel it that way. This is what I feel (*at the moment*) and this is the way I play." And that's it... Then Ashkenazy again, putting a finger exactly on the nature of a Richter performance. "I don't often agree with him after the performance, but during it I can see that everything fits together and is completely sincere and devoted, and that wins me over."[30]

In this artistic playground, if you cannot accept your own special way of doing things, from how you sit at the instrument to how you "hear" the music, you won't be loved for who you are but who you'd rather be. This is true no matter how facile you become in turning out the notes, how smoothly the music flows from your fingers. You may fool some of the people all of the time, and perhaps all of the people some of the time...Oh, you know the rest. It is particularly true for your own perception, your own appreciation of this experience.

When you are playing a piece for someone—and that time will surely come—you must listen attentively to what you are doing and attempt most purposefully to please yourself, not even considering for a moment the aesthetic needs of the other person. Do what is most delightful, most stimulating, most novel, most balanced, most fun for your own sensibilities. Do not rush. Revel in this moment, then the next one, not even considering whether the listener is interested or even there. If your focus is on whether the other person is captivated by what you do, you will, paradoxically, reveal less about your imaginative processes. I am tempted to draw a sexual analogy but I will resist the temptation except to say that if you are able to do this thing, if you are able to musically love yourself, you will be taking great strides towards liberation and joy. And, curiously enough, in so doing you will allow the other person to appreciate more fully who you really are.

Teacher

Remember that to change your mind and follow him who sets you right is to be none the less free than you were before -
Marcus Aurelius

They know enough who know how to learn -
Henry Brooke Adams

Those who trust us educate us - George Eliot

Everywhere, we learn only from those whom we love -
Johann Wolfgang Von Goethe

Frank Wilson, the neurologist who writes so persuasively on all of us having the gifts and the necessary equipment for the making of music, also has it right about the teaching experience: "No single decision you make will have greater impact on the outcome of your musical aspirations, and probably no single decision in a musician's life is made so naively."[33]

Going to the Well(s) One Time Too Many.

Howard Wells, an immensely satisfying pianist living in San Diego, performed many times at the Words and Music Book Gallery—a glorious book store and performing arts center that we shall visit later on. Howard, on a given night, could play with the angels. (For future reference, please make note of the company.) He was, on those evenings, with his unique gift for being with an audience, the equal of any performer anywhere.

After being in the presence of Howard on one of those occasions when he turned all our heads, I decided, what the hell, despite my misgivings about taking lessons—I last had taken lessons almost seven years before—despite my reluctance to give my trust to the unknown qualities of yet another teacher, if this great man would have me as his pupil, I'd take the plunge.

Why would this even be a question? One would think this a rare opportunity. And it was. But no decision that you make concerning your musical experience is as important as the careful selection of a teacher, and about no decision do I have such a mix of feelings.

For now, let us reflect on the source of this ambivalence, the seeming advantages and possible pitfalls of the teacher-pupil experience. Afterward, I will tell you what happened at my first piano lesson with the remarkable Wells.

From an apparently unrelated sector, let's look at the results of some rather dismaying research. Psychological investigators have long known that roughly one-third of the people who turn to counseling for problems in living will receive relief, another third will experience no change, and the rest will actually be worse off! The more surprising finding is that the outcomes are about the same or better for those individuals who share their problems with bartenders, hair stylists, and, most importantly, friends!

As noted previously, I see the function of the music teacher as roughly paralleling that of the counselor, albeit in a musical context, and I would like to suggest that the chances of your getting an effective, thoughtful and caring piano teacher are nearly the same, i.e., about one-third of the time, and, without going into it here, for much the same reasons.

Since the odds are somewhat daunting, and since you may not have enough information to tilt the chances in your favor, what should you do? How will you find that one musical counselor in three who can provide a positive experience for your considerable enthusiasm? And, if I may challenge the conventional wisdom, should you even be looking?

Let's take up the last question first. Most people feel a need for substantive direction and an even greater desire for having someone to "report" to, and be with, in their early and uncertain musical trials. Others, on the other hand, prefer working things out for themselves. If you are in this latter group, if you have always preferred only a helpful nudge on your bike to stay erect, you might, surprisingly, be better off going it alone—at least for the time being. This is particularly true if, having interviewed a number of candidates—I will supply a list of pointed questions for that critical interview later in this chapter—none seems to satisfy some kind of intuitive comfort zone. Better to wait. Much better.

To be sure, with the right teacher, lessons can be a joyous experience contributing dramatically to your feelings of musical well-being. But the wrong teacher...*I* know you can do it. But what is important at this stage is how *you* feel about it. Starting with an unsympathetic or ineffectual teacher can have a disquieting and even terminal effect on the most musical of hearts.

Thus, a great deal of caution and enlightened self-interest must go into this choice of musical counselor. For some inexplicable reason, Charles Cooke, in his otherwise wonderfully satisfying book, *Playing the Piano for Pleasure*, devotes surprisingly little space, a scant one page, to the subject of teacher selection, dismissing its importance with the ready assurance that there are thousands of qualified persons easily found "just waiting to help you."[6] That is like saying that now that you are an adult, there are thousands of eligible helpmates just waiting for your hand. While technically true, nothing could be further from a thinking person's reality. Until you find the right teacher, one who embodies a mix of nurturance and wisdom, it is incumbent upon you to practice musical celibacy.

Frank Wilson suggests that your musical leanings need strong consideration:

In my view, your training must *from the very beginning* deliberately guide you toward the goal of making your own independent judgments about the quality of your playing [Emphasis added]. There is a serious threat to your growth if this does not occur, because if your interpretation must always be approved by someone with greater knowledge, your music ultimately can only be imitative. If this happens, you've missed the boat.[33]

This sentiment, of course, does not argue for having or not having a teacher, but it is clear that the choice, from this point of view, must be one that involves a very special person, one who can reinforce the uniqueness of the student, even in the early stages of his or her development. In the real world this very special person is not one easily found, Charles Cooke notwithstanding.

John Holt, one of the outstanding educators of our time, has made a life-long study of the teaching process and has concluded:

> The trouble with most teachers of music, or anything else, is that is that they have in the back of their minds an idea that: "Learning is and can only be the result of teaching. Anything important my students learn, they learn because I teach it to them." It is not enough for them to be helpful and useful to their students; they need to feel that their students could not get along without them. All my own work...has led me to believe quite the opposite, that teaching is a very strong medicine, which like all strong medicines can quickly and easily turn into a poison. At the right time (i.e., when the student has asked for it) and in very small doses, it can indeed help learning. But at the wrong times, or in too large doses, it will slow down learning or prevent it altogether. The right kind of teacher can be a great help to a learner, particularly of music. *The wrong kind can be worse than none.*[15]

Holt took up cello in his forties. This experience convinced him that:

> ...the teacher I need must accept that he or she is my partner and helper and not my boss, that in this journey of musical exploration and adventure, I am the captain. Expert guides and pilots I can use, no doubt about it. But is my expedition; I gain the most if it succeeds and lose the most if it fails, and I must remain in charge.[15]

Now, finally, with John Holt whispering in one ear, Frank Wilson in the other, I rang the bell to Howard Wells' apartment for my first lesson. In that briefest of moments I thought about past teachers. Moving about from one city to another, I have had the best and, possibly, nearly the worst of them. One made me so keenly aware of my deficits that I quit for 17 never-to-be-recovered years, yet was totally reclaimed by another. It was, it seemed, a throw of the dice—as with any relationship with so much at stake—which added no little uncertainty as I heard Howard padding to the door.

Bear with me, however, before he opens the door for there is more that you should know. Part of not being in a more trusting frame of mind had to do with that last teacher back in Albuquerque, New Mexico. No, it was not an experience that left a bitter taste. Far from it. It was the best teaching imaginable in or out of musicland!

Everyone Should Have an Angel on His Side

Her name, in fact, is Rita Angel and soon you will know more about her. I had not studied since that time, almost seven years before, and, in fact, had not even looked for a teacher in our new home of San Diego. I thought it was time to rely on my own musical capital without an Angel to watch over me, and besides, I did not think it probable to find another like her. Not even when his name was Howard Wells.

While in the midst of my reverie, Howard opened the door, and we made our way into his living room; from a corner a Steinway was vying provocatively for my attention. First, however, Howard and I had to chat about the worrisome ground rules. Did we have the same "manual?" Was he a right and good thinker? Would he be sensitive to my delicate condition?

Nothing must be left to chance. Perhaps Howard needed help on the care and feeding of the journeyman piano student even if he were not so inclined. I should be ashamed to describe the mini-lecture I gave this most charming man on what I wanted, needed and demanded in a piano teacher. It was mostly a list of not-to's: he was not to help with technique without invitation; he was not to coach me on interpretation unless he could take it no more; he was not to be active or quick to interrupt my musical "storytelling" efforts.

What was left to do? Lest he become comatose, I had to allow some room for his role in this arrangement. Well, said I, pursuing a measure of generosity, he would be encouraged to talk about style. He would, should I not notice their presence, be allowed to correct wrong notes. Certainly words of praise were not unwelcome. Perhaps that was enough.

He listened patiently to my outrageous exercise in intimidation with his usual quiet charm. He was agreeable. He had passed the first hurdle beautifully...whereupon I sat at the promiscuous Steinway and played a reasonable rendering of the slow movement of Beethoven's *Pathetique Sonata*, the one Karl Haas plays so bravely as his musical logo. To his credit (to my way of thinking) Howard said not a word. Had he successfully negotiated the second hurdle?

Well, not quite. After an implausibly long silence, his first words: "You can't play like that."

You know, I can still hear them. Listen... "You can't play like that." And then, a recital of my sins (how do I count the ways?): from hand position to phrasing, tone production to principles of style, and on. It was a scene from Pinter, so absurd I was removed from possible harm, both of us playing out our parts for the rest of this one-act play.

We spent another half hour together, talking pleasantly about distant things. One thing, though. I remember not being able to hear very well. There were these sounds, an echo. I listened carefully. There it was again. "You can't play like that."

And so I was on my own once more, and that was OK. Until the right one comes along, I am content. I have firmly in my mind how Rita would respond to my playing these days and that still sustains me.

Subsequently, on another wondrous night of Howard's playing at Words and Music, I was able to tell the anecdote from the stage for everyone's, including Howard's, amusement.

There were other times, other teachers. I had started at the Cincinnati Conservatory of Music with Donald Van Horn, a dear man who gave me a much needed boost in terms of self-confidence; with Robert Goldsand, a virtuoso type at the Manhattan School of Music; Stewart Gordon, then head of the music department at the University of Maryland; Ralph Berkowitz, accompanist of famed cellist Gregor Piatigorsky, and for moments, it seems, a few others, most of whom needed to tell me, because they had the "keys" to this wondrous kingdom, how pieces ought to be played.

I enjoyed them all for their strengths—although not usually in piano pedagogy—but never entirely, because I knew, down deep, something was missing. Between us? In me? In them? I remember Berkowitz, who grandly earned his teaching fees with stories about his friends—Leonard Bernstein, Aaron Copland, Joseph Gingold, Rudy Serkin, heavyweights all—telling me how a piece of music clearly indicated, in no uncertain terms, its directions and meanings, that "the way" has already been revealed.

How did he know? Because it was there before me! Somehow, the notes and all the rest(s) communicated clearly, unambiguously, from the page to Berkowitz—and most others of his musical generation and repute—just how they should be played; when it was just as clear, to me, that there were other paths, perhaps less traveled, certainly unauthorized, for playing the same notes. But the force of authority that such individuals bring to this experience is intimidating beyond reason. Just look at their friends, the lineage, where they have studied. Look at the years of experience.

In fact, this is why I quit music for so many years. There were these secrets I was not privy to. There were these revelations from the sainted composers to be divined only by the chosen, the Goldsands and his kind—actually, Robert Goldsand must serve as unlikely villain of this piece, courtly, conscientious, and well intended though he was—honored members of the inner circle of sensitive artists, membership of whose ranks I could never hope to attain. I felt this way early on—although Van Horn was wonderful in helping me through this period—not sensitive like the other students, not knowing what they seemed to know, not knowing what "correct" playing was all about. In a medium that should have provided a sanctuary for freedom of expression, doubts of my person were intensified.

"Louder, Margolis," he shouted from across the room, a cavernous divide in space and artistry. Goldsand knew—from his position in the classroom, from his place in musical history, from his musical rank—how this piece should sound even though I am the one playing and he is seated far away, head nodding, bored beyond belief, experiential dark years across the many tabletops and chairs.

This unquestioned authority manifests itself in many fields of teaching, but in a field of artistic expression it is particularly heinous, and needs fists banging on desks from our side of the great divide to rid ourselves of its unconscionable oppression. It took someone like Rita Angel to awaken me—at that time, only dimly—as to what is possible, what is rightfully demanded from this experience. Only years afterwards has it occurred to me with re-sounding clarity how Rita Angel and her kind have placed themselves squarely in the Carl Rogers humanistic approach to counseling and teaching.

What has Rogers to do with it? Once upon a time there was a man named Freud. Do you believe in Freud? He thought he was God, or at least his disciples did, and he created, almost out of whole cloth, a "science" of personality development, out of which came a "science" of diagnoses, out of which came the "science" of therapy* known as psychoanalysis. It explained everything and it explained nothing. Freud/God somehow was able to take a promising and salutary art form—the golden promise of psychotherapy and counseling—and by a reverse alchemy transmute it into a "respectable" scientific discipline, the proper purview of learned doctors of medicine.

But it more closely resembled science fiction with innumerable, unproven hypotheses accompanied by unsuccessful attempts to cure the "neurotics" among us. Far worse than a passing fad, its unfortunate ideas have permeated much of Western culture. It took from medicine (or perhaps strengthened) the idea that the doctor knows insufferably best, that your problems in living stem inevitably from your early experiences, and, without the good doctor to guide you towards health, you shall surely wallow in your own neuroses. Moreover, whatever problems in living you run up against may be likened to some medical dysfunction, dressed in psychobabble terminology, and you, dear patient, cannot begin to make curative headway without the trained hands of the philosophical descendants of the great sorcerer of pseudo-sexuality.

Along came Carl Rogers—with the wisdom and the courage to go against the prevailing trends of early 20th Century thinking—who assert-

---

* This attempt to reduce the complex mysteries and wonder of the human creation to a system of sexual and other primal impulses had unfortunate consequences for the therapeutic encounter itself. Instead of allowing the healer to come closer to his subject—a requisite in this loving process—analysis created an awful and artificial distance between the healer on high and the "pitiful sick wretch" below in his (the healer's) care and obligation.

ed that each person must be considered an unique and a valuable resource for finding his or her own way.[26] Moreover, each person (or at least most of us) has the potential to do just that, to strive towards growth with all that that portends. Instead of a pathological pull, implicit in virtually all of Freud's writings, dragging us to mean and uncomprehending depths, there is in the vast majority of individuals a natural, even awesome, tendency towards positive growth. When coupled with those elements required for survival—food, shelter, security—all that is needed for the full realization of one's extensive potential is the nurturance that our fellow humans, when on their best behavior, can provide.

These ideas derived from the world of counseling and psychotherapy are clearly applicable to teaching (music and otherwise), parenting, and, in general, our capacity to nourish one another. For what can be more nurturing than to feel accepted, respected, and honored for one's mode of expression, one's individual style. What more emotionally sustaining experience can one imagine than to have one's inner feelings and expressions affirmed as valid, as significant, as worthy of a hearing. In what other experience of life is one as likely to acquire a more lasting confidence, a fullness of self, the energy to persevere as when one is fully affirmed for what one shares from within.

When I began this section it had been my intention to recount a loving series of anecdotes illustrating how Rita Angel exemplified the essence of ideal music teaching. But as I read the paragraphs above, I find that I have already accomplished my purpose: that to describe what happened in those years would inadequately portray the power of this experience. The relationship between teacher and pupil was correct, affable but not particularly social, yet by her total acceptance of my efforts, so artistically and personally affirming. In the pursuit of my goals in music, and more, it has sustained me all these years. If you will reread those few paragraphs before, you will know why my time with Rita was one that I shall always treasure. Let me, with all the feelings that this means to me, wish the same for you.

Oh, and one other thing. When Howard made his pronouncement—you remember the one—he never laid a glove on me.

Just as there has been a salutary movement away from authoritarianism within the mental health movement during the latter half of the 20th Century, there have been similar rays of enlightenment in other disciplines, particularly those of higher education. Student-centered learning has been a powerful force among progressive academics for some time and it is good to report healthy inroads in some rather unexpected areas.

In the authority-laden halls of medicine, for example, even with the good doctor of the scalpel, there has been an increasing acceptance of a more egalitarian working relationship between healer and patient. A person going for surgery these days is now more likely seen as an unique individual, a person with questions, a need for knowledge, fears, hopes, a desire to be heard, all of which, if elicited and made overt, can contribute to the recovery process.

Well, if it can happen in that last bastion of authoritarianism, certainly the music teacher, a respected member of the humanities, should not ask the piano student to interpret great works of art without attention to his or her feelings on aesthetics, on music making, on his hopes and fears of performing, on his self-image and, most importantly, on the personal vision that he brings to the music performance.

Let us pause. I've wandered across the disciplines concerning the potential role of a music teacher in your life and whether at this point you even need this kind of figure. If your answer remains yes—I want someone who will act as guide, or collaborator, or loving friend, perhaps all of these—then it is time, indeed, to get on with the search process.

The first thing to remember is that the ability of the teacher/candidate to perform, no matter how impressive, must not be the litmus test upon which this decision turns. Too much fame, too much artistic accomplishment in that corner, may foreshadow the correctness of *your* interpretation to reside unimpeachably in the guide/teacher as protector of our "precious" musical heritage. What you most need at this point, or, indeed, any point, is one who will appreciate you for the unique and sensitive ways you have for perceiving the world, and the difference you will make as you struggle to find your own voice within this artistic medium.

To Find That Teacher

If you know other people, particularly adults, currently studying with a teacher/candidate, ask them to describe the experience: (1) Do they love going to the lessons? (2) Do they feel inordinately nervous when they play for their teacher? (3) Does the teacher encourage participation by the student in the selection of pieces, in the trying out of original interpretations, in the creation of different work habits or methods of practice? (4) This may be the big one: Does the student leave the lesson with a charge sustaining his enthusiasm and his attraction to the keyboard throughout the week? (5) This may be an even bigger one: Does this experience, when all is said and done, make the person feel better about himself? If the answers to these questions are to your satisfaction, then the teachers in question are solid candidates.

Unfortunately, you may have to carry out your search by means of the Yellow Pages, or by other equally blind methods. Not to worry. You have time, and after consideration of the issues raised in this book, you will have plenty of questions.

When you have your first appointment with a likely candidate, be prepared to ask some of these questions: Does the teacher feel strongly about the sanctity of the musical manuscript? Since most will, be prepared to evaluate this as a matter of degree rather than a black or white response or you may run out of candidates. Does the teacher have inordinately strong feelings about the way he or she would have you approach the keyboard? Be particularly watchful for those birds. They seem incredibly blind to the marvelous diversity of the human condition. And worse, it presages other areas of musical intemperance.

Will the teacher allow a certain amount of freedom concerning choice of repertoire, practice methods, and, most importantly, the issue of platespinning? (Sorry I haven't been more clear about that. We'll get to it, I promise.) He or she must understand that you are not interested in the "Row, Row, Row Your Boats" of the beginners' musical world but the stuff that has moved you as a thinking, feeling adult; further that you are ready to take on these pieces before getting much older.

I needn't tell you this but here goes anyway. As your teacher fields your questions, which may well be a new experience for him or her, and which may take more than one session if you are not as aggressive as I, the important thing is not so much the answers (the words) but the vibes (the music, if you will). As in any important social scene, the words that don't mesh with the music are the ones to flee from. Don't settle! Not here!! Not anywhere!!! If you will not seek the best for you, who will? And who, if I might ask with the passion this printed page permits, deserves it more?

Structure

But keep to the work: it is a glorious end in itself as it slowly but surely improves your playing and thereby intensifies all your enjoyment of music. The work's the thing! - Charles Cooke

Practice done in the spirit of why-do-I-have-to-do-this is worse than none at all. The only good practice is that done with zest and enthusiasm - John Holt

The student should practice exactly what he wants to learn and—if the practice is to attain maximum efficiency—only what he wants to learn. Put differently, he should examine his goal and let the obstacles that keep him from it be what he practices - William Newman

Quoted earlier: "Don't you wish that your parents had made you take music lessons when you were little? The answer is, no, I don't. I think that such forced exposure probably would have turned me away from music, as it has so many others."[15]

I could not agree more. Taking up music late in life has meant a number of unforeseen advantages for which I am intemperately grateful. This is not a case of putting the best face on an unfortunate reality. True, I will not become a classical pianist of note, nor play with a band like Duke Ellington's (both of which I would give up 34 minutes of my life for). But the personal meaning of making music could not be greater; the commitment to learning, more intense. Perhaps it is true that one who has studied for a lifetime derives equal pleasure. It is unimaginable, however, that those who do this to keep bread on the table can rival my relish of the practice session, or the pleasure in absorbing the latest piece learned into the depths of my being. The difference between having to and wanting to in this sphere of life is the same as in any other except that here it is amplified by the lens of one's personal expression.

I was not abused as a child. Nor am I a son of an alcoholic. But, I was reared as an aesthetically deprived child, Lawrence Welk and Sammy Kaye being the upper limits of progressive musical education in our home. And, like the child raised in a poor environment driven to accumulate wealth in a way that the born rich cannot appreciate, I am driven to make up for all the beautiful sounds that I have missed. And that is a good feeling, not one to regret. For one thing, I never feel that learning about music and practicing are things that I have to do; rather, they are what I want to do, now get to do, and thrive most joyously in the doing.

Too, this being a member of the late starters' club has forced me to create systems of practice and ways of thinking about things, musically, but then generally, that, had it been easier for me, simply would not have happened. By the time I started really studying piano seriously in my second pass at the thing (first pass, as a nineteen year old, second when I was 39 with 17 years off for bad behavior),* I had learned a fair amount about how I like to learn and how to maximize that learning. One of the really important things to note, for example, at least for me, and I'll bet for you, too, is how much faster and more confidently I learn when I love what I am doing and when I am generously rewarded for my efforts.

By the time that I got to you through this writing, I had developed a system of related principles of practice and a general philosophical approach which, I believe, will take anyone to competent and satisfying music making. All of the elements that go into this endeavor have been painstakingly thought through and tested** for their motivational properties. Actually, these latter, if I am to be completely honest (I need to practice this from time to time), was completely unintentional. It is only in retrospect that these motivational properties emerge and take on the importance that I now believe them to have. Fortunately, and almost coincidentally, they have proven to be consistent with effective learning—possibly, even, the best way to learn. It was as though I had

* Someone else's. I have already recounted this sordid tale in the chapter on teaching.
** On my own person. This is a small sample, I'll grant you, but it is remarkably skewed.

said to myself, "let me think of all the things that will make this learning situation pleasurable and rewarding so that I will have no choice but to stay with the program."

All of the elements of this system, in fact, are not the result of a rigorous and knowing discipline on my part, but of a reaching toward pleasure with the end only dimly perceived. The only discipline that I seemed to possess was a proclivity for making certain that the learning process was a pleasurable one. I am absolutely a musical hedonist, and so it turns out, happily, that the "no pain, no gain" school simply does not apply here.

The pleasure in this approach begins almost immediately when the new student learns that he or she will not be subjected to a lot of meaningless drills and exercises bound fast by the timely chains of the heartless metronome. Those mind numbing activities, perpetrated by (usually) well-meaning, dedicated musicians with an insufficient zest for living, are, for the most part, unrelated and irrelevant to most musical masterpieces. In other words, you can "practice" a musical life quite nicely without them. A satisfactory technical competence can be achieved in much more interesting and goal-directed ways, and I intend to present a number of these for your consideration.

The next revelation, in this Epicurean* approach to musicmaking, is that your personal relationship with the great composers will be initiated very early in the process.** Naturally enough, the pieces will have to be relatively simple, but they do not have to be child's play (technically or spiritually) or simplified (edited) into a state of musical ennui. You will be able to play meaningful and appropriate music early on because there is plenty of such music in the repertoire available for these purposes, and because you will choose a teacher who will support this plan. As a result of efficient practice methods and rewarding principles that I am going to be sharing with you, you will be wading into the great masterpieces much earlier and more effectively than you in your wildest would have thought possible.

---

* Epicurus, Greek philosopher (342-270 B.C.), held that the highest good in the external world was pleasure.

** Brahms or Chopin or Beethoven, not the *John Thompson Modern Course for the Piano* lineup of Biehl, Gurlitt, Concone, and Spindler.

A blue print for practicing will be furnished for your consideration which will allow customization of the general principles for your kind of person with your kind of schedule. You won't, for example, have to wonder about how much time to spend on a piece or, more importantly, how much time to spend on the difficult sections of a piece.

Attention will be paid to how you pick out pieces that you want to play and, perhaps most significantly, a great deal of emphasis will be placed on teaching you how to keep a number of these all going, figuratively, at the same time. This is where the platespinner will make his presents (sic) felt.

And finally, you will be given some helpful hints on how to focus your attention. You will learn how to stay in the hear and now—a musical residence of immense pleasure, making possible the rapid learning one hopes for and deserves.

And finally (I know I said that above, but I wanted your attention badly), you will learn the secret of happiness as it applies to learning to play a musical instrument and possibly its adaptation to other, albeit less important, areas of your life.

When you have experienced the full impact of this kind of structure, you will see how piano playing can become not only a passion but an enchanting addiction. When I am done with you, you will be practicing so much that you will be alarmed by the pull of the experience—and so will your family and friends. The computer will not even be in second place and golf, bridge or whatever it was that previously had a hold on you, forget it. It is inexorable and terminal. Because of this pleasure-seeking, engaged practice, you will make steady progress, and that will inspire you to practice more which will lead to still further progress and that's the name of this tune. (The music goes round and round, ♪ oh, oh, ooooh, oh, ♩ and it comes out here.) You will come to understand how a musician can practice eight to ten hours a day and not want to stop. Of course, professionals also do it because they have to, because of the intensely competitive nature of the field, and because of the demands of the public for perfection in their art. But you will be doing it, my unsuspecting friend, because you are a gone goose.

To be sure, playing a musical instrument has a kind of romantic allure to start with. It is romanticized in the movies, in fiction and even by real people. But all of that falls away unless the structure of the practice, the means of getting there on a moment to moment basis, is sufficiently engrossing, rewarding and so clearly leading to success that one is swept along by its currents. All too many people start this potentially life-nourishing endeavor only to fall by the wayside buffeted (again?) by feelings of personal incompletion. We are going to make sure that this does not happen to you. The rules that allow you to function without having to worry about choices, the games that allow you to feel good as you move from piece to piece, even measure to measure, the emphasis on unconscious learning and performance, all will give you freedom of expression in a language that will astound and delight both you and, much sooner than you would have guessed, those around you.

I have in these previous paragraphs hinted at some of the elements which contribute to the positive structuring of the musical experience. At this point I had intended to list, in order of their importance, the full complement of these reinforcing agents, and to elaborate on their separate contributions. But I must pause. Before I get carried away with the promises that my enthusiasm produces, before I begin earnestly preaching that what is good for me will, for that reason, be good for you, I must step back and give heed to a measure of caution. And I must attempt to pay closer attention to the conclusions drawn by that remarkable student and educator, John Holt.

> Part of the art of learning any difficult act, like music, is knowing both how to teach yourself and how best to use the teaching of others, how to gain from the greater experience and skill of other people without becoming dependent on them. For few people are likely to become good at music, or anything else, who do not learn how to teach themselves. What we can best learn from good teachers is how to teach ourselves better.[15]

Rereading John Holt's words provides much needed braking power to my runaway enthusiasm. Although the things that I have devised to keep my practice motor running have been marvelously effective for me, they may not work the same for you. I offer this system humbly, then, as an integrated model with a number of potentially helpful tips, but, more importantly, as one that will spur your imagination for finding that which works best for you. It is, if you will, a menu with substantive choices but with ample opportunity for personal substitutions.

I suppose that most of the practice methods I have devised could be evaluated with scientific rigor as to their various contributions to pianistic progress. More likely, however, there is no right or wrong path but only that which, by its goodness of fit to your way of doing things, facilitates your being able to stay with the program. I believe that my ways of thinking about this experience have kept me practicing all of these years in a way that following other's precepts—even if shown to be objectively superior—may not have. After all, who is the ultimate customizer, and who knows better what feels good, for this first person singular.

Too, I have a stake in what I create. I have an incentive to make it work since it comes from *my* think factory. The lesson? As you listen to what I have put together, as you hear me surreptitiously trying to convert you to my way of doing things, pay more attention to the process of system building, of learning how to learn—that's where the real game is played—no matter how well I may make the case.

OK. I've made the mandatory disclaimer. Now, let's stop trying to be so damned fair-minded. It's time to discuss the elements of practice that have worked so effectively for me over the years in order to find the ones which will work to your best advantage. The list presented consists of conditions designed to make music making not only possible but more probable. They are created to reinforce your natural inclination to express yourself and, in particular, your readiness to do this in a musical language. After I present this list—it is in descending order, the most important elements at the beginning—there will be a discussion on how each works within the system and how it may be modified for your individual use.

Some last prefatory remarks. There are what I would call ten relatively important elements in this group with two additional, albeit, uncertain candidates—elements about which I have some ambivalence. I had a difficult time ranking within the top ten those which take precedence over the rest. The top five, however, are all nearly equal in impact and stand squarely above the bottom five. Since the system would be decidedly poorer without any one of these, all must be deemed "most" important.

*****

(1) Platespinning

In first place, the feature that separates this approach to music making from all others, and the element that gives rise to the name of this book, is the art of the platespinner. A platespinner, as the name would suggest, is a juggler of sorts with his stock in trade being a number of plates kept spinning atop vertical sticks for much the same reason that his more traditional cousins keep a number of balls on the fly. What this has to do with rewarding the piano student can easily be learned by turning to the chapter of the same name. Some of you, however, particularly those who have actually witnessed this lively art, will already have guessed.

(2) The Secret of The Happiness Scheduler

Also in first place is an eccentric, whimsical, but incredibly motivating method of scheduling, of allotting time for the completion of tasks or the realization of goals, that gives rise to an unreasonable amount of happiness. Unless you are into pathos and think that becoming an artist requires sustained frustration, emptiness and pain, you will enjoy this idea which goes curiously against the usual motivational grain.

(3) Thoreau's Drummer

Certainly a candidate for top honors is the principle that the expression of music must in no uncertain terms be reflective of who you are. How to pay attention to the special rhythms of your own drummer, while screening out the enervating effects of the many rhythms from without, is the focus of this discussion.

(4) Being With Those You Love

Nothing is more important than this one, the sentiments voiced above to the contrary. If we do not play pieces that reach into our souls, move and uplift us, express who we are, then why have we bothered? To some degree, this is a derivative of Thoreau's Drummer but sufficiently important to elevate it to its own talking point.

(5) Keeping Your Eye on the Ball

This is really the big one. You need to stay in the hear and now to get this thing moving. Easier said than done, however, but with Gallwey's help via *The Inner Game of Tennis* and our collective I.Q. points (your's and mine) we'll figure out a way.

(6) Keeping Your Musical House in Order
So that you can tell whether it is you or your instrument that needs work, keep the instrument A-1 and the tune unwavering.

(7) A Rational and Relevant Road to Technical Know-how
Out damned drills, away superfluous exercises. You *must* have better things to do than play scales.

(8) No Brainer Practice Methods
Spend your practice sessions doing, not thinking about what to do.

(9) One Thing at a Time
We're talking about a complex learning task here. I plump for separating the learning of notes from the practice of what these notes mean. You may feel differently.

(10) Give Your Tush a Break
Unfasten that seat belt. Standing makes sitting a good thing. Going at it slowly and with plenty of breathing space will get you there more quickly. There is time for all of it.

Those are the top ten. Perhaps there are things that leap out at you by their omission. If so, then you have already begun the customization process. You have thought of something that will keep you going that either has not occurred to me, or might not work for me. If this hasn't happened, not to worry. You and I might be more alike than it looked at the start.

Oh yes. There are those two other elements of the music work-experience that I shall label alternates for this list. As noted, I have ambivalence about their inclusion, but as long as they are qualified so, they can be addressed. The reason for the ambivalence is that these elements can be rewarding or punishing to the student depending on the circumstances. I speak in the first case of the choice of teacher. As is covered in the chapter on this subject, whether you even require a teacher is up for grabs as far as I am concerned. After obsessing about it, however, I have come down on the side of having a teacher/collaborator if the choice is well considered.

But even the best laid plans for picking mates, friends, or mentors can go astray. If you have made the good choice and defied the odds (see the chapter on teaching) by having it work to your satisfaction, you can most assuredly put this element down as belonging to the structures that will keep your musical journey on track. However, having chosen poorly or unluckily, divorce that sucker before you finish this chapter. Do not assume that it is you. In some mystical, philosophical, and yes, even rational sense, this cannot be. The longer that you stay with what doesn't feel right for you, the longer will you be denied the joy you deserve. 'Nuff said.

The second alternate is a suggestion to gather a number of people together into a group that play for each other on a regular basis. Getting together with others who are going through this same adventure can be a richly rewarding part of your week or month, depending on how frequently you get together. I have formed a few of these groups over the years and, if you choose the membership oh-so-carefully, such a group can not only help you get over your fears of playing for others, it can serve as a forum for talking about the joys and problems of this learning experience, and, perhaps most importantly, it can provide an opportunity for the forging of life-long friendships.

If you decide that getting together with others for these purposes sounds attractive and useful, there are a couple of things I would counsel. The first is to set some ground rules as to proper group comportment, most particularly around the issue of the critique. Actually, there is only one way to go on this: no critique is the best critique. To consider this experience a place for "constructive" criticism is to pave the way for the early demise of the group and the friendships therein. Along with trying out of your wings in this relatively safe environment, the focus must always remain on what it is like to play for others, hoping that the sharing and accepting of these feelings will be helpful to all concerned.

The second suggestion is to begin this experience in a gradual manner, playing for just one other person at a time. You might try this simultaneously with several others, that is, having several two person groups—always yourself and one other—until you see that these are persons who you feel could all work together. In your first trials at this sort of thing, of course, this will also be easier on your nervous system. If your best guess is that these other persons can all live and play in harmony, well then, you have the solid makings of your first musical support group.

Now, in a quasi-systematic fashion, I am going to present that list of the ten rewarding elements to show how these unite and conspire to produce practice sessions of pure pleasure, and have, separately and in concert, created the practice junkie you see before you.

(10) Give Your Tush a Break

Unfasten that seat belt. Standing makes sitting a good thing. Going at it slowly and with plenty of breathing space will get you there more quickly. There is time for all of it.

Sitting at the keyboard for too long a period, concentrating on making every moment count, the ambitious pianist can experience tension levels and fatigue quite incompatible with effective learning. As in circumnavigating the globe, the path to the most effective use of time at the keyboard can also be one of great indirection. Taking frequent breaks while practicing can get you there faster and in better fettle than senselessly keeping your fingers to the ivorygrinder. Getting off your duff is kind to your back, good for concentration—which for most of us turns out to be realized in pitifully brief moments—and allows for much longer periods of quality practice within the same time frame. I would be embarrassed to tell you how much of my practice sessions are given over to striding about the room. On the other hand, every time I sit down, I feel renewed and ready to add impetus (spin) to my charges, those awesome plates under my care.

If these mini R & Rs between practice segments appear a sinful waste, put them to good use by alternating them with chores that are crying for your attention, or another artistic endeavor that you can pursue in like fashion, such as writing or quilt design. Think of yourself as the tortoise, making good time slowly, plodding determinedly towards the goal, expanding the session with its curious alternation of task completions that keep you interested and on course for hours into the night, until the race is won. Thus, simply by engaging in the process, you become a winner.

Anyhow, that is item number ten—rewarding because it keeps one vitally interested in the task(s) at hand, maintains energy at near peak levels, and allows you to alternate this activity with other pleasurable (or loathsome) activities that need attending to. If this doesn't seem a compelling approach to music practice, remember that it is only number ten on my list. Perhaps number nine will be more promising.

(9) One Thing at a Time

We're talking about a complex learning task here. I plump for separating the learning of notes from the practice of what these notes mean. Others feel differently. I'll give my side, and then a brief look at the other.

This element is the most controversial of the ten. Before I continue, moreover, let me clarify the issue at stake. When one learns a piece of music, there is much to attend to: the notes, the rhythms, the harmonies, the meter (speed), the phrasing, the breathing spaces (silences or subtle pauses), the use of pedal, the balance of the voices (the relative loudness of notes played simultaneously), the shape of the melodic line, the key signature, the mood, the style, the meaning behind the notes (or the stuff between the lines), the intention of the composer in terms of emotional content or aesthetic contribution, and probably more, depending on the piece and the sensitivity of the player.

Wow, when I started the last sentence, all nine lines of it, I did not fully realize all that one has to consider. It is not unlike the hoary story of the millipede who, if it considered what it must do to move one inch forward, must certainly perish from complications of the self-conscious. And I can imagine that for the newcomer this extraordinary list of things needing attention is likewise cause for pusillanimous pause. Fortunately, in practice, it is not as daunting as this analysis would convey. Much of what goes on in the learning of a piece occurs on a gradual, almost unconscious level, and we are better off for this naturally bestowed kindness.

Perhaps more importantly, all of the elements of a musical composition can, at a first stage of classification, be divided more simply—as is true of so much of life—into the technical side (how things work), versus the feeling components (how things really work). On the technical front are the notes, the timing of the notes, and anything to do with the correct mechanical delivery of the notes by the player.

Although not as clear-cut as this portrayal would indicate, the complement to technique—the other side of this musical coin—is the meaning of the notes, the feelings one wants to convey, the sensitivity which one imparts to the music. This latter is, of course, the subjective and more inherently fluid side of the musical experience, especially when compared to the stark realities of the black and white notations.

When one takes on the learning of a new piece, one can logically proceed on one of two paths, or, of course, some shading between. The first is to attempt to swallow whole all that has gone into a composition, blending the mastery of technique and the consideration of interpretation as one process. After all, the proponents* of this approach argue, the two sides are integrally related, one having no existence without the other. It is, they would continue, like separating the structure or function of a building from its aesthetic impact. Too, they maintain, practicing notes or passages in a strictly mechanical fashion must lead to playing in an artificially stiff manner in performance.

In fact, as I study the arguments of this moral musical majority, I am impressed with the correctness of their position to the point that it seems nigh uncontestable. I can't imagine how I will have the courage to take up the other side.

And, as if more argument was needed, it might be instructive to think about an actor learning the lines of a play. These lines— composed of words, organized into sentences and paragraphs, then into scenes and acts—can be recited mechanically, as one would nonsense syllables, without heed for their meaning in the play; or, more intelligibly, as elements of descriptions, stories, and communications laden with the

---

* Almost every other existing musician.

variegated colors of the human landscape. Put in this context, it seems clear that the more natural approach favors combining the learning of the words with an appreciation of the soul of the piece.

And yet, I feel strongly about the way that I have resolved this issue for my own comfort, sanity, and, importantly, with regard to learning potential...which is to separate musical considerations from technical practice. Thus, immediately upon taking up a new piece, I strive to learn (memorize) the notes reasonably early in the process and, in a natural complement to the memorization process, have a go at the technical difficulties. Only when I have gotten to the point where the piece is, relatively speaking, mine, one that I am comfortable with in terms of playing the notes accurately, and in time, do I allow myself the luxury of thinking about the musical possibilities. In the beginning stages, at least for this piano-player, thinking about the seemingly infinite variation of musical interpretation is simply too distracting.

Giving a time frame for how long one remains on level one—technique only—for any piece is, for obvious reasons, impossible. Some pieces are much longer and/or much more difficult than others. You might be working on a large number of pieces at the same time—as you will learn, that would be my preference—or you may not have the time to practice that mastering certain compositions require. The time, then, in working at the technical level before "graduating" to a more expressive one, can range from a few weeks to a *few years*. The rationale for this somewhat idiosyncratic behavior, perhaps my defense, is that only when the piece is truly mine will I have the freedom to "ignore" the notes, as it were, allowing for the unbridled freedom to go where the music takes me, reacting spontaneously to the moment. When I give technique this kind of temporal priority, it is not with the idea of having it overshadow my artistic intentions; on the contrary, it is to make sure that the means of music making will be as inconspicuous as possible, that as I attempt to serve the cause of beauty, you will not "catch me in the act."

Actually, unless you are capable of inordinate concentration, it is virtually impossible to play without some musical response to a piece right from the beginning. There is really nothing to worry about since the development of your interpretation will occur naturally over time, as you practice the piece, as the piece annoys you (or you, it), as you attempt to make practicing the piece more interesting, etc.

It is simply easier for me to concentrate on one dimension at a time, to gain mastery over these elements in an orderly sequence.* Otherwise, it feels like I am in an encounter group with the notes where I am constantly asking of them, or of myself, what they (or I) are really like. A certain amount of just flexing the notes, as in exercising, is satisfying on its own terms, and makes it all the more pleasurable when it is time to turn to matters more musically interesting and passionate.

What is more, the opposite is true. When I am attempting to breathe life into the phrases of a composition, I cannot be distracted by the search for elusive notes, by a recitation of time values, by a consciousness of what key I am in, or what the chordal structure is like. All of these elements have to be consigned, by dint of diligent practice, to a part of me as though genetically cast. I have found the only way for me to function in full aesthetic mode is to experience the beauty of the music not complicated by an awareness of the mechanics by which one achieves its expression.

Trying to make progress by the more traditional mode of practice, that is, considering notes and feelings as one, makes the conquering of technical difficulties not only more trying (particularly for a person who has trouble walking and chewing gum in the same rhythm) but, in terms of the pure mastery of the notes, a more prolonged affair. Thus, progress does not seem to be made at the same rate or in the same time frame. The single most effective reward, the one reinforcement that brings me back to the practice session with enthusiasm day by day and even hour by hour, is the knowledge of the "note worthy" progress I am making. This reward of mechanical competence, not mucked up by the vagaries of interpretation, is a real confidence builder. When I see (hear) this happening, and it is much easier to record in the technical quarter than the slippery area of the soul, I am closer to freeing the musician within.

Since I bring to this arena more passion than substance, I suggest that you give both approaches a reasonable trial and to trust whichever feels more addicting. Remember, it is the pleasure pull of these ele-

---

* Returning to the play for a moment, reading the lines as though we have entirely digested the nuances and subtleties of the play from the beginning, while we are concerned with where the furniture is and the choreographed movement of the principles, also seems an intimidating jump.

ments, the compelling arguments to return to the keyboard, that will sustain you over the long haul.

(8) No Brainer Practice Methods
Spend your practice sessions doing, not thinking about what to do.

(7) A Rational and Relevant Road to Technical Know-how
Out damned drills, away superfluous exercises. Tell me that you have better things to do than play scales.

I have joined the two elements above for discussion in the following paragraphs:

Every time you sit down to learn a piece of music, there are many organizational decisions to consider. How difficult a piece should you be working on? Should you start by working on the hands separately? How fast should the tempo be? How long should you practice on a piece and how long should an individual session be? Should you be looking at the music or at the piano or both? But, although the list seems endless, the question that causes the most indecision in a practice session—thus wasting the most time—and the one about which there is very little consensus, is the question of what to do when you make a mistake. Surprisingly, there is very little agreement about the most effective course of action when an error has been made beyond the obvious fact of setting it straight. But fix it how? With one correct playing? With 100 repetitions? With whatever number seems to feel right at the time? Should it depend on how often you have made that mistake before or be more closely tied to how much practice time you have available this day?

To begin with, let us define what we mean by "mistake." In the context of working on technique, it is the playing of a wrong note, or the playing of the right note at the wrong time or with the wrong time value. *Since making mistakes is the most valuable thing that you will do in a practice session—perhaps correcting them could be considered even more valuable—and since making mistakes is an activity with which you will become intimately acquainted, it is critical that this experience be turned from one that is often punishing to one which is mysteriously, indeed, almost perversely, looked forward to.*

I assume you read the phrase "making mistakes is the most valuable thing that you will do" with some puzzlement. But, of course, it *is* negative feedback, or the mistake, that drives the learning experience. It *is* the error that keeps you on track, that gives you information about what needs to be done, that directs you to where the lion's share of your time should be spent. Of course, to make it truly a positive learning experience, one which consistently leads to behavioral change, you must also be (1) extremely vigilant (2) (un)forgiving, and (3) ready to respond appropriately. Here is Frank Wilson, the eminent neurologist, on the subject of mistake making, who in this following quote also introduces the advantages of learning, as we do, in small increments:

> This brings us to a fascinating paradox. Since learning is a process intended to produce change, it is essential that we learn to embrace our errors, indeed to treasure them and rejoice in them, rather than deny or despair in them. For it is our mistakes, when we understand them, that instructs us. As you venture into the world of music in order to refine your own motor skills, remember the paradox, and take heart in your own tendency to improve at a snail's pace: Our physiologic makeup ordains us for a process of change and improvement that take place in steps. As we discussed in the chapter on the motor control system, it is because of this arrangement that improvement becomes stable and dependable.[33] [I would like to add here that we actually must go further than embracing errors. For efficient practice, we must encourage a structure that produces errors a rational and reliable percentage of our time. This will be explained in the chapter on practicing.]

Since this is an inevitable consequence of your learning efforts—in fact, as noted, an integral component of the practice system presented in these pages is the directive that mistakes must happen regularly and in a reasonably predictable ratio—it is clear that one should not be in the position of wondering what to do when those things happen. In other words, the precise behaviors one is going to perform at the point of a miscue should be in place, ready to be activated, as though waiting for their turn.

To find out the specifics of this system, the precise behaviors recommended for responding to the inevitable and necessary errors of the practice session, please read the relevant sections in the chapter on practicing. While you are there, you might want to discover why I believe it to be an outrageous waste of time for the serious (amateur) student of great music to be involved in the incredibly time-consuming task of scale playing, or the mindless performance of repetitive, abstract exercises neither of which is directly related to the playing of most compositions. I expand on the importance of not getting involved in these enervating and, for the most part, highly questionable behaviors in no uncertain terms. Needless to say, it is the absence of these behaviors, when you stop to think about it, which I do whenever I want an extra spritz of endorphins, that is rewarding; the absence of time-wasting, fatiguing, meaningless drills, that is so good for the soul.*

(6) Keeping Your Musical House in Order
So that you can tell whether it is you or your instrument that needs work, keep the instrument in A-1 condition and the tune unwavering.

One important way to structure the practice experience which will unquestionably improve the odds of your frequent return, and the one most often neglected by many amateurs, and even some professionals, is to keep the piano in tiptop service and in as good a tune as your pocketbook will allow. While the piano is a magnificent instrument with many advantages—I've already mentioned the incredibly rich repertoire left to us by the giants of this realm, almost all of whom were pianists, Beethoven, Mozart, Chopin, Brahms, Bach (a keyboardist)—choosing this mode of expression presents disadvantages not immediately apparent. The first is that you can't, unless you are a Paderewski or a Glenn Gould, take it with you. As a consequence, after getting nicely settled on your own instrument and learning a piece somewhere in the vicinity of flawlessly, what you often find at someone's home where you

---

* I am willing to concede that these activities may be indirectly related in the sense that if someone is willing to involve himself in the execution of years of work on scales and intrinsically meaningless exercises, it is a clearcut indication of that person's motivation to succeed.

have been invited to play is a wholly uncooperative instrument not tuned since Jimmy Carter was our chief, giving off sounds unrelated to the keys put in action.

Moreover, the pianist, compared to virtually all other musicians, has but a distant relationship to the inner workings of his instrument. Almost no pianist tunes his piano and must, when he can take it no more, pay for the restoration of harmony. To play a piano which is out of tune, which is virtually every piano all of the time, is to be unfairly penalized for your accurate play. Conversely, when the piano is in tune—a miserly short time it does seem—you will practice in blissful contentment marveling at your own progress and sensitivity. Like that first bite of a sandwich or your lover's first touch, there is nothing quite like it.

The curious thing about the piano is that although it begins to fade before your very ears almost immediately upon its being tuned, it loses this state of grace quite gradually. As a result, one gets used to the changing condition, adapts as one does to displeasing odors, so that this unsuspecting evil is upon your person long before you sense the need for an auditory mask. The recovery of harmony by the miraculous tuggings of the piano tuner is shocking, as though something had been altered inside *your* being, your fingers more accurate, your playing more soulful.

As it so happens there is an excellent remedy for this dilemma. Actually, there are two. The first is to learn how to tune your piano. Before you dismiss this possibility out of hand, let us remember that the pianist is virtually the only musician who shuns this honest work. A guitarist, for example, adjusts his strings many times at a single sitting, often in the middle of a piece. True, his instrument will go out of tune faster than the pianist's—it is a function of the physical design with the pegs not nearly as tightly "locked in" to the main body of the instrument—but he would still tune frequently, because he can, because it is doable, there being but a tiny fraction of the number of strings to keep in balance. Now, however, it has become possible for the pianist as well. With the aid of an electronic device designed for this purpose, one that actually "reads" the number of vibrations that a string puts out per second, almost anybody can gently rough up the piano while staying on friendly turns.

The other remedy for maintaining an instrument with a cheerier, in tune, disposition is to consider the electronic keyboard. Personally, I was an insufferable snob in favor of acoustic instruments before trying the Yamaha Clavinova.* True, it doesn't in all respects resemble a piano, particularly in the sustaining of a note, but the advantages, depending on your situation, are many. For instance, if you live with somebody or near somebody, and most of us do one or the other, and you need to turn the sound down so as not to disturb the neighbors or, more importantly, not to feel self-conscious when you practice, this feature of aural invisibility is outstanding. You can even put ear phones on, having it silent for others, while letting out all stops for yourself.

Another advantage from musical new age electronics concerns the attribute of touch on a keyboard instrument. An even production of tone made possible by an even resistance from one key to the next is of critical importance to a pianist. Because of the simplicity of their design—there is no throwing of hammers towards distant strings—the electronic keyboards decisively have the nod on this score with the additional virtue of being miraculously maintenance free. I have had my instrument now for five years without even an imagined problem of any kind. This in contrast to any acoustic keyboards from my past which have kept me, as a kind of musical hypochondriac, on the edge of atonal despair.

You can even take your Clavinova with you. Although it is bigger than a bread box, my instrument can "accompany" me to far off places, thus maintaining the home court advantage. Too, because it takes up so little space, you can put it virtually anywhere in your home. And there is more. For example, you can play with a number of timbres which by their variety evoke more interest in the practice of some pieces. I frequently put on the vibes sound because of its soothing effect, and it is really quite interesting to hear the same notes decked out in different tonal colors.

But I have saved the big one for last. It is *always* in tune. I still can't get over this, I mean, always! Of course, say you. Well, I had

---

* This is not a plug for the Clavinova. It happened to be what was in the nearest showroom for pianos when I was trying to figure out what to buy for the confines of a small condo. In the movies, however, when you see a coke bottle in a scene, money changes hands for showing these "random" bits of our everyday environment. If the Yamaha people are sufficiently sensitive and caring, moreover, my address is easily attained from my publisher.

never thought of it. After all those years of being annoyed by the lack of consideration of my Baldwin to maintain its social manners, what a pleasure to know that when you sit down for a practice session, the instrument, at any rate, is going to be the same. It is like the kind of friend that we all want, consistently there for you. Wait...there with consistency for you. Since that is so, I, of course, find myself constantly wanting to be there for it.

These are all illustrations of the powerful effects of the consonant reward of tuning and why this item, number six on the list, almost made it to the top five. Now, however, let us move into those more highly rated elements to see why they have made the final cut.

(5) Keeping Your Eye on the Ball

This is really the big one. You need to stay in the hear and now to get this thing moving. Easier said than done, however, but with Gallwey's help via *The Inner Game of Tennis* and our collective I.Q. points (your's and mine) we'll figure out a way.

All would agree that the act of concentration is vital to efficient progress in any sphere of learning. How one can achieve this heightened degree of focus will, because of its importance, be the subject of a separate chapter, heavily influenced by the original writings of Tim Gallwey. Here, as preview, are a few lines by the estimable Mr. Gallwey: "Concentration is the act of focusing one's attention. As the mind is allowed to focus on a single object, it stills. As the mind is kept in the present, it becomes calm. Concentration means keeping the mind now and here. *Concentration is the supreme art because no art can be achieved without it, while with it, anything can be achieved.* [italics added]...By learning to concentrate while playing tennis [piano], one develops a skill that can heighten his performance in every other aspect of his life."[11]

Gallwey's most important contribution, moreover, is that he goes far beyond describing the importance of concentration to the learning process and to being able to perform—which, to some degree, everyone is already aware—to giving intriguing ideas on how to achieve and maintain this incredibly elusive state. It is one thing to understand its critical nature; it is quite another to develop strategies sufficiently engrossing to sustain one's focus over the long haul and to which everyone can put to immediate use.

Although Gallwey formulated this approach with tennis in mind, or at least with tennis as vehicle for its discussion, it seems particularly applicable to the process of learning and performing music. So apt is the fit, in fact, that another book utilizing this general approach has been written by Barry Green, working closely with Tim Gallwey, called *The Inner Game of Music*. It should be noted, moreover, that this is not a simple reworking of *The Inner Game of Tennis* in musical clothing, but a complementary effort that expands the original book's principles and practices and is therefore quite worthy of investigation in its own right. Interestingly enough, Gallwey was sufficiently intrigued with this new direction and with Barry Green's particular handling of the subject that he began his own amateur career as musician.

Both books are persuasive, as is my own experience, that one is amply rewarded, in terms of pure learning, when following this creative path towards functional concentration. And while this is, as one would expect, enormously satisfying, an interesting byproduct is that the act of pure concentration, with or without tangible results in the real world, can be rewarding for its own sake. Gallwey, in the quote above, seems to be describing some altered state of consciousness where time is irrelevant, where being is sufficient unto itself. After reading my chapter on concentration, do read Gallwey's book *The Inner Game of Tennis* and be prepared for an altered consciousness of your own.

(4) Being With Those You Love

If we do not play pieces that reach into our souls, move and uplift us, express who we are, then why have we bothered?

Although there is no more rewarding work than this, it is hard work requiring not only high levels of concentration but a seemingly unending number of repetitions. If a composition is not one we truly care about, our involvement with it can only diminish. A distance develops not only from that piece but the keyboard, itself.

The object of our work must matter. It must be meaningful. It must command our deepest and most profound attention and love. For who (to wax lyrical) is more motivated than the person in love. Who will more quickly rise to the challenge, take on greater risks, defy the odds, and, finally, stay the course with more ardor and focus, than one caught in the commanding passions of love?

If it were simpler to master the playing of an instrument, if you could, with the greatest of ease, digest large portions of the repertoire, the selection of which pieces "to marry" would not be of such far-reaching consequence. But for me, and most likely for you, taking on a new piece, particularly if it is a major work, represents a commitment of epic(urean) proportions taking weeks, months, even years before lying comfortably under your hands; it can also mean working through countless obstacles, even blind alleys before yielding to your personal vision. Unless you feel a compelling passion for what a piece is all about, you must not lightly get involved. True love, yes, but infatuations of the moment—no matter how giddy the pleasures—must be regarded as sirens on rocky clefs.

Let me call upon Tim Gallwey once again as he would help us focus on the tennis ball: "As silly as it may sound, one of the most practical ways to increase concentration on the ball is to learn to love it! Get to know the tennis ball; appreciate its qualities. Look at it closely and notice the fine patterns, etc., etc. Allow yourself to know the ball both intellectually and through your senses...do anything to start a relationship with it."[11] Well if you can do that with a tennis ball, you're a better person than I, but with a Chopin ballade, or Brahms intermezzo, ah, that is the stuff of enchantment. You don't have to learn to love these profound works of art; you have to decide to which of all the miraculous pieces out there you will limit your promiscuous tendencies.

(3) Thoreau's Drummer
How to pay attention to the rhythms of your own drummer, while screening out the enervating effects of the many rhythms from without, is the focus of this discussion.

Actually, this topic is so important to the proper expression of an art form that not only is a chapter ("Drummer") devoted to it but the entire book is driven by its energy. If you promise that you will not neglect this element, I shall for the moment pass on to the next one on the list, the irrepressible "Happiness Scheduler," something I have looked forward to sharing with since we began.

(2) The Secret of the Happiness Scheduler

An eccentric, whimsical, but incredibly motivating method of scheduling, of allotting time for the completion of tasks or the realization of goals, that gives rise to an unreasonable amount of happiness.

Although especially true in the early years of my learning how to learn, to this day I still devote generous amounts of time not only to the practice of my instrument, but to the thinking that frames the doing of this activity. Anything that might affect the path towards the final goal is looked at, turned over, punched, pinched, pondered, tasted and tested. Whether we are discussing the physical approach, the kind of instrument, the choice and sequence of musical materials, teachers, aids to concentration, the configuration of the planets, in short, any and all things that would affect the progress of that session are considered. And with all, I have found none more important than the state of one's mind at the beginning of a practice session.

I'm now going to tell you something that I have never told anyone before. It is about how I schedule the time that I am going to spend practicing, and how that decision will nearly always lead to success and good feelings about myself.

Listen up because what I am about to tell you is big. I've already told you it was a secret. But it's not just any secret; just as you are not just anyone to tell. And it happens to be that I am one of the few, perhaps the only person in the civilized world, who knows about this. So draw closer, and don't let anything distract us. I'm telling you, it's that big.

Give yourself more time to do something than you need. *That's it.* That's the fabled concept. The formal name for it, of course, is the I've-got-so-much-time-and-so-little-to-do-principle.(My appreciation to Roald Dahl for sparking the idea in *Willy Wonka and the Chocolate Factory*).

Possibly you are underwhelmed. The principle stated baldly is deceptively simple and, if I may say so, deceptively powerful. I suggest that if it is not a great discovery, it is certainly not how most people proceed when they are trying to accomplish a task, particularly when that task involves the learning process. For I contend that most of us have, whether consciously considered or not, a time frame allotted for each activity scheduled in our daily rounds. Further, our current state of feelings is somewhat determined by the dimly perceived success or failure of straying from these allotted boundaries.

So, for example, in a practice session I suggest that you give yourself more time to make something happen than is reasonably required. On a larger scope, assign, in a conscious and disciplined way, less things to accomplish in a day's time than you think reasonable. This is to be accompanied, of course, with a firm commitment to realize these assignments. Since the projected list lies by definition well within the comfort zone, this commitment can be easily granted—and met! Let us look at an hypothetical scenario which limns out the differences between the usual approach to productivity and the one being put forth here by the happy scheduler.

First, the traditional (or, catch-up) approach: You arise in the A.M. determined to have an unusually productive day. You consult your organizer and jot down those things you feel you can reasonably accomplish before nightfall; and then, you make the list *longer*. This way you insure mega productivity. This is, after all, the first day of the rest of your life and you are determined to set an example for all those others to come.

Unfortunately, we invariably come up against unforeseen—indeed, overscheduling is midwife to the unforeseen—events we hadn't counted on: a voice mail's menu depositing us in a maze of misleading choices no matter the bends we round in the electronic highway; the traffic jam that made us wish we were still in the maze; the appointment that kept us waiting. Through no fault of our own, and through our own faults, the list that we thought easy to digest becomes a thing looming large, one impossible to swallow. Our list was six items long but we get to the finish line with five; we have once again fallen behind. We give ourselves a just passing grade with feelings to match.

Now let's approach the same day using the Margolis Happiness Scheduler: You get up thinking the same thoughts about wanting to be productive. You go for your (now very receptive) organizer. You decide, looking at this day's activities, that you will be able to accomplish six items relatively comfortably. Instead of writing these six down—much less the added one for good measure—you select only three. Accompanying this unimaginably rational act you say, "It will feel wonderful to get these things done." Let's say it together. "It will feel wonderful to get these things done." Then you say, there is always tomorrow. That's OK. We don't have to say that one. I think you're getting it.

Now you're into the day, and by two-thirty you have completed the elected three tasks. It is about the same time as in the first example, but notice that you are no longer running behind. Do you relax for the day complacent with success? Well you can. You have earnnnned it. But where is it written that you can't do something, or even a couple of somethings, that you were planning on doing tomorrow. Now we have gotten four, possibly five items accomplished, considerably more than we needed to reach our criterion number for complete success. In fact we are operating at anywhere from 33 to 50 percent in the black. We are wonderful.

With my keen eye for the obvious I would like to compare these days. On each we arose with the same eagerness to be productive, with the same number of things in our life that needed to be done. On each day we accomplished the same number of projects, even the very same projects. With mind set number one we felt our old feelings of incompleteness, of falling short of expectations, while on the other we were smugly proud of our resourcefulness and productivity.

Wait, you say. The story is not that simple. The person who puts more on his or her plate is fueling the probabilities of accomplishment. Perhaps piling it on can heighten one's sense of purpose. If one does not shoot for the stars, one can never rise to the top of one's potential. And so it would seem. And so I once thought.

Now what I think is that being productive is at least partially to do with your state of happiness, with the absence of overweening stress, with the rewards that you build into your activities. And this is particularly true of the long haul where cumulative effects of stress begin to make their presence known in most uncomfortable ways—like avoiding the causes.

Perhaps, you think, this kind of structuring has differing effects on different kinds of people. Possibly this kind of setting up of expectations, of projecting high or low levels of anticipated accomplishments, will have different consequences for people who are high achievers as opposed to the rest of the crowd. It could be argued that different expectation strokes for different folks is the operative concept. Well maybe. In fact the whole thing remains theoretical since I am unaware of any proof for these musings on one side of the issue or the other. But my bet is that it is the very person who needs to achieve a great deal who will benefit most from this kind of altered planning. I have always been one of those highly driven individuals who milked some degree of success out of my very slender talents. And then one day I tried this "underachieving" motivational scheme. It has changed everything.

And now that you are primed, here is how it works in practice. I have as one of my projects today a Brahms intermezzo. Based on the last few times that I have practiced this piece, I know, with reasonable confidence, that it will take between fifteen and twenty minutes to deal with any problems it has in store for me. On this day I have only one short hour to give over to practicing. Actually, instead of the one Brahms piece, I have three pieces of equal difficulty that I was hoping to cover, three pieces that should each take roughly between fifteen to twenty minutes to cover. Let's see. If I am right about my projections, that comes to somewhere between forty-five and sixty minutes for all three. If everything goes according to par, that should be just about right. Now, do I proceed with this relatively modest goal as my agenda? All together gang. Hell no! I decide that I will be more than pleased to do an honest job on just two of these within the 60 minutes I have available.

What happens now is simply playing out the game. I approach the keyboard utterly relaxed in terms of expectations. I have built in plenty of time in case my projections are off. If I decide that one of the pieces needs a little more work, I can go in that direction: I can practice the piece more slowly, with more loving attention than I had anticipated.

And...I will succeed. I will finish in a timely fashion and likely have some left over to "play with." What's more, if I want to start that third piece, perhaps not finish it, but at any rate get started, I can award myself bonus points for having so clearly surpassed my sincerest expectations.

Please note that this approach involves a fair amount of self-deception. If you have a problem with self-deception, you are either (a) deceiving yourself or (b) need to get some help on this one. We all can use some of this salutary ingredient to get through this life of ours, although it may take some of that old time religion to get the proper practice effects.

As I read the above (and I must say I have enjoyed trusting you with my secret), I wondered if it sounded like the devil's temptation towards idleness. Would you be concerned that this kind of relaxation of the great overseer—some call him superego—would start you towards the couch where potatoes dwell? Since I had some extra time left (I gave myself two weeks to write this section, it took only one), I would like to disavow you of the apparent ease of the happiness scheduling approach. It is not simply a case of applying this principle in an offhand manner. For it is well known that to avoid seeing things as they really are, a disagreeable habit at best, requires great vigilance and rigor.

As a final riposte, then, setting a time limit, even if it is too long, perhaps too liberal for the realist, is a way of setting goals in a manner conducive to your mental health. Notice that this way to learning is paved by the act of being more than generous with yourself. Indeed, what better habit to get into?

Writing about the happiness scheduler, which depends on the thoughtful, and largely imaginary, manipulation of time, is so rewarding that I am having a difficult time moving on. We must, however—as once was heard in the old movie travelogues—take our leave of this peaceful clime, this verdant isle, this place of *just rewards* and move on, for there are other lands to visit, other times to be together. What makes it easier, even exciting, is that the place where we are headed is the most rewarding stop on the tour. Ladies and Gentlemen, with a fanfare due his station, I give you The Platespinner.

(1) Platespinning

In first place, the feature that perhaps separates this approach to music making for amateurs from all others, is the element that gives rise to the name of this book, that of the platespinner.

What in the world is this business about the platespinner and what could it possibly have to do with the playing of a musical instrument? I know I have been throwing this term around insensitively without even a hint of its meaning to the practice of music. I hope it has piqued your curiosity, because, despite what I might have said about the other four (of the short list), this is, indeed, the most rewarding element. And I am about to launch into a complete description of what it means and why it is so important; only I am going to put it all in the next chapter. It is long, deserves its own space, and is but waiting for a turn of the page.

Plates

We study the piano in order to play, do we not? I grant that browsing and ensemble playing and accompanying are pleasant and soul-satisfying results of piano study. But I feel that playing pieces is indubitably the major and most gratifying goal of study of this essentially solo instrument. You agree? Can you explain to me, then, why piano teachers thoroughly teach fine compositions to their pupils and then complacently let these compositions slip through their pupils' fingers? Or, worse, partially teach fine compositions to their pupils, drop them, and go on to new work before the old work is done? - Charles Cooke

As Cooke notes, when a student has achieved a level of mastery over a great piece of music and allows it, however inadvertently, to slip "through his fingers," it is a regrettable and perplexing experience. No one suffers more than the hardworking amateur not able to call forth a cherished work into which he has poured so much of himself. Bad enough that it is not available for playful reminiscence; worse, it has the effrontery to decompose at a depressingly rapid rate. Unfortunately, it is not as though one can put such beauty away for safe keeping. Once courted, seduced and won, it is not forever his possession. As in any love relationship this friend/object needs consistent fussing over, and more.

Enter, The Platespinner.

It occurs to me that I have not told you who or even what a platespinner is—for it is both a person and a calling. If you are younger than I, you may not have seen this person. I'm not even sure he still exists, but I hope so, for I would like you to meet this individual who is going to contribute so much to the pleasure of our musicmaking. Describing him will not set your pulse racing—life was simpler then—but you may take my word for it, his show was a gentle kick.

To begin with, this energetic fellow would have a large number of rods—the number, as is usual in such stories, grows as time passes—anchored to the floor and reaching a vertical height of nearly seven feet. He would place an ordinary looking plate on top of a rod, giving it sufficient spin to keep it "aloft"; then a second plate, placing it on top a second rod, repeating the process, occasionally returning to the first in order to refuel its purposes. His pressing goal was to keep each plate's momentum going *and then some*.

This metaphor is, of course, all about keeping the momentum going *and then some*. Early on, however, his primary intention is to get the second plate "up to speed," almost certainly the derivation of this phrase. Getting it to this state, apparently, was more difficult, more time consuming, more a delicate balancing act than keeping it there, a fact with not unimportant consequences, especially for the practice of music.

And then, of course, a third plate was started, a fourth, and so on, all the while having to divide his time—the plates, like hungry young birds, relentlessly demanding his attention. By dashing adroitly from one to the other, refreshing each with a firm but sensitive touch (lest he knock the damned things from their tenuous hold on reality), he was, by the management of the many plates whirling all about, able to create a great deal of excitement.

Between the number of these plates propelled into their varying states of (e)motion and the distance this spin commander had to travel, the objects of his affection would sooner or later arrive to what must be their last revolution, poised to plummet to certain shardom, their spinning beauty but a memory. But our reliable hero, always sensitive to the plight of his charges, would arrive at the dramatically correct moment with the precise energy for driving each plate to a more balanced version of its wavering reality.

Of course, with a different strategy, one calling for far fewer plates, the spinner could maintain more order in the ranks. With additional time for bonding, each plate could hum a happier tune in a higher key. Our friend would not have had to dash so frantically—each plate more safely ensconced, less vulnerable to disaster, perhaps aesthetically more attractive in its spinning attitude. But then, who would have cheered?

The reason that this unusual way of making your way in the world has stayed with me these many years is not altogether clear, but I'm delighted that it has. Fairly early in the game I decided it would be wonderfully rewarding to have memorized, and ready to play at a moment's notice, many of the fine pieces in the piano literature. At first I assumed that this would happen as a matter of course, that after a few years of diligent practice I would show marked improvement, that part of this improvement would involve a natural building up of a sizable repertoire.

Well, it didn't turn out that way; not by a long shot. And so I had to ask myself—given the complexity of the learning task, the constraints of my schedule, the technical demands of the pieces, and the rapid rate of deterioration for repertoire neglected—how would it ever happen?

Each time I puzzled over this seemingly intractable problem, I would hear in the distance sounds of the calliope, then the image of this fellow dashing from one plate to another. He was able to keep everyone's attention—a not unimportant characteristic to me at the time, perhaps even now—by concentrating on an improbable number of these ill-mannered objects "at the same time." In his dynamic domain none of these fugitives from the cupboard received his whole regard, but neither were they ever quite out of mind. And he kept them all whirling about in their varying states of accomplishment, coaxing them towards a kind of stabilized perfection by his persuasive manner.

The platespinner approach graphically suggested that if you were prepared to make certain tradeoffs, you could pay attention to a larger number of things at the same time, or thereabouts. It seemed to promise, for this impoverished musician, at least, a model for keeping many piano pieces alive in their various stages of development, thereby accumulating an extensive and dynamic repertoire, one whose pieces would be available at the "spinner's" behest.

As noted, having such a rich collection is important for a number of reasons,* but the most compelling is a characteristic we all share,

---

* Here they are: 1. For varieties sake, as described above; 2. For working on a number of technical problems concurrently, replacing scales and other such nonsense; 3. For having a number of pieces to play for others—in other words, to make an awesome impression; 4. For achieving immortality; 5. For keeping you off the streets and out of other people's houses.

namely, a need for change, an almost insatiable hunger for variety. Always with us, this characteristic becomes especially salient when we are involved in the learning process. In order to be aware of all the rich possibilities inherent in the play of a musical composition, it is essential that these pieces we study, and spend so much time with, retain their sense of romance, their ability to engage and beguile us. Once these characteristics are gone we do not approach the pieces with the same interest, dedication or passion. Of course the compositions do not change. It is what happens to us and the way we structure our "play" that allows the sparks to ignite or the embers to cool.

If suddenly asked to sit down and play, most amateurs, even after years of serious study, have virtually no pieces they can get through from beginning to end. Those on which they are currently working are not quite ready for a confident run-through—or they would not still be working on them!; the pieces that they have "mastered" *and put aside* have a more or less neglected feeling about them and "respond" accordingly.

Because of the complexity of learning a piece of music—the motor coordination, the memory work, the balancing of the sections, the proper phrasing—it simply takes a great deal of time, a large number of repetitions, hours and hours of unflagging concentration, before one can truly call a new piece his own. Of course, if you had eight to ten hours a day to study, the length of time to learn a piece, perhaps several pieces, would be considerably shorter, at least when measured in days. But that's not where you are, at least not yet—you might have a job, a home to care for, or loved ones to consider, those bothersome things we must learn to accommodate between rendezvous with our instrument. Withal, it invariably takes much longer than you had bargained for to learn a piece to your satisfaction. This usually leads to one of several responses, none of which is terribly effective or satisfying.

The first is that you stay with the piece until it is utterly and completely yours. If you have chosen this course—and few do, that is, few stay with a composition until it is really mastered—it is likely the piece will have lost much of it attraction for you. If this is the only piece that you are practicing or, at any rate, one of the few, and you seek out its company each day, every day, the excitement once so palpable is simply not there. You may begin to work with it less—certainly with less enthusiasm—than your early and naive explorations into its technical and spiritual mysteries.

This is particularly true if, while in these doldrums, you happen upon a new Chopin prelude or scherzo whose impression will not go away, or recall a Beethoven sonata you have always wanted to play. It truly is the first-bite-of-the-sandwich syndrome—there is nothing like it, the enjoyment of even the second and certainly the third are but distant pleasures; perhaps more dramatic, the first touch of a new love partner—for here the excitement is uniquely intense, a state never reclaimed. So it can be with a new piece of music, even from afar. Like a young person in love, you know this ballade beckoning you will bring you happiness—the melody so moving, the drama more than you can bear. You must have it even if it means dropping your current working partner who, at any rate, has been hard to get along with of late. You leave, promising to return.

As a matter of fact, you can begin to wonder what you ever saw in this altogether ordinary piece of music you have pursued for such a long time. (If this sounds like young love gone awry, the story line is surprisingly familiar.) The functional sirens of novelty have lost their sway. An additional consideration is that while you're working the same piece relentlessly towards its moribund state, anyone hearing you practice may be refashioning his opinions about your person.

Or... The second course is to put the current piece aside while it is still in your good graces to return another day, refreshed and ready to tackle anew its once unforgiving difficulties. This solves the problem of indecent exposure but introduces a second problem: you do not renew an acquaintance as though nothing has happened in the time away. While there will be many fond memories, the relationship will have lost something in the bargain. How much will depend on the depth of your (kinesthetic) feelings and the time elapsed between meetings.

It is true, as Charles Cooke says, that "The forgotten-ness of those pieces will turn out to be only partial. Any piece once learned, even if it was learned twenty years ago, is easier to memorize and retain than a new piece of equivalent difficulty."[6] But this rationalization (sorry, Charles) can be overplayed. While it may help to know that it won't take long, in terms of days or weeks, to bring something up to speed, of what good is that when you are traveling in Casablanca and happen upon, in of all the gin joints in the world, that special person you've not seen since Paris. You need, without apology, to play (again), before time goes by, her favorite Chopin prelude on the old upright sitting in the lobby of Rick's Cafe. It is about that moment you've dreamed so long. It is that moment that most needs your attention and your music. If you need a couple of days to get the damned prelude ready ..... she will fly off with Victor Lazlo all over again, or he'll walk off to begin that wonderful relationship with Louie (Claude Rains). (Sorry, from my vantage point, it is difficult to tell your choice of gender.)

An associated difficulty of staying with a single piece, or a limited number of pieces, is that while you are practicing the piece of the moment, mastering its challenges as best you are able, the technical progress made in works put aside will begin to unravel. In other words, to argue the reverse, practicing many kinds of pieces "all at once" has you working on many kinds of difficulties, practicing a variety of skills, ever raising your confidence level. With this latter strategy in place as you take up new pieces, you are better prepared for their, now, familiar technical circumstances.

Think of going to a gym and only working on one piece of apparatus for one set of muscles, versus moving from one kind of machine to another with the obvious value of preparing your body for a variety of challenges. And this varied approach to muscle groups and exercise motions maintains interest, reduces fatigue and, for these reasons, provides a buffer against exercise burnout. If I had not used the pumping ivory metaphor in the first chapter, this would have been a good place to flex its possibilities. And for added weight training, here is Charles Cooke: "Repertoire should be stressed, for memorizing and retaining pieces lifts the general level of playing faster than any other one thing, through developing so many different things: technical ability, touch, ease and confidence familiarity on the printed page and on the keyboard with recurring passage-work patterns and chord sequences, and so on."[6]

The third alternative is a combination of the other two, that is, practice each day your most recent works while fine tuning, in stolen moments, pieces already in progress. Ostensibly, these latter works should not take the same level of care. Remember, plates, once set in motion, tend to take on a life of their own, particularly if you take them for an occasional spin. While sounding eminently sane, the problem with this solution is that there simply is not enough time in the day for even the most disciplined and well-intentioned amongst us.

Clearly we must play with time. One way of making this precious commodity more available concerns speed of practice. An obvious way of getting through more repertoire is to play the pieces as fast as you are able. But speedy play may not get you there first, or, at least, in the most finished state. When you become familiar with the work habits of the great virtuosos, you will learn that slow careful practice is the approach most championed, being particularly valued, interestingly enough, for its effect on one's ability to play rapidly. But what a bind. If you truly practice with discipline in terms of slow and careful repetition, particularly if you would model yourself after the great pianists and the exaggerated slow pace that they advise, you will cover very little ground in the time that you have.

We are back to the same place. There simply is not enough time in the day. And if you say that enough times—there is not enough time in the day, there is not nearly enough time in the day—you are bound to arrive at the answer. After a brief interval for stage setting, we will come back and see if your answer looks like mine, and whether we can do anything about this time thing that appears so impossibly limiting.

Stage Setting

A beginning musician might tolerate the ennui of playing the same pieces over and over again. As in my own case, he or she reasons it can't always be this way; surely this is part of the dues structure. When I improve, says he, I will be playing lots of things and more easily. While this has a good ring to it, and while, as noted, I certainly felt this way at an earlier time, it ain't necessarily so. Few amateurs, no matter the length of their study, achieve this fantasized state of holder of a rich, diverse repertoire. Because of the inherent limitations of the usual approach, they begin to alternate joylessly between the objects of their practice. And, with the continual revisiting of the same material comes a tendency to lose focus, not only on the working out of technical problems, but even more in the critical area of interpretation. As the fingers become more grooved in their automated rounds, the player is more prone to not really listening to his or her efforts—a most serious problem in making good music, as you can well imagine.

This discussion may also have relevance for the well-known plateau phenomenon that supposedly besets all students of music—and anyone else, presumably, involved in the learning of a challenging psychomotor skill. It is a concept used to "explain" why a student seems stuck at a certain level of accomplishment. It is supposedly a place, more accurately, a time, where you reside languishing without improvement; where, no matter how hard you try, progress seems just out of reach. You are told that until your hard won gains are "consolidated" (whatever that means), it will be difficult to move on and, further, that it happens to everyone. It is a reasonably apt protective device (I'm being held prisoner by some kind of neurophysiological process which afflicts all, even Rachmaninoff!), but it may be a theory without sufficient basis in fact.

I propose a simpler and less mysterious explanation: prolonged exposure to too few challenges with a corresponding dearth of stimulation. Attending to these few sources with a consistent level of vigilance becomes increasingly difficult. The scanning mechanism that promotes maximum engagement simply shuts down when variety is in such short supply. Add to this that you may be trying to make too great a leap in improvement, too quickly, by attempting to batter these current technical difficulties into hurried submission. Your only measure of progress, in that short interval, is whether a particular problem is giving way; whereas, if you are playing many pieces with a broad range of problems, you will be inching up on at least some of them, thus always making gains somewhere. The fact that one challenge or another does not willingly submit seems of little consequence. This is not only good for the hands, it refreshes the spirit.

Playing the same piece every day will affect even the most tolerant craftsperson, the most inventive of artists. Surely this is not the intended effect for a piece you had so longed for. By contrast, coming back to music played earlier is invariably refreshing, even allowing the player to hear things and to play things "not previously there."

Well then, the answer must lie in practicing material that is always new or, at least, seems to be. But how does one maintain novelty with material that must be played over and over in order to be absorbed.

There *is* an answer. That's why I wrote the damned book. What is required, however, takes a daring break from the norm and a dazzling degree of trust.* To cultivate a rich repertoire, one that allows you at any one moment to choose a piece from among many "won over," you need but two ingredients: the first is to work on a number, even, one might say, an impossibly large number, of pieces "at the same time."

And the second ingredient, the one which will allow you to take on what otherwise would be considered an overwhelming agenda, is to let go of the day as your basic unit of work-time. That is, you must discard the idea that it is essential to practice the same things every day, or even every other day, or even every third day to maintain or improve on what you have learned on day one. The linking of the amount you can digest and learn, to the day as standard unit, is completely arbitrary, whereas the acceptance of some time frame that is longer, perhaps much longer, will, over time and with a great deal of patience and humility, solve this age-old problem—one plaguing the repertory hungry musician since the reed players of Cleopatra's court.

Of course you will have immediately spotted in this strategy what appears to be a short-term weakness (I prefer long-term tradeoff!): the longer interval between practice visits to a particular piece, inherent in this approach, will result in a longer period of time, measured in weeks and months, to master that piece. Absolutely right. But that does not take into account the bigger picture. To clarify the difference in outcome between this approach and a more traditional one, and to show it to best advantage, let us now go through an example using the expanded time frame suggested above.

Suppose you have decided to learn ten short pieces, one of which is by the Italian composer, Domenico Scarlatti, and you set as your basic unit of practice an interval of four days duration—instead of the traditional single day. This means it should take no longer, and probably no less, than four days to work through the "spin cycle" of these ten pieces. I will, in the chapter on practicing, give a specific, step by step description of what it means to "work through" these ten pieces. For now, suffice it to say that it means playing slowly through each piece

---

* The trust that I refer to here has to do with the individual's ability to learn and retain skills and patterns incremented gradually over fairly widely spaced intervals.

from beginning to end *one time* only, in *strict* tempo, correcting *all* mistakes using a no-brainer correction formula, and *never* looking back. If all goes reasonably well, it may take, since you are coaxing them along at nearly the same rate of improvement, six months to learn all, and therefore any, of these pieces. This means, to bring Scarlatti back into hearing range, that it has taken six months to have learned this short piece to an acceptable level, a piece which you might have otherwise learned in three weeks, perhaps to a more finished degree, if studied without the "company" of the other nine pieces.

No thanks, say you. Why should I wait six months when I can accomplish the same thing in just three weeks? A fair question. But consider: how many pieces would you be playing concurrently with your usual approach? In other words, besides the Scarlatti, what else would you have had to show for your efforts? Moreover, using the traditional approach, will you still be studying, or even performing, the Scarlatti after six months or will you have moved on, other pieces crowding it out for playing time?

In contrast, using the four day cycle, platespinner approach, and balancing the ten pieces on their own time poles, you have them all up and running at roughly equivalent states after the six month period. And...and this is the punch line, you now can start another plate spinning without in the least disturbing, in fact, with continued revitalization of, the first ten. It is by this time undoubtedly taking you only three days to get through the original ten, leaving you one glorious day to add the next piece, perhaps two or three. And on. And on.

From your excitement, I'm confident you are with me. If you can, by organizing your time, bring ten pieces for six months on their separate stations up to a reasonable state of repair, you will have much more to show for yourself, and to others(!), than with the more traditional learn-one-piece-after-another approach. And while the traditional approach will possibly achieve a greater gloss for a particular piece at a particular time, your repertoire at that glossy moment will be very skimpy, indeed. And *that moment*, in some sense, is all we ever have.

On the other hand, only you can decide how long a period is acceptable to wait on having in your possession a "finished" product. Using the single pole, and not being concerned with numbers of pieces, you will have a greater chance to hone in on a composition's intentions, more time for polishing and looking after nuance and control. Thus, if you would be satisfied with playing very few pieces at a time but with pride of your craftsmanship more easily expressed, well then, the single-track, single-day approach is your ticket. This is not to say that you would not arrive at the same level of artistry if you stayed with the approach of my friend, the platespinner, but it will take longer—longer than you might want to take.

You see, the one characteristic that you must possess, using the platespinner plan, is a healthy talent for delayed gratification. Getting all those plates up and running simply takes a great deal of patience. And so while the scenery is breathtaking, and the treasures worthwhile, we're talking signing onto a leisurely trip over a moderately long haul.

I know you can play only one piece at a time. I also know that no one listening to you will have to know that you're repertoire is near the poverty level. It might well be, given your particular slant on things, that playing only a few pieces, but playing them really well, is all you require for complete musical happiness. But, unless you are one that needs no variety for spicing purposes, and prefer *Leave it to Beaver* to *Streetcar Named Desire*, playing just a few pieces will not sustain your musical appetite for long.

And the advantages to platespinning are manyfold and glorious. To play such a great variety of pieces, to luxuriate in the (almost like) new tonal bath of each piece come back to (where familiarity has not been overdone and contempt is unthinkable), to anticipate the practice session with gusto *every* time out, to realize a repertoire of great pieces that you will not soon grow tired of, all of this gives me a rush just to place it before you.

And while I am unapologetically rhapsodizing about my own approach, let me put before you this mesmerizing quote by Charles Cooke:

It is the moment when, having memorized a piece and placed it on his "to be retained" list, he turns to the treasure house of piano literature to select the next piece that he will make his own. He has behind him, at this enviable moment, work well done. He has before him, within reach, no matter what the level of his technical ability, a display of priceless treasures that out dazzles the loot in

Ali Baba's cave. He runs his eye over the exhibits which glint like diamonds set in platinum. Excited by his opportunity, he considers long. He will not take this one just now, nor this one. He will take that one. Yes, that is the one he will now add to his precious collection. And, curiously, after he has made it intimately and permanently his own, it will still be there for other treasure seekers like himself to take....Moreover, the amateur pianist, leaving Ali Baba's cave with his new piece of treasure, exults in the knowledge that he will come back later for some of the others.[6]

This metaphor of Cooke's reminds me of the Greek myth where travelers—secretly they are Gods—stop at an impoverished farmer's home who, despite his penury, graciously treats them to milk, and suddenly finds that his pitcher—courtesy of his mysterious guests—is always brimming full no matter his frequent outpourings. Rejoice! The Gods of music history have done the same for you and me.

Getting back to more earthly matters, let us now consider what is for you the optimum length of time to cover your complete working repertoire. This is, obviously, an individual question and depends on your tolerance for making progress with individual pieces, how much time you have available for practice each day, and how many pieces you would like to keep in your active repertoire. Your best bet is to begin gradually, starting out with two days as your basic time/work unit, then three and so on. When you see that this plan has merit, when you find that you can trust yourself to retain newly acquired information over longer periods of time, when you accept that small increments are the watchword to the final solution, you will lengthen the time unit to accommodate the size repertoire to which you aspire.

When I had this idea some years ago, I thought, given my propensity for leaning to the left, I would test it with a five year plan. I picked a fairly large number of pieces, given the time I had available for practice—no more than two hours a day and on many days far less than that—and set as my goal to be able to practice, and then play, all of these pieces "at the same time." (By now you realize that this latter quote is Platespinnerspeak for keeping all of these pieces on an active roll.) As I recall, it was something like forty or fifty pieces, some of which are relatively undemanding—three Chopin preludes, for example, which are short and straight to the musical point—but some of which are extremely ambitious: Beethoven sonatas, Chopin ballades, Chopin's *Barcarolle,* and Brahms' *Variations and Fugue on a Theme by Handel.*

Of course I didn't start all of these plates going at the same time. I really don't remember what number I started with, only the time period of one week. I simply took my list, starting from the top, and played through as many pieces as I could, going only as fast as my formula for correcting mistakes would allow. I may have only gotten through a few of the pieces that first week, but perhaps as many as twenty. If that sounds like a lot, remember that at that point I was not a beginner although neither was I very advanced. Also, some of those first twenty were already revolving about their poles, albeit in a reasonably unstable fashion. Perhaps over the course of the next couple of years I got the full fifty pieces rotating in a one week period. Of course, at that point, and to some degree, still, we're not talking quality so much as incredibly interesting quantities for a person of my rarefied gifts.

To Illustrate

To give you a closer look, allow me to take you through a portion of my practice week. Let us choose the first piece on the list, a Chopin prelude, and assume our week in question started on Monday the 7th. I will play the Chopin prelude through just once, stopping to correct any errors, again using the correction formula covered in more detail in the chapter on practicing. But for now, to give you some idea of this regimen, any missed passage, any error in technique, is gone over until I can play that passage a set number of times consecutively correct. (Although I hate acronyms and initials as much as the next guy, "consecutively correct" is just too much— hereafter, it will be known as a CC.) If I make an error in the passage while I am trying to correct it, I have to start that passage over again until I achieve the criterion number of CC's, however high a number that may be. Let us say for purposes of this example that the missed passage must be played three times in a row without error. And, of course, when I speak of errors I mean only errors in technique—right versus wrong notes, as opposed to "errors" of interpretation, a much more subjective judgment. Having played through it either perfectly, on those places where I could, and imperfectly, but reaffirming the missed passages with an appropriate injection of CC's, was my way of giving this musical plate additional spin, enough to carry it through the week *and then some*. Although by next week's time this plate will be slowing to some degree from the neglect engendered by this expanded schedule, it should, if I have done my work properly, be incrementally improved over this week's edition.

At they end of the day, it is music to the ears of big time financial investors if their gainers have outnumbered their losers. This is precisely what the well-heeled plate spinner must realize at the completion of his spin cycles. Inherent in this approach of rare visitation rights is the fact that losses from week to week are considerable, but, and this is the important point, the gainers should have more than compensated. If this sounds like double talk, that is my intention. It is the balancing of opposing forces. Here is what I mean:

To remind you, I practiced the prelude on Monday the 7th and did not take it up again for a week. Next Monday, the 14th, I was not able to play the prelude as well as I would have, had I practiced it in the days between, as on Tuesday the 8th followed by time spent on it Wednesday the 9th, and Thursday, etc. In that sense I lost a great deal of potential gain. But after the second Monday's practice, the 14th, I was, nonetheless, able to play it better than the Monday before, by some rather small increment. And that small increment, you see, is all I needed to run with. If all the pieces could advance by some small increment each week, the plan would work: gains would consistently outdistance the losses (theoretically) taken. And look at all the pieces I am in touch with during this long interval. I was so sure that I was onto something, that I was prepared to risk the next five years in this improbable experiment. Only then would I come up for air and evaluate what happened and compare it with what I think would have happened with a more traditional approach. Not exactly scientific stuff but I doubted that the National Science Foundation was going to fund any controlled studies. Twenty years later and I am still tinkering with the variables, still honing the parts, still playing with time, but convinced that this is a workable and, more importantly, rewarding system that will keep you hanging around the keyboard.

John Holt seems to support this idea by characterizing the way that a baby learns:

Some like to say that we have to learn to walk before we can to run. Not so; babies start trying to run while they are still very clumsy and uncertain at walking. The growing baby *advances into the world on a great many fronts, doing as many things as he can, none of them very well, but all of them a little bit better each time.* It is the same for the novice advancing into the world of music.[15]

In the beginning my goal was to crowd all fifty pieces into that weekly time frame just as soon as I could. I would simply go over each piece in a way that was, at the same time, reasonably disciplined yet not too demanding. I had given myself years to bring them all to an acceptable level, remember, and I could always address any lingering doubts about my ability to learn, and the system I had chosen, by reminding myself that this was an experiment leading to what I "knew" would be the grand result after the five year testing period.

One more advantage of the plate spinner approach, then, is this not unimportant psychological one. If you are working on a large repertoire and bringing them all along slowly, you are more tolerant of your daily and weekly progress, more protected against nagging feelings of short-term failure. You can say to yourself quite legitimately that this slow progress is a result of a Faustian pact with the time unit devil, that if you wanted to you could have played several things perfectly, you could have polished them into jewels, you coulda been a contenduh.

You let yourself off the hook, therefore, quite reasonably. You can even suggest to others that they should lower their expectations for the same reason—that they should be impressed with quantity for the time being while you are dashing about getting your house of plates in order. Some day, you tell yourself, and anyone who will listen, that all of those plates will be humming, and that the sounds that emanate will be as impressive in quality as they are in their number. The lack of pressure on the perfection of each plate's spin allows for a more relaxed and pleasurable practice session. It makes a lovely game, one that never, ever ends, and that everyone who plays will win.

In fact, I had to do a lot of experimenting over the years, with both the number of plates I could keep spinning, and the number of days that seemed optimal in terms of the tradeoffs. At times I was sure that a week was too long, that I must cut back the days—and hence the pieces that I could keep spinning—and other times I traded for more days, thus slower overall development. That led recently to a refinement that makes a lot of sense when I have the discipline to carry it out: to give some pieces, those that are going reasonably well, an occasional week off from the spin cycle. This wrinkle, however, is a hard one to stick to. I love all of my pieces—else I would not be playing them—and not hearing one for two weeks is a tough assignment. (Well, do I want a larger repertoire or don't I?) Too, I am not yet entirely confident that advances will always outgain losers over a two-week fallow period.

At the present time I remain on a weekly schedule and play fifty-seven pieces per week on a daily average practice of nearly two hours. My goal is to stretch the cycle, over time, into a two-week period while simultaneously increasing my daily practice. This should result ultimately and joyously in a doubling of my repertoire. (Perhaps you will tell your friends about this book and they will buy a copy. The more copies that sell, the more time I will be able to give over to my practice. It seems the least you can do.)

There was much time given over to the decisions involved. It is these kinds of things that will allow the person of no talent (myself) to play (someday) like an artist. It is these methods, strategies, systems, rewards, call them what you will, that I believe will free me, to the extent possible, from my limitations.

And I am telling you this—and this *may* be the last time—because anything I can do, you most certainly can do better. It is as though I am lovingly maneuvering myself (yourself)—by trickery, by structure, by rewards—into this state, a state where I (you) will be everything that we musically can be.

Incidentally, there is another major advantage to this approach that we haven't even touched on. Surprisingly, it is perfectly all right to miss whole days of practice. If you have a finite amount of material to cover in five days and you get it done in four or even three and want to take a day or two off, or you need to practice some days as much as three or four hours and do much less on others, it is not a problem. No nagging guilt about goals unfulfilled for missing daily practice will assail you. Now I don't mean to say that spreading it out in uneven proportions is as good as playing every day, but once you get into this way of looking at things, you can generally stay on track in this user-friendly schedule. There is a larger degree of freedom inherent in this elongated time unit which can feel surprisingly important.

And on this subject of degrees of freedom, it is not at all critical, although there may be some tiny advantage, to play the pieces in the same order from week to week. If the next piece to practice was supposed to be Bach but, with the rain softly running down the window panes, felt more like a day to keep company with Chopin, well then, put Bach aside till tomorrow. Picking a piece to work on that fits your mood is a nice refinement and adds that little extra to a practice session.

The Mesh of Time

Of course, all of the principles that are presented within this system were "designed" to be in sync with each other. For instance, the time unit—time given to get through all the plates on a regular basis—must not be at loggerheads with the so-called happiness scheduler. In fact, it is critical that your time unit, whatever its length, be long enough for you to *effortlessly* tend to all of the spinning plates, taking into account all interruptions, expected and otherwise, from the rest of your life. If you learn through repeated experiences that you have too many pieces for the time frame you've picked, it is time for a modification in short order. Either lengthening the unit, if that seems commensurate with your capacity, or reducing the number of things that you are working on are the two most obvious remedies.

You could, of course, simply forget this imposed temporal organization and play through the repertoire repeating the group of pieces without concern for how long it takes to make it through. But then you would not be "playing with time." The game would be over. The chance to earn bonus points gone. Unthinkable! Those bonus points are what will keep you coming back for more. Please, no more idle speculation of this kind. Let the games continue!

Having made sure that you schedule a longer interval to go through your cycle than it will actually take, you will usually have a little time left over near the end of the period. (If you are playing the game properly, however, this bonus time will always come as a reinforcing surprise!) When faced with this extra time, you may choose one of three luxurious possibilities.

The first is that you can simply take off the rest of the time left in the cycle, making yourself ever more eager to get back to the keyboard when the next unit begins. Personally, I have never been able, or even wanted, to consider doing this. I mention it because you may not be the addict your author is.

Second, if you are a well-balanced person, you can cheat a little by starting the next cycle earlier than scheduled, keeping, however, the end point fixed. In other words, you add the left over time to the beginning of the next cycle thereby giving yourself longer to accomplish the same material the next time around. (Think of the bonus points with that setup!)

Or third, you can do some really helpful things like taking up new repertoire, or practicing sight reading, or revisiting the hard parts of the pieces that you are currently playing. Of course, if you are consistently too far ahead of the unit—no one needs or deserves that much reinforcement—you must adjust by adding more things to do within the unit or by shortening its length. This tension between how much to do vis a vis the length of the chosen time frame will joyously and annoyingly go on for years.

The Mobile Effect

Speaking of uneasy tension, the attentive platespinner needs to do a balancing act on many levels. The primary level, the long arms of a mobile, as it were, consists of deciding how many pieces one should keep going. Even this first level decision, which on its face is a fairly simple one, requires much thought and experimentation. To repeat ground already covered, too few pieces will lead to more rapid success on each individual piece but then not to a very grand total. On the other hand, if you find yourself being intolerant of small but consistent gains, launching a large number of plates is clearly contraindicated. It will keep you insufficiently rewarded over the short haul, and, remember, for reinforcement purposes, the short haul cannot be so lightly ignored. However, this balance between size of repertoire and increment of improvement is one that you will come to, in terms of your own personal bias and balance, along the way, and needn't concern you at this point, except to be aware that you are in charge of which way it goes.

But, not only does the platespinner juggle his schedule to fit in the great variety of pieces, but other kinds of conflicts have to be taken into account. Perhaps more accurately, a balancing act must go on within a balancing act much like the inner arms of that mobile we are perilously hanging on to.

One such inner arm is the question of how much time to give to each piece. The time spent on a piece varies directly with the amount that you need that piece to improve on each visit to its realm. Curiously enough, you have a reasonable degree of control over this improvement rate. While your limits are somewhat fixed by your capacity to advance neurophysiologically, they are also a function of how you go about your practice, how much time you give over to it in a particular sitting, and how stringent you are with regard to the "fixing" of troublesome spots— what Charles Cooke calls fractures.

Let me elaborate. As you will read in my chapter on practicing, in the section on how to respond to mistakes, you are asked to play the problem passage X number of repetitions consecutively correctly *every* time you make an error. The X is up to you—although I will have some advice on that score—but it really depends on how much of an increment you are wanting to annex. The larger the number of CC's, remember, the larger the increment for that session, and the more prepared and confident you will be the next time you meet that same passage. But with the larger criterion setting (repeated playings) comes exponentially longer periods of dealing with the missed passage. To be specific, it is much easier to do a certain passage twice in a row flawlessly than three times. Raising the number to four creates a whole new ball game. And while dealing with an error with a rarified criterion of four CC's will most certainly result in accelerated learning of that section, what about the rest of the material that you have scheduled to cover during the allotted time unit? Have you sacrificed too much length in your quest for the big score? Of such things do I spend my time worrying.

And now I would like to ask the reader's indulgence as I paraphrase a paragraph from the introduction. It is important to me and there is at least some chance you have forgotten.

I began playing music as a way of learning something that would solve this mortality problem that we all seem to have. It clearly was something that you could do into your old age and beyond, something that if you played your notes right could actually extend the time limits, that if you saved your musical stamps and if your collection just grew and grew, you would live forever in harmony (or at least until the coda).

In that section I used the concept of stamps, since that seems to convey so quickly the idea of collecting, of having within one's grasp an incredible variety of sizes, colors, patterns, pictures, allusions, illusions that would tend to delight, to engage, to comfort and that would, most importantly, help me in my reasonable pursuit of immortality. (If this is truly not possible, I would prefer not to be enlightened.) Unfortunately, as a metaphor, the time-bound stamp lacks the attribute of kinetic energy needed to convey the dynamics of a musical composition. Thus the plate spinner came even more to attract my attention. If you will see his plates as I do—all different sizes, colors and patterns—it will serve us well. And, if you listen carefully, you will hear the music of his Plate(onic) choir reaching an unforgettable crescendo of excitement.

Which is why a warning needs to be sounded. The platespinner can never stop. Once he decides that this is his ticket to immortality, once his fingers and ears have savored the richly spinning delights of his handiwork, he may never turn back. Having fashioned a trap of finely tuned happiness, the platespinner, like the dancer in the story of the red shoes by Hans Christian Andersen—or that highly energized drum beating rabbit—must keep going and going and going.

Ya Just Gotta

In closing it is clear that with the judicious use of time, the concept of the platespinner can be widened beyond the learning of pieces of music to a position where many interests, projects, and activities can all be kept spinning at a merry clip and, of course, "at the same time." Perhaps now is the very time to start other plates going, representing all the things that you have wanted to do but never made time for. Before you complain—there is no time, there is no time—I want you to listen up. Scientific studies have shown that people who take up things that they have always wanted to do, who live out their fantasies and are not afraid to reach for the brass ring—in today's parlance,"go for it"—turn out to live longer, happier and more prosperous lives, have more time at their disposal, make more friends and, generally, are in tune with themselves and the world around them. If you ask me where I got this information...Well...I made it up....But isn't it so?

Surely you and I are together on this. Start a book, paint, play the piano, change jobs for one you would enjoy, learn to play tennis (especially the inner game), read, keep them all going, round and round they go, they are all precious, all the more so because you have never made the time for them. Tell you what, if you put them off until you have more time, your time will be up. There is no later. There is only now.

Do it!

Concentration

At my recitals no one listens more attentively than I do -
Ferruccio Busoni

I remember reading Busoni's quote many years ago, well before I became this very serious player that I have introduced you to, and being struck by its surprising revelation. What, I asked myself, is this music maker doing listening so "attentively?" Shouldn't he be focusing on his performing skills? Shouldn't he be putting his energies into reproducing what he has practiced so assiduously to achieve: a burnished, ready-made copy of what he has lovingly stored in his wondrous personal storage bin. If he is so busily involved with the listening process, how can he possibly do justice to the satanic demands of playing? It seemed a contradiction, an act of self-indulgence.

Of course, I feel quite differently these days.

Just Follow the Bouncing Ball

One day while I was practicing I found myself humming along somewhere in the musical neighborhood of the piece I was working on. It was an unconscious, without rhyme or reason (or melody), going-along-with-the-program, sing-along kind of thing. I'm not sure what got me started. I am *not* a singer by nature having been disabused of this misdeed by my fifth grade teacher and every significant other in my life to this day.

Except that I will admit to a certain amount of serious imitation in my time. I used to think that whatever the really fine musicians did, or wore, felt or said must have something to do with the mysteries of their talent. And one thing I noticed about them that seemed different from you and me—particularly among the jazz players—was that many sang during their playing, even in live performance. Monk did it. Diz hummed tunelessly along. Hamp almost drowned out his playful vibes sound. And Glenn Gould, forget it. Hey, if it could work for the good guys, why not me and you?

So there I was, singing along, hoping some of the trappings of The Musician would provoke a miracle within—doing anything that would take me from humdrum to hummable, mundane to musical.

I must confess that in my less fantasy-ridden moments I thought of this sing-along as no more than a harmless diversion, accompanying, but not materially effecting, the effort required for the playing of a piece of music. It was possible, however, that it could encourage and facilitate one's ability to feel *and stay with* the pure music of a composition, helping to illuminate the phrasing, thus the meaning of a piece.

It turned out to be far more, a personal discovery of moment, or so it seemed at the time, with interesting and unexpected consequences. I began to notice that something else, something wonderfully unlikely, was happening beyond the pleasant exercise of being with the music. Although initially I couldn't be sure that what I was experiencing was "real" (meaning lasting), I became convinced that when I was in the humming mode, my *technical* accuracy improved, and did so dramatically. After a number of practice sessions with this delightful effect continuing in evidence, I became increasingly confident in its reality. I began singing with every piece of music that my hands would play, confirming repeatedly and happily that something extraordinary, indeed, was going on. I was definitely playing with more accuracy, particularly, it seemed to me, on leaps—those consecutive and distant notes on the keyboard essayed without regard to one's personal safety. I had also—at least to my measure—leaped over several tall buildings at a single bound.

Of course I had to ask myself, am I being taken in once again by the subtle effects of Hawthorne? The Hawthorne effect is one discovered in psychological research where a variable introduced into an experimental study, such as vitamin A into the diet, will have a measurable effect, such as improvement in work output, not because of the variable itself, the vitamin A in this case, but because it represents a change in conditions, a change from the status quo. Later on, in fact, the reduction of vitamin A might have a similar positive effect on the same work because of *its* change in the new status quo. In my search for the magic formulae that would help me master the seemingly infinite technical challenges of playing the piano, I had been seduced by the power of Hawthorne all too often.

Thus, I was excited but wary. Excited for obvious reasons. Accuracy of this kind in the real world of the practice studio is typically won only after much struggle and many, many failures. Was it really possible that simply by humming a happy tune, I was going to improve my leaps and bounds? What about the dreaded Hawthorne figure? I had been put through his deceptive maneuvers too many times. I had previously found the "secret" to many technical problems only to have them disappear mysteriously into the unforgiving Salem graveyard. Through with being the public fool, I would not discuss my discovery with anyone.

But a week went by and I continued to play with uncanny accuracy completely and willingly under its mysterious spell. Whistle while you work, that's the ticket. It had to be real. Hadn't Sleepy and Dopey and Doc been there. And Hamp and Dizzy and Monk. I knew something that was going to put me into the select company of all the guys. I wasn't sure how it worked, only that it did. I hung on for dear life and sang my naive head off to the despair of those who once had loved me.

And so with great excitement I brought the news to my then teacher, Ralph Berkowitz. Ralph, truly a musician of many parts, had been Gregor Piatigorsky's accompanist for most of his professional life and Dean of the Tanglewood Music School following Koussevitsky's reign. Ralph knew everybody in the field of music and all their secret rituals. If he was impressed with my discovery...

He wasn't. His bored but kindly response was that everyone knew my "secret." Everyone sang while they played, said he. Wait a minute, said I. I've been to many concerts where the musicians are not singing. Why some of them even have instruments in their mouths while others, not so occupied, are clearly staid and silent with hands busily applied. Inside, said he. Inside. They are all humming to themselves, inside. It is a common practice. Why didn't you tell me? I asked. I thought you knew. I thought everyone knew, he said gently, but with secret wonder at my questions.

All right. I could accept that. Who would know better than Ralph? I was still, if belatedly, working towards membership in the distant and hallowed ranks of The Musicians' Society. I had learned just a little bit more about their secret rites. Just keep on singing—and progress and repertoire and artistry would eventually be mine.

Time passes and things (as they will) change....

Some Hawthorne effects are more subtle than others, the illusion more complete. When the magical effects of singing evanesced like the melodies on which they were borne, the disappointment was not music to my ears. Wait a moment! Singing still helps. But perhaps only if taken with "vitamin A." It *was* the magic of change that carried the day. The improved accuracy was, in large measure, a function of my believing. This mysterious surge in my technical prowess would remain that, a mystery, a help, but not *the* answer. It certainly increased involvement but the magic bullet, the wondrous discovery of this effect, was more and more missing the target; and with less accuracy came more skepticism and with more skepticism came less confidence ultimately resulting in a downward spiral of missed notes and misplaced chords. And yet...

Is there not more to say? If it was not the final solution, and it clearly was not, there was something here beyond old Hawthorne that needed more time. In fact, I have been haunted ever since by this melodic experience that turned my head all too briefly.

And so we shall return to this mystery. But first let us move on, to where this chapter should have begun, and most certainly would have, if I hadn't been distracted by this rather confusing story on humming. The subject we really need to focus on, the phenomenon that is so elusive for the struggling student of any discipline, the characteristic that is the sine qua non of the successful performer is the ability to...is his facility for...for, hmmmmm....By golly, I seemed to have lost my way. Where was I going?...Oh dear, this *is* embarrassing. Right in the middle of this discussion I seemed to have wandered onto a different train of thought taking me far from our destination.

For a moment, just for a moment, as I was writing, I found myself thinking of my lovely wife Ann, wondering how she was feeling... thoughts of the deer who came to our back window for breakfast this morning....where's that mailperson? He certainly was late. I worried about how much writing I would get done.......the virtues of the jump shot...what can I get from the refrigerator to munch on. And that is all that I had time to get down on paper. Actually, images flowed through the little grey cells faster than I could haul them on board.

As we all know, it is incredibly difficult to stay focused for any measurable time no matter the task. But that is precisely what we must do to learn anything of great moment, especially something as complex as playing a musical instrument and, should I ever get back on track, that is imprecisely what this chapter will cover.

It can be absolutely maddening for most of us to maintain a consistent level of concentration for any reasonable period of time, no matter how we are feeling, no matter the importance of the event. Moreover, probably the most discussed topic by, and about, most first-rate performers is their ability to attend to the task at hand in a disciplined and tenacious manner. Despite the story that Arthur Ashe tells—that as he was serving match point for the U.S. Open Championship, he was thinking about strawberries and ice cream—it is unquestionably the ingredient that separates the very best in sports and the performing arts from the rest of the crowd.

I'm sure you have noticed how easily and mysteriously the mind wanders—and to inexplicable places—no matter our desperate attempts to stay on track, no matter the critical nature of the events we're involved in. Try, for example, with all of the discipline you can muster, not to think about your most cherished dream come true as you arrive, unsteadily, to the end of the next sentence. The ability to focus, of course, varies between people (did you succeed?) as any other personality trait, but just how difficult it can be, for almost everyone, may surprise you. If the criterion of staying on target is rigorously defined, that is, if staying focused means few or no lapses into extraneous thought or image, the length of time that all but the most disciplined among us can control our wanderlust will, on our good days, be measured in seconds, perhaps even less.

Perhaps those with a reputation for being highly focused are different only in being better able to rein in, that is, to return rapidly and repeatedly to the task at hand. Or maybe, just maybe, those who have a reputation for being able to keep their eye on the ball have a different genetic makeup—they seem to be finding everything else in those little rascals these days. Finally, perhaps there are some who have found ways of achieving focus of which we are simply unaware. That's one we better come back to.

Again, even as I write, even as I try with both sides of my brain to keep my attention consistently on what I am telling you, even at this very moment while I am considering its importance and lamenting its frustrations, I find myself thinking of events and ideas that have no bearing whatever on the topic at hand and would, if I let them, defeat my efforts to stay with you. Since all distractions have in common that they work against our "getting there," we must, if we are to succeed, learn how to come to terms with this problem. We must learn how to maintain the thread—the damnably delicate, tenuous thread.

I Can't Remember Where or When

In order to be reasonably accomplished in this musical endeavor, you've really got just two kinds of experiences to negotiate. One is the time devoted to practice. The second is playing for others. For both, the ability to concentrate is essential. If you can't stay focused when trying to get a piece ready for performance, that piece will lead you a merry chase to the finish line. If, on the other hand, you lose focus when playing for others, forget it. And often you will.

Each circumstance, practicing by yourself and playing for others, has its own set of distractions with, of course, "intruders" wandering in on either level. It is time to look more closely at both of these experiences and to identify for each the troublesome sources of derailing effectors. Perhaps that will help us to combat their mischievous presence.

Perhaps.

On first consideration, you would think that staying in focus during a practice session would be quite a simple matter, certainly when compared to the awful complexity of playing for another person. When you are ready to take that giant step of playing for others, for example, you have to contend with lapses of memory, with self-consciousness, with some one else's expectations, etc. This working on your own, on the other hand, why this should be a snap.

Well, maybe! But let's take an in-depth look. Let's say that it is time to practice and no one's around. You've got at least an hour to go at it. You are alert to all the wonderful possibilities. Your mind is clear. You are definitely ready to stay in the "now." What can possibly interfere with your making great strides? What can prevent your putting all of your attention to the task at hand?

You gotta be kidding.

For instance, here's one distraction that may not have occurred to you: the act of repetition, or more precisely, the fallout of repetition. Unfortunately, in the learning experience there simply is no substitute for this means of accumulating and reinforcing information. In order to memorize you must play the same material over and over, and the same is true for coaxing the fingers to do things for which they don't seem capable, or are dead set against. But, utilizing repetition, for whatever good purpose, can and will summon the familiar experience of ennui, an incessant craving for something more lively than the stimuli you have exhausted. Although repetition is an essential part of the learning process, certainly when it comes to learning a musical instrument, if it is not thoughtfully incorporated into the practice structure with enlivening and creative tinkering, it will derail the most conscientious of efforts.

While much of what we are doing during practice, if it is to be productive from a technical standpoint, is repetitious, and while the burning in of patterns will, in terms of efficiency, take hold in no other way, the conscious mind tends to reject this way of doing business. Repetition may be effective in helping the nervous system (and supporting cast) acquire acts of coordination—particularly if we can trick it into attending relentlessly to the required patterns—but it lacks the coloring, the variety needed to feed the voracious, curiosity-seeking higher cortex. The brain, if it is to keep our head from bobbing and weaving to delta rhythms, needs more to do than processing this set of movements over and over again. The mind will not only wander, it may lose for the time its wakeful interest to the world all around.

Moving from the numbing effects of monotony, let us consider a distraction of a more psychologically creative sort, one at the other end of the distraction spectrum—I speak of fantasy land—good, perhaps, for mental health, not so useful for efficient learning. If you are wrestling with intractable problems of technique, problems that you feel should have given way to the relentless hammering you have subjected them to, it may be seductive, even nourishing to attend to the internal movies your restless cerebral neurons seem ever intent on running in the background. Although a legitimate addition to the list of distractions, a good fantasy life has saved many from the enervating feelings of failure. Surely a short respite cannot be harmful and may even rekindle the creative juices for solving the problems at hand. Probably more could be said about this. Whole books are written about such psychodynamic tampering, but just starting this kind of discussion and I have started to nod off.

Perhaps that is a signal to move on to the next source of distraction, which is another unwanted but even more damaging kind of intrusion— actually the list is incredibly long, the items specified here, but a sample. This semi-intentional diversion, which comes upon me more than I would like to admit, is the intensely nervous-making fantasy about playing this piece for a live audience, that is, a kind of checking to see how I would do if this was actually "show time." When looked at naively, this appears to be a rational way to test your progress. In fact it is anything but, since when you fantasize about another time—that time when somebody else will be listening—you have effectively removed yourself from this moment's version of the here and now, the only one you've got. And it is the here and now that one must "live in" to make effective progress. This continuously testing of one's progress can be a crippling exercise, not unlike the proverbial pulling the vegetables out by their roots each day to be certain they're still growing.

And then, of course, there is a whole class of distracters which can be grouped together as a kind of current-state-of-your-mind-and-body category, that is, those things that you carried into the practice session with you that day, or developed while in the act, in response to biological or psychological prodding. These things can range from personal problems, or other sources of stress, that you haven't been able to stop thinking about, to those positively exciting things in your life (that you haven't been able to stop thinking about). You might be hungry, in pain, sexually aroused, or exhausted, etc. Almost anything can and will serve to take you away from the rigors and repetitions of practice if you are not well prepared to stave off their relentless bullying tactics. Not to worry. By the end of this chapter we shall have you better armed for their disconcerting demands.

Before we go onto the distractions of live performance—a shaky giant step above and beyond—I will add one more to the practice types, even though for many of you this one is probably not going to be of great moment. It concerns whether anyone is able to hear you practicing and how important that is to your state of comfort. Arthur Rubinstein confessed that even if a maid in a hotel was working in the next room, he would shift from the diligent practice mode of high discipline—repetition, working on difficult passages, slow and methodical progress through the score—to that of performance mode (not stopping for lunch), this after fifty years of playing concert after concert for thousands of people. If you have some Arthur in you, it may be distracting for you to practice with friends or relatives close by (or, if you are really disturbed, by people that you don't even like).

A Monumental Shift

Now that we have catalogued a partial list of factors that make concentrating during a practice session all but impossible, let us move to the stage where staying focused appears wholly inconceivable, the playing for others, The Performance: the time when you ask others to stop, look and listen, quietly, respectfully, thoughtfully, to the amazing progress that you've made.

Finally, after all of the struggle, the dedication, and the joy, it is time to focus all those practice hours into an audio snapshot of your efforts, those playful experiences where, if you have chosen your friends wisely, they will absorb with equanimity the wonderful and awful times you will visit upon them.

Have you ever thought what it would be like to hear your name called to accept an academy award? Have you wondered how you would make it across the lonely stage? Walking, for those of us lucky enough to take this for granted, is a behavior pattern we pretty much have down pat. It becomes, early on, the most automatic of habits, close behind breathing and sleeping, unfolding in its way, not demanding one's careful attention. How you go about doing this thing is not of great concern most of the time. But put yourself in that place where Oscar is celebrated: the long walk down to the stage, the steps to negotiate, the striding across the floor boards, footfalls echoing, people watching from too many rows, and through antennaed boxes from God knows where, all making up their minds about your (now) odd way of getting from here to there. If one's confidence can so quickly be shaken with your most automatic behavior on review, think what it is like to perform a language which (to make the best showing) should be memorized and "spoken" through your fingers.

And that doesn't even count the major distraction implied from the "Oscar" story. Drum roll please, as you make your tortured way: this part of becoming a musician, this playing for others, this thing called Performance will bring you face to face with the most serious distraction of all, the raised consciousness of Your Self. If you made it across the stage to pick up your Oscar without a second thought, you have nothing to worry about. But the rest of you; how will you go about ignoring the critics, real and imagined?   How will you have the courage of your musical convictions?

Of course, it is this raised consciousness of self that is primarily responsible for the performer's nervousness. And talk about distractions! Will you, out there, so very far away, like what you hear? Will you think me musical? Will you spot my uncertainties? Will I draw you into my world, or will you grow distant and cold?

And, as if all of the above is not enough, let us not forget one of the more potent sources of distraction, even trauma, for which concentration is a necessary but not sufficient antidote. Memory! Just bringing the subject up can bring beads of condensation to the coolest of heads. To some degree, I believe, this response has to do with the particular nature of memorizing music, which in large part involves kinesthetic memories and, as such, remains "unknowable" to the conscious mind. It is pretty frightening to go out there in a public way and play something that relies heavily on patterns that you consciously recall only as you see them unfolding before you.

Certainly fear of memory loss is one to take seriously. In fact, it is so troubling to most performers that a chapter will be spent on its vagaries. But perhaps it is not memory per se that needs our concern, but the adequacy of preparation and, further, the criterion for measuring this adequacy. Possibly thinking about memory in some unusual terms will help to get you over this hurdle. I would like to offer the following quirky, but reasonably uncontestable, argument as a possible salutary response to this whole memory business.

Imagine yourself a contestant on a nationwide television quiz show with a million dollars on the line. You are asked to name the capitol of the United States, or to name the country that makes up the northern border of the U.S., or, for the big money, to recall your own name. The point is that no amount of nervousness, no amount of pressure as to what you will win or lose, could send the right answer from your conscious reporter. You are so prepared, or over-prepared, for these "feats" of memory, that no distractions or self-consciousness or fear of memory loss could shake those answers from your grasp. If you accept this absurd example as having some validity, it is incumbent upon you to (over)learn a piece as though it was your name. Then your fingers don't have to consider the multiple choice of notes looking up at you from the keyboard. They go *automatically* for those in the same way that you respond unfailingly when called by your name.

But let us return to the more general problem—the endless ways we can be thrown off course not only by real world considerations but by thoughts, fears and fantasies within. The list is interminable. The chances that you can keep your mind on the task at hand, minuscule. To plug one hole in the dike is to ignore the other rivulets testing your defenses, waiting impatiently to burst forth, sweeping your concentration downstream. Many a great person has been rendered senseless over this thing. Is it worth it?

You bet! It *is* difficult to stay with a line of thought, to battle the dark and unrelenting forces of distraction, but it is doable and most certainly worth it. But not because you wish it so. It needs work. It needs creativity. It needs Tim Gallwey.

Concentration is the supreme art because no art can be achieved without it, while with it, anything can be achieved.
From Tim Gallwey's *The Inner Game of Tennis*

You remember Tim Gallwey, of course. I have brought him into the discussion a number of times (wherever I sensed your attention flagging), but it is his creative exploration on the subject of concentration where he stands supreme. Earlier, I recommended the reading of his book, *The Inner Game of Tennis*. Some of you may have resisted the suggestion. Well, now it is time. We are talking serious impact here. It is in the area of concentration that Gallwey is most eloquent, most persuasive, most on the money. And, his approach seems particularly apt for the study of a musical instrument. (Barry Green obviously agreed and was moved to write *The Inner Game of Music*.) In the performance of this complex operation of music making, where all manner of distractions are eagerly ready to bring you tumbling down, every possibility of assistance must be examined. In *The Inner Game of Tennis*, fortunately, we have a richness of ideas to explore and, even more importantly, a methodology to build upon.

Gallwey is a font of creativity and, while he doesn't put it in these terms, his most important contribution to the learning process is an ingenious methodology for the distracting of distractions. While admittedly an awkward phrase, it seems to capture the essence of his approach to the problem of maintaining one's focus, particularly while under duress. The vehicle upon which he has borne his ideas is tennis, but the principles generalize, happily, to most learning situations. Gallwey has fashioned a number of exercises which engage the mind on some relevant aspect of the (tennis) environment thus precluding other thoughts and images—the dreaded Group from Distraction—from interfering. He doesn't, in his search for the calm and focused mind, spend much time on ancient causation. His is a most useful approach precisely because he concentrates, in the best sense, on simpleminded, practical solutions. In short, he proposes that the player creatively home in on some engaging aspect of the relevant environment that will successfully compete for his attention, quieting his higher and more critical faculties, and allow his wondrous computer-like organism to do its usual reliable job.

Better than reading his book (which I am tired of recommending already), if you have the opportunity, watch his superb TV series originally broadcast a number of years ago. Also, be sure you tape these invaluable lessons before getting in touch with me. I have been watching for it ever since viewing them in 1976 and would reward you handsomely for a copy. As an example of his magic, I will describe a demonstration he presented on one of the earlier shows. It is not in the book, and it illustrates his approach remarkably well.

It was live in front of a studio audience (courtside) with television cameras "rolling." Gallwey picked a woman for the demonstration—a pointed decision, as you will see. He positioned her some thirty feet across the court and facing him. He told her he was going to toss her a tennis ball; women are not usually as practiced at playing catch, at least back in 1976, as your average guy-person. He tossed it in a relatively easy loop and, since it was a tennis ball, it did not hurt when it bounced off her chest. He did that several times with this same woman who occasionally caught the ball but always in a nervous, clutching manner.

Then he changed the conditions, but apparently only slightly. He asked her to count the number of times the ball rotated as it came toward her by watching the seams of the ball. This was to be the focus of her attention; catching the ball, by inference, was simply to be what happened, if it happened. Her primary task was to be aware of how many times the ball turned over from the time it left his hand until it reached hers. That was his only suggestion, the only difference between tosses. But apparently, that was all that was needed. On the very next trial, not only did she catch the ball, but looked quite at home at it. Her form was more graceful, her face more relaxed. He had, by gently shifting her focus onto a concrete and doable job, removed the distractions swirling around and within, eased her anxiety, thus dramatically smoothing out her performance.

The Inner Game of Tennis has a great deal to offer, but for me this was a very special moment, this insight into stage fright, this key to performing under pressure in a relatively comfortable manner. I was hungry for more. What other bag of tricks did Gallwey have up his tennis jacket sleeve? It turned out there were many, and I would like to share a few of these with you. Although they are, of course, grounded in tennis, their implications go far beyond that performance stage. Perhaps one of them will inspire you to the creation of your own ingenious device for staying with the music.

Love (1-2-3) Thirty

One simple but marvelously effective example has the tennis player occupying his mind with an engaging verbal/visual task that keeps track of the usual events taking place during a tennis exchange. As the ball hits the opponents racket, you begin the count (number 1). When the ball makes contact with the surface on your side of the net you advance the count (number two), and when it, hopefully, makes sweet contact with your racket, you count off (number three). Since I have a Ph.D., I took the liberty of adding a fourth count. Number four, of course, is the ball hitting safely on the other side of the net from a ball struck well at juncture three. This pattern is repeated until the opponent, presumably not reading the right books, can stay with the program no longer. This counting strategy is fairly engrossing—the first 14,000 times—and satisfies one very important psychological requirement for maintaining interest, namely, the utilizing of novelty within the context of familiarity or sameness. The sameness is the counting to a maximum of three or four (depending on your educational status)—the novelty is supplied by the particular look (tennis snapshot) that the number is attached to.

An interesting effect, of this imposed organization on the visual components of hitting the tennis ball repeatedly, is an apparent slowing down of time, thus allowing you more of it for whatever needs doing on your side of the net.

Or, Gallwey would have you imagine that you are some professional player of note, whose style and form attracts you, being that person as much as powers of imitation and imagination will allow, thus acting the part. This parallels the well-known phenomenon reported by actors that they are less nervous when taking on the role of another than when called upon to be themselves—as they commonly are, for example, in an interview.

Or, perching, in your imagination, astride the tennis ball, careening gaily across the net; or watching the arc described by the ball, not the ball, to be sure, but the arc traced by the ball as it gets sent back and forth to meet its traumatic comeuppance on both sides of this punishing affair.

All of these strategies take you "out of yourself." All, like a magician's misdirection, reduce the conscious mind's attempts to manage the learning experience. But there is more. Not only does a heightened awareness of self introduce troubling distractions, but higher levels of consciousness are not especially adept at the rapid processing of complex acts of motor coordination. This is particularly true in the playing of a musical instrument. If you attempt to track what is happening on a conscious level—as opposed to allowing your well-trained fingers to take over—the playing of unusually fast passages can become a bewildering mess. Gallwey's strategies, his emphases on staying with a becalmed mind and a "lower consciousness," are facilitative towards this more efficient working of the neuro-muscular system and thus the automatic play that must take place.

Deprived of Gallwey's philosophical approach or neighboring mind-sets of Far Eastern persuasion, musicians have been forever aware of the importance of maintaining concentration, attempting endless stratagems for improving their facility in this critical area. All manner of things have been tried, e.g., hypnotism, psychotherapy, drugs, behavioral modification, and many, many others, with varying degrees of success. The hope, by the uninitiated, is that there are well guarded secrets known by the professionals of the field—the virtuoso, the great teachers—who will mercifully pass these secrets on when the player has completed his rite of passage(s).

While they are waiting, however, the most common device for maintaining a high level of concentration for many has been the very one with which I introduced this chapter, the almost natural tendency to sing along with your musical output. After a quite decent run based more on belief than neurological underpinnings, it has lost much of its charm for this player. Still, it should not be dismissed, as it may work wonders for you. My astonishing lack of facility for staying on pitch or to even sound halfway musical certainly doesn't help matters. Those who are able to be tunefully involved, and they are legions, swear by its efficacy. Both in the jazz and classical music fields, there are a number of people who in live performance and even on record can be heard humming aloud, not always in tune (that doesn't seem to be required *for them*), all the while in the throes of success.

Slam Stewart, a jazz bass player of note from the forties and fifties, used it so prominently that it became his signature, a part of his artistic profile, and a not unimportant reason for his fame. Glenn Gould can be heard quite audibly and disturbingly on many of his records, again, his particular accompaniment rarely in tune but truly participatory and probably facilitative. What is so rational about this approach is that it is supportive to what you are doing mechanically, and it is always being with the music, always residing in the ever changing now. And although the following sentiment by that renowned teacher, Leschetizky, is somewhat tangential, I include it for whatever relevance it might hold for my readers: "If you can tell when someone is playing that he is singing the music in his mind as he plays it, it is a good performance, and if you cannot, it is a bad performance."

For many ideas that were developed by a musician—instead of a tennis player, although the tennis player (Gallwey) worked with the musician on this book—for the purpose of quieting the conscious mind and for heightening musicians' powers of concentration, let me repeat my earlier recommendation of Barry Green's splendid book *The Inner Game of Music*. In it you will find many options some of which may be compatible with your approach to this learning experience. And if it doesn't turn out that way, I offer you one more, one with which I have been working for some time.

Togetherness, Then
Selective-Combined-Tones Listening

I must confess that this following discussion will not be as relevant to the absolute beginner as I would like, but for those of you who have progressed past that point, or intend to in the near future, I offer it for your consideration. I don't mean to neglect you new guys. It is only that the task of listening in the way described might be a bit of a burden at first. I do invite you to read through the material now and to come back to this point when you are ready to take it on—which shouldn't be all that long.

What works best for me, when I am trying to stay "tuned in," is to listen to the combined sounds of the important notes being played together. Usually these are notes of the melody line as they sound "against" (with) the bass. And this usually happens on the beat, sometimes every two beats, sometimes even less frequently, all depending on the tempo and complexity of the piece in question. This, surprisingly enough, means that I tend to listen in a vertical or chordal sense rather than in the more common horizontal or melodic one. And, I must add that I focus on these combined notes only as I can absorb them comfortably. If the music is rapid and I can only grasp this combination on the first beat of every measure, well, so be it. But if the music is slow enough, then I listen to a greater proportion of these combined notes involving, again, the melody with the bass wherever they are played together.

If you are having a difficult time understanding what I am talking about, I apologize. It is difficult to convey as it is not the usual way we talk about listening to music and may even sound quite foreign. Do me a favor and read the above paragraph again and see if it doesn't begin to make more sense.

I have found this technique, this way of being with the music, wonderfully effective. If it is a case of another one of those damned Hawthorne effects, it has me completely taken in. Since faith carries this skeptic a woefully short distance, I suspect that I am onto something quite important, at least for me (only a fool would argue with that one). If you try this approach, however, and it doesn't seem comfortable or effective, please remember that in the end each person may have to devise his own complex of defenses against Demon Distraction. In fact, while most of Gallwey's and Green's suggestions are marvelously creative, I have had a tough time even staying with some of them for the duration.

For example, the suggestion that Gallwey made that seemed to promise most and, in fact, netted(!) the most return(s) for this hacker's opponents, was the watching of the seams of the ball arcing its way towards your racket. He characterizes watching the seam's contour as being a more engaging task than attempting to focus on the whole ball, particularly when charged with the additional task of counting revolutions. But, as Gallwey points out, even with this enhancement, the fascination for this pleasant little ball will eventually fade.* The number of rotations you will count in the brief interval between racket hits is, after all, quite limited, and soon you will need something more subtle

---

* Gallwey's imagination doesn't stop with the physical world. In extending the boundaries of ways that will keep us focused, he shamelessly asks us to think about loving the object that you would be involved with. "As silly as it may sound, one of the most practical ways to increase concentration on the ball is to learn to love it! Get to know the tennis ball; appreciate its (her?, his?) unique qualities. Look at it closely and notice the fine patterns. Allow yourself to know the ball both intellectually and through your senses...*Do anything to start a relationship with it.*" ["her?, his?" and italics added by fascinated author!][11]

and/or engrossing to keep your attention. Your brain simply needs more stimulation always and ever. As it voraciously devours the ingenious games you may con it into buying, it endlessly seeks, like the diabolical swinging plant of *The Little Shop of Horrors*, almost more than you can provide. While this does put a premium on creativity, at least you have been put on notice as to what is required.

I am pleased to report that my distraction filter, the two sounds together, remains reasonably interesting and therefore invaluable to me (please, for God's sake, don't disturb this delicate balance that I believe in, there is little enough in life that one can rely on), since, as of this writing, I haven't had to create new ways of staying with the music for years. Because the sounds are constantly changing, even from how well the instrument is tuned, but more commonly from the width of the interval (the distance between the two notes), and the order of their sounding, the possibilities *seem* infinite. It is like watching a fire which, while exhibiting a terrible sameness, provides constant variation.

Somehow, the concept is right for me, but you must find the strategy that works best for you. If you can benefit from my approach, great, but it may very well be an individual thing for which there is no universal solution. Incidentally, the oddest device of this sort that I have heard was one used by Glenn Gould. When he found himself in a panic state, having difficulties with passages that formerly he had been able to easily negotiate and not knowing what else to do, he would turn two radios on as loud as possible. This forced him, since he could no longer hear the piano, to rely on automatic playing, that is, the playing of notes habitually controlled by the hands and the muscles—so called rote playing—with little or no help from the conscious mind. He called this the method of last resort since it usually rescued him when all else failed.

Having previously said, somewhat apologetically and safely, that my approach might not work for you, I would hastily like to return and promote it for its other wildly improbable benefits. It has so fascinated me over the last years and been so incredibly helpful that I might be able to impart some enthusiasm for its use to some of my uncertain readers.

Remember, I am not trying to hear all of the tones that sound together, only those on the beat or those that seem important. I am trying to "stay with" a procession of vertical tone rows, as it were, as opposed to riding the crest of a melodic line. My rationale suggests that if I am able to make each vertical combination in the series sound its very best—(1) by hitting the individual notes accurately and together (thus sprucing up the technical side of things), and (2) by arranging that the sound levels of the individual notes, relative to each other, are in proper proportion (so as not to neglect the musical aspects)—then the melody line will take care of itself. That is, the rise and fall of the melody, and its corollary, the shaping of phrases, will take place in a kind of unconscious manner, much like what happens when you are speaking.

This may appear contradictory to the importance of phrasing in music, which implies looking at a bigger picture, i.e., through a wider time lens, but the difference is only apparent. It is really more a matter of order—what you are trying to accomplish in the early stages versus what is to follow. This particular technique of concentration may realize its maximum potential in the early phases of practice, as one gets the sounds in one's head, as one, more importantly, gets the notes in one's fingers. It is only later that one can pay attention to the real sense of the piece, the serious apperception of the musical language and its overall story. Perhaps then one can widen the musical lens. Everything up to then has been preparation, a number of freeing techniques, freeing of the earthbound constraints of the piano technique, of the slavish getting of the notes precisely right and in time and in balance. And if this approach to staying with the music furthers these preparations, you will be in a position to widen the scope of your attention and to bring what you feel, as you feel it, to your interpretation of the bigger (musical) picture.

The oddest and happiest discovery of this approach is that it seems to have helped me to become technically more accurate. (Does it sound like you've heard this story before? But this time it has lasted for years, so get away.) If, when I reach to hit a note with my right hand, perhaps a jump made perilous by the distance of the leap, I focus at the same time on listening for the note occurring in the left hand, usually a bass note, the accuracy of this leap is substantially improved. Just thinking of this "right hand" note in isolation, while the left hand is left to fend for itself, is definitely second rate by comparison. There is something about coordinating the effort by the way one listens to its combined effects that allows for smoother flow and greater accuracy. It may have something to do with keeping more of the body involved at the same time, some kind of respectable gestalt principle. Having said that certainly does not explain it to me; clearly I am groping to make sense out of something that is beyond my ken.

Another interesting and facilitating by-product, of listening to these pairs of notes as they "go by" together, is that it tends to impose an unifying organization on the material. When you listen in this way, you hear the piece in outline form, since you are tending to excerpt the salient sounds from the whole, to listen in a way that "gets rid of," i.e., reduces in importance, any but the most essential notes to the overall structure. You will tend to hear the notes in groupings much the same way that you memorize, usually unwittingly, such things as telephone numbers. If you try to memorize the number, 2954921, for example, it seems far more difficult than memorizing 295 4921, while easier still would be 295 49 21, particularly if you accent the first number in each sub-group. In like manner, this organizing facility tends to arrange musical material in groups making them easier to remember and to process in terms of their musical values.

Creating such a shorthand memory device allows the musician, not unlike the miracle of the centipede, to produce complex effects without much conscious effort. While this short-hand or short-circuiting (in the best sense) effect is potentially valuable on any kind of musical material, it is absolutely essential on technically complex passages, those, for example, where many notes need to be played rapidly. For even if you wanted to "elevate" all of the notes to a more apperceptive or conscious state, you would find this task, in a great number of cases, to be all but impossible. It turns out to be extraordinarily difficult for the conscious mind to "keep up" with the number of notes that your fingers can negotiate in a given time, particularly after many repetitions have led to a pronounced automaticity of these passages.

Again, to do this, you needn't try to focus on every note in your right hand, only every so many, perhaps those that are on the beat or every other beat, those that seem to sound well with the bass notes. Since you are organizing them in a temporal manner and reducing the apparent load—by the selection of key notes only—you get a better feel for the outline of the piece. Then you can focus on this outline, this kind of extended musical acronym, while letting the musculature take care of the connective tissue in between. You must trust your mind\body on this one. You really have no other choice.

As a matter of fact, many pianists actually take the chordal progressions—those underlying the running patterns—that composers use over time, and put them into block chords as a way of delineating what is happening harmonically, as a memory aid, and as a way of raising consciousness and control. I do not recommend going overboard in this way for reasons to do with overanalyzing an art form, a subject treated in more detail in the chapter on practicing, but it really is not so very different from what I am doing with this focusing technique of mine, and I won't be put out with you if you decide to go in that direction.

Another benefit of the selective-combined-tones listening method is that it seems to facilitate learning to play more rapidly. I put this forward tentatively as I am unsure of my ground here. One does not listen to all possible clusters of sounds but only those that are easily managed, beginnings of phrases, beginnings of measures, etc. This heightened sense of focus seems to have a similar effect—distortions of size and time—to those reported by professional athletes. Athletes will describe the baseball or tennis ball as seeming larger and therefore easier to hit when they are "in their zone" (see below), or of having plenty of time to accomplish an act of coordination because time has apparently cooperated by slowing down. As a matter of fact, I sometimes do get a glimmer of this effect—the slowing down of time—when I am most focused in my keyboard playing, and when that happens, it does seem that I have time to get things done that formerly I had to scramble for.

When an athlete is riding on the wave of an uncommonly long "hot streak," when a basketball player actually believes he cannot miss a shot, the words most often used to describe this sportsperson's nirvana are "unconscious," "he's playing out of his mind," "he's playing over his head," and the most recent variant, "he's in a zone" (unconscious zone?). Here is how Gallwey, who must be credited for this prior characterization, talks about this "condition":

Reflect on the state of mind of a player who is said to be "hot" or "on his game." Is he thinking about how he should hit each shot? Is he thinking at all. Athletes in most sports use similar phrases, (like unconscious), and the best of them know that their peak performance never comes when they are thinking about it. Clearly, to play unconsciously does not mean to play without consciousness...But the athlete is not aware of giving himself a lot of instructions, thinking about how to hit the ball, how to correct past mistakes or how to repeat what he just did. He is conscious but not thinking. But, can an athlete learn to play "out of his mind" on purpose? How can you be consciously unconscious? Perhaps a better way to describe the player who is "unconscious" is by saying that his mind is so concentrated, so focused, that it is still. It becomes one with what the body is doing, and the automatic functions are working without interference from thoughts. When the player is in this state of concentration, he is really into the game; he is at one with racket, ball and stroke.[11]

This strikingly resembles the description of a baby's learning to walk. Both Gallwey and John Holt use the baby's manner of learning as illustrative of the absence of self-consciousness of this age. For example, when a baby begins to walk, he is so self-absorbed in what he is doing, so focused, so uncommunicative in terms of verbal skills, so uncritical of his failures—e.g., the continual falling down—that he is in a protected zone of his own making, and the learning process is allowed to proceed in an optimal fashion. To a lesser degree—unfortunately as we begin to mature, our self-consciousness and self-criticism develops at an alarming rate—children seem to maintain this facility until they get over being children.

Remember, the general idea is to keep focused on the *hear* and now, honing your powers of musical observation, so that the learning process will proceed in a quiet and orderly fashion. Thus, when I focus on the sounds of two tones *right now*, I am focusing on what is, not what came before, which is utterly beyond my control,* nor on what is yet to be.

---

* This is particularly true of the piano as there is, when compared to many other instruments, precious little that one can do to alter what has already been played.

In some very real sense, neither of those exist for the player or the listener. If I can attend with a studied vengeance the series of discrete here and nows, simply noticing the quality of each pair—loudness, tuneness, length, simultaneity, clangor, dissonance, or consonance—not really identifying these things discretely, just letting the mind lock into these qualities as they take my fancy, then what is happening along the horizontal path of the musical experience, i.e., the melodic line and its organization into phrases, will take care of itself. At least, that is my faith!

It is important to point out that I am not really listening to two things at once—probably in the psych labs of the world considered impossible anyway. This is not a juggling act with the attention span balancing the disparate stimuli. When I talk about listening to two notes sounding together, I am really only listening to one thing, one resultant sound, a resolution of the two notes playing off one another. And when I am doing that successfully, there are a number of things that I am not able to do. I am not able to worry about how you are feeling about me or my playing. I am not able to be concerned about how well or poorly it has gone so far, or about the tough spots to come. I am not distracted by any of the other potentially disruptive thoughts already discussed in this chapter, or whether I am straying too far from the literal reading of this composer's intentions. I am simply listening to a succession of sounds, noticing their qualities each as they come before me, letting my physical apparatus do the rest without being concerned about how well these marvels are doing their astonishing work. If I have prepared adequately and if I am staying with the succession of sounds, it will go as well as I am able and that is all that one can ask.

If my approach intrigues you, fine. If Tim Gallwey or Barry Green comes closer to how you learn, that is wonderful. If you can invent your own strategies, even better. The point is that you must have at your disposal some way or ways to restrict the various distractions in an unthinking (automatic) manner. With this process in continuous operation—or as close as our frailties will allow—you can listen intently to what you are doing and bring all of the love and sensitivity that you have for this music into play.

*****

At my recitals no one listens more attentively than I do.
Ferruccio Busoni

Ah, this is where we came in. It now seems self-evident, does it not, this proclamation by Busoni, a thing as essential for performance as the thousands of hours of preparation. Of course the performer must listen with all his heart and intellect. It is the only way that he or she can fully express his love for his listeners. Absorbed listening by the player to what he is producing will paradoxically give the audience what it most needs from the performance. It is the assured self-acceptance by the artist that will allow the audience to be with him and to know fully his musical conception. Eric Fromm almost had it right: to love others you must first love and accept your (musical) self.

Memory

Even those musicians who agree that a fear of memory slips is the chief cause of nervousness would still defend the virtues of playing from memory - Seymour Bernstein

Memorizing is the soft spot, the place of greatest vulnerability, for a surprising number of soloists. It is a process executed by most with great inefficiency and with little confidence. Not a few live in absolute terror of having a devastating memory lapse that ends a concert, even a career. Some have given up public play over such concerns.

Consequently, when someone of musical aspirations hears that I may be of some small help with this intimidating process, her interest typically quickens. She might even listen with close attention to a detailed description of my somewhat unusual response to the problem, express heartfelt appreciation, and go off for a crack at it.

Never to be heard from again.

Once, I was certain that anyone using this rational approach would be inordinately grateful for the dramatic progress she would most certainly make.

Not so.

Actually I don't bring the subject up much anymore and try to change it when others are not so polite. To be fair, my approach is an unhappy, mechanical process—perilously lacking in meaning or interest—the fact that it works, its only saving grace. Moreover, there are certainly less tedious ways of going about learning and retaining musical works which produce, if not equivalent results, then those more happily achieved.

Having indirectly apologized in this way, let me suggest that there are a number of benefits to be had by the early use of my approach to memorization. Further, if it can be incorporated comfortably into your mode of learning, this admittedly mechanical method will surely help you get from here to there more quickly.

The remainder of this chapter, in fact, will be devoted to how you can make memory work more efficient, and why you might want to memorize early in the process of studying a composition rather than later on (the usual route). At the end, for those who see the logic but are less masochistic than your author, a compromise strategy will be offered combining moderate effectiveness with reasonable comfort and meaning.

It is important to note, however, that should you remain unpersuaded by the importance of early memorization—it may not be appropriate for your situation—you must absolutely ignore my efforts to sway you into its participation. Much better to follow your own path, for that is one which will take you unerringly to your comfort zone.

In fact, should this be your resolve, and to convey an *apparent* sense of balance and objectivity, I will present two reasons for choosing an alternative approach. The first has already been addressed: because of its mechanical nature, my approach is not very pleasant or even remotely musical. These shortcomings are not to be dismissed lightly. Even though it may receive high marks in efficiency and its benefits readily demonstrated, the sustained use of my approach comes into sharp conflict with the important pleasure principle already discussed, to wit, most, if not all, of what you do in the learning of musical skills must be swiftly rewarding. In plain terms, it should feel good right now. Whether you decide to make this a part of your program, then, should depend on whether the rewards of learning something relatively quickly and efficiently are sufficient compensation for the tedium and somewhat anti-musical nature of the process.

The second drawback to memorizing, particularly in the early stages, is that you will invariably spend less time looking at the printed score. The consequence of this behavior is that you will spend considerably less time in sight reading—the practice of watching the music while directing your hands unsighted to the relevant portions of the keyboard. Of course, if you are sufficiently disciplined, you can remedy this deficit by regularly putting aside time for this activity alone. Most students, however, find it a notoriously difficult habit to maintain, particularly in the religious manner required.

Curiously, the habits of looking at the score and playing from memory fight each other. Not only may memorizing seem difficult when one is used to looking at the score, but conversely, reading from the score becomes difficult after one gets used to playing from memory! In fact, students often note that they undo their hard-earned memorizing by returning to the score for a time.[23]

This is not an easy choice. For instance, you might some day wish to get together with other musicians in small groups and play things with which you are not familiar. You will find that if you can't sight read in a reasonable way, no one will come out and play with you. (I guess we all remember how that feels!) Also, sight reading is a marvelous skill to have handy if you just like browsing through stacks of music, discovering works that are meaningful or just plain fun, thus deciding what pieces you will want to spend more time with in the future.

While sightreading is a skill professional musicians usually cultivate—depending on their role in the market place—and while this capacity for reading from the score is championed for their students by most teachers, the skill of memorizing is, perhaps for this very reason, slighted to an alarming degree. And this is true even though all music teachers know that their students could perform the pieces they are working on better, both technically and musically, if they would but commit them to memory.

A couple of factors, however, enter in, which keep teachers from being as aggressive on this point as they might. The first, which may not advance my popularity with this group, is that most teachers, themselves, have a devil of a time with this operation. Oh, they will talk about the three major approaches to memorizing and how these complement each other, and so forth, but precious few are really facile at negotiating this difficult step in their own play. Here is how Lloyd describes these three approaches that teachers talk about easily but employ with uncertainty:

Most musicians use a combination of the three main methods of memorizing. For muscle memory the performer plays or sings the composition so many times that it is remembered as muscular action (like walking and riding a bike for instance). Persons who have a so-called photographic memory can memorize a page of music just by looking at it; their brain seems to take a picture of the page. In analysis, the third method of memorizing, the performer studies the work in great detail, often before playing it. He sees how it is put together, section by section; he learns the harmonic plan of the work [for those of you who are not familiar with this fact, this study of the harmonic plan is how, in fact, jazz musicians are able to stay together] and what the principal tones are. Analysis calls for much musical experience, but once this method is mastered a performer can memorize long works in a short time. He also knows much more about the music.[19]

Let's review these three approaches briefly. We can dismiss the one about mentally taking a picture of the notes as it will not have much bearing on the subject for most of us. If you can do it, fine. Do it. By the way, most people can see some of the notes in their imagination. The trick is seeing them all, particularly in long complex compositions. It does not help much to see some of them!

The discussion of analyses of compositions as an aid to memory work gets very low marks from this corner even if it is "cost effective."* While it certainly is the most respected of approaches in academic circles, it is too calculating, too bloodless, too anti-musical even for my taste. And, committing the ultimate heresy, it is not really appropriate. If you want to hear more along these lines, complete with some degree of animus, please consult page 218 in the chapter called "Practice." For the sake of the present argument, however, I ask you to consider the act of analyzing, in grammatical terms, any speech of emotional import for the purposes of memorizing that speech, e.g., a proposal of marriage. I suggest that attempting an analysis of this sort is an insult to, and a detraction from, beauty and love and art. For even more diatribe, do see page 218!

The second reason that teachers don't push memory work is eminently sensible and we have already touched upon: the greater the time put into memorizing, the less skilled the student becomes at sight reading.

Alright already. Enough! What's with all the mixed messages? If it is so bad, why bring it up now? Why not put the "thing" in the appen-

---

* And in my mind, if in no other, there is room for argument even on this score.

dix—traditionally an intimidating and unread portion of a book—for those who are interested in its pursuit?

Well, one of the important reasons you may want to memorize—thus escaping the possibility of appendixitis—is that it simply makes the playing of the piece that much easier. Look, the coordination required for a new player getting most of the notes right, in time, and with some modicum of spirit involved, is tough enough. When all of that is overlaid with your having to find those notes on the keyboard "blind," it clearly becomes too much to ask of the relative beginner. This is, after all, a pattern of learning which has been called the most complicated task that our species takes on. Admittedly, it does mean you will have to suffer the concerns of memory loss, but, as you will see in a later chapter, this may not be the worrisome problem that it would seem.

As you will learn when we come to practice methods, the speed of learning a piece of music, in the sense of getting the notes right and on time, is directly related to the care and creativity of your practice. Without getting into the details, the governing principle for maximum efficiency posits that you spend the lion's share of your time on the parts of a composition that are most difficult, i.e., those passages where you tend to make the most errors. A highly specific method will be presented on how to implement that approach, but the first order of business must be to make sure that the technical difficulties are isolated from errors brought about in other ways—e.g., those caused by having to attend to the manuscript—so that you are not confusing digital problems with your ability to keep your place on the printed page.

On a higher level, and probably the most important argument for learning to play by memory is so that you can concentrate on the sounds and messages you are creating, that is, your interpretation or reading of this composer's intentions, and of your own unique expression concerning these sounds and messages. It simply makes good sense that if you are preoccupied with the mechanics, either from the reading process, or from other technical difficulties, you cannot give full attention to the soul of the piece.

Finally, memorizing is an undeniable advantage as well as a convenience to artistic playing. The elimination of note reading and page turning allows the performer to devote just that much more attention to his performance. It also permits the music to be called forth from inside oneself, as it were, so that the notes are assimilated before rather than while they are performed.[23]

You may have noticed that the super advanced players seem able to simultaneously read and "interpret" reasonably successfully. But please remember the ease with which they are, in a sense, almost bypassing the complicated operation of sight reading. In their long experience with the feel of the keyboard comes magnificent awareness of where their hands are, thus little need to devote precious energy to the mechanics of the finding act. And even in their case, I would argue, and I think most would agree, they are far better served when the music comes from within, with a chance, then, for individual processing, reflecting on, even "romancing" before releasing the new mix upon the grateful keyboard. And I'm sure in this complex interplay that you and I would lose even more of our expressive potential, a loss which at this point probably neither of us can afford to bear.

If you think about an actor with script in hand, or watching cue cards while playing out a scene, you recognize immediately the importance of memorizing from the audience's point of view. Even in the unlikely event that the actors could involve themselves into the scene with the same level of commitment, the illusion to the audience will never be the same. Instead of conveying the essential element of spontaneity, that is, that the actor is responding appropriately, in the present, as his or her character would demand, the audience has been forcibly reminded that what it is hearing was composed at another time and place and has really very little to do with these people still working on their craft.

Perhaps you are resisting this analogy. You may feel that people in a string quartet, for example, cannot possibly be engaged in the same kind of interplay as actors in a play. Yes they can (he explained).

Speaking of string quartets, Norman Lloyd suggests that "chamber music players usually do not memorize their parts, because of the risk of a memory failure that would disturb the whole group. String quartets memorize their programs only if they are going to play the same works many times on a concert tour." If this argument were truly a logical one, actors in a play should always have their scripts handy. One of them forgetting could certainly leave the rest of the acting ensemble out on a shaky dramatic limb. Oh, well. Musicians always have had interesting views on their practices.

Symphony members can watch the notes because it is not their soul they are consulting during the play of the music. Musicians in a large orchestra are almost never given voters' rights for how the music should be interpreted. That would be a nice democratic ideal, but great orchestras are closer to dictatorships, with the dictator—called the conductor for reasons of propriety—often memorizing the score, even when he seems to be following its intentions in front of him. In this way he or she can be assured that everyone is playing his concepts in the way that they had "agreed" on in rehearsal.

If, in spite of the warnings that my memorizing approach in its purest form may be dangerous to your musical health, you decide to give it the good try, and I think that there are a few of you who will do so for reasons that are obscure to me, I would like to hear from you. I need to find someone willing to do this thing besides myself. It's lonely out here. In fact, I have been close to jumping ship a number of times,* but if I have some good company and I am buoyed up by your success stories, I may see out the rest of the voyage in your good company.

Well, here we go. Clearly, with all of the buildup, it can only be anti-climactic. But if you suspect that I have practiced a kind of reverse psychology, you have done both of us a disservice. What I shall talk about does seem an original contribution to the discussion of memorizing music. But brother, is it tough to put into practice. With all of these mixed messages, I am sure my reader is curious as to my purpose. I do think this a sensible if painful approach. But the main reason to learn its outline is to have room and knowledge for a fallback position which is still moderately efficient and useful.

Seize, Overlap and Keep Going

To memorize a musical composition earlier in the learning process, thereby allowing you to watch the keyboard while working on technical

---

* To take up sail on the slightly compromised version.

problems, as well as later on when playing for others,* you may want to take advantage of the (1) Seize, (2) Overlap, and (3) Keep Going memorization approach.

Let us look at the elements of this approach in turn. The first, the so-called "Seize" principle, suggests that a unit of musical information to be memorized should, in terms of its size and complexity, be one that can be committed to memory with incredible ease. Thus, whatever else it may be, it is amenable to being seized and deposited into your memory banks without further delay.

The "Overlap" principle, on the other hand, declares that the unit to be memorized must be large enough to share some of its information, usually in the form of notes, with the next unit in the sequence. This characteristic is important for the providing of connective tissue between these two units.** Note for the moment that these first two principles are in apparent conflict with each other.

The essence of "Keep Going" is that one never looks back on one's completed rounds. The student simply plows ahead trusting that his nervous system is doing what is required for making progress.

I was tempted to call these units of material to be learned *bytes*—this being the age of information and the byte representing, at one level of computer analysis, the basic unit of word processing—but it seemed more sensible, because of the picture of selecting material of an easily digested size, to use the homonym *bites*, which in this aural context has naturally and happily evolved into sound bites. Of course we have learned during the last few years, particularly in the political arena, that a sound bite is an attenuated news clip that a politico hopes will have a telling impact on the six o'clock news. The fact that this phrase already has a shared meaning in our culture has not stopped your intrepid author from this flagrant appropriation.

* Clearly essential for at least the first few years of your training. You might be surprised to learn that Arthur Rubinstein retired at age 93—after playing on the unchanged keyboard for 88 years!—not because his hands gave out, not because he was tired of the demands or the tour, not because he wasn't playing as well as ever, but because he could no longer see the keyboard clearly.

** Charles Cooke speaks, charmingly, of passages, in a composition where frequent errors are made, as fractures. And he talks graphically about the fixing of these fractures as a process of splinting. Splinting, then, is another way of thinking about putting these memory units together whether problemed areas or not.[6]

Since I think the phrase "sound bite" fits so well in the present context, I shall redefine it to mean a sequence of notes which is instantly retained by the memorizer, but which, at the same time, is of sufficient substance to satisfy the principle of overlap-ability. Clearly the length of the sequence will be an individual affair. What is easily retained by one person can be another's overwhelm.

Before I give an example as to how Seize, Overlap and Keep Going actually works, let us, as a way of making some comparisons, look at other ways musicians actually—as opposed to what is bandied about—approach memorizing musical materials. Since I cannot communicate through these pages by sound, and since many of you do not yet know how to read music, I shall make graphic use of the printed language for this presentation.

The quote at the beginning of this chapter reads:

Even those musicians who agree that a fear of memory slips is the chief cause of nervousness would still defend the virtues of playing from memory.

If our task is to memorize the page where this quote is found, one possible approach would have us reading the full page from beginning to end, over and over again in its entirety, until we could actually recite its total contents without referencing the page. Words that are difficult to pronounce would receive added attention, of course, and we would stop to consider the emphasis that certain thoughts or phrases needed, but essentially it would be a matter of getting from beginning to end in as expedient a manner as possible within a reasonable time frame.

This approach may sound unlikely and inefficient (I certainly hope so), but is, in fact, the typical "method" of memorizing used by most musicians. That is, they play a piece, or sections of a piece, over and over again until they can play it "automatically." (Are there those that would deny this as a most common strategy?) Of course, as implied by the example above, they are also working on other facets of this learning process, e.g., technique and interpretation, at the same time.

In fact, generally speaking, they are not trying to memorize the piece at all, but find that, if they are very patient, they can accomplish that "goal" as a byproduct of so-called incidental learning and with the soundless assistance of their rote memories. The reason I have put quotes around the words "method" and "goal" is that while memorizing in this way is not the direct intention of this approach, it is, at the same time, one of the hoped for results. (What else am I to do?) Unfortunately, for many people this does not happen for a very long time, if ever.

Of course, they have several support systems, already mentioned, that are of some help in this, for the most part, unsystematic process: images (for some); aural memories, although how this works is unclear to me and even to the people who use it; and knowledge of the harmonic structure, which the trained musician will recognize and which can help in the learning process. But most of what is happening, I suggest, is the getting of the notes into the hands—a kind of learned chain reaction of kinesthetic responses. By the way, learning by rote, the views of the professional community notwithstanding, is a perfectly acceptable strategy as a part of the picture—indeed, it may be, as an essential building block, the only communality to all approaches—and plays a strong part in the method I intend to present. But playing the piece over and over again, hoping the memorizing process will somehow happen as a matter of faith is, I must repeat, a hopelessly inefficient, if ultimately successful, strategy.

Probably the most common approach to memorizing any sequenced material intentionally and directly, whether music, verbal text, or a coordination sequence in sports, is to go over a small amount of material enough times until you have it memorized, then to go on to the next small amount of material attaching it to the first batch; then after reassuring yourself that you have this entire bundle together, adding the next chunk, and so on down the line.

To illustrate this generally accepted model, using the same sample page as above, you would memorize the first sentence, "Even those musicians who agree that a fear of," etc., or part of that sentence, until you knew it cold. Then the second sentence is memorized and attached to the first, checking to see (hear) whether the two can be "replayed" together. Then the third sentence—or clause, if the sentence is too long—is incorporated in the same way always going back to the beginning to make sure the entire block of material is holding together. While being psychologically reassuring, this approach is staggeringly inefficient—a characteristic which does not seem to overly concern most who go this route, principally, I would guess, because it also seems to work! (What else am I to do?)

However, one sees immediately that while you are making sure that you have the target materials properly intact, you are spending a vastly disproportionate amount of time on the early portions. It all comes down to the very human quality of not trusting yourself to have learned something unless you can actually hear reassuringly, all of the evidence (not) before you.

Of course, using this approach to learn music presupposes that you can play the notes in a reasonable fashion, that you can string together the elements well enough to present them to your memory catcher. That is why the pieces are generally played for a long period and many times over *before* memorization is attempted. But, as you can well imagine, this effectively finesses one of the previously noted advantages of early retention: to be able to work on technique without the confounding effects of watching the printed page.

Let's now consider how we would approach this same material with the Seize, Overlap and Keep Going approach. Our first job, now that we have a specific example, is to determine the actual size of our basic building blocks, the sound bite. Again, this will vary from person to person. And, unfortunately, each sound bite—because the words are not uniform in nature, nor if it was music, would the notes likely be—is also going to be a different size, even for the same person. If this sounds overly complicated, it really isn't. Each sound bite is determined as you go along, and I am going to show you how to go about it.

In ascertaining the correct bite size for you, let us utilize a criterion measure that makes the process semi-automatic. I have decided for no particular reason (and feel dogmatic about it, to boot) that an expedient bite size is *the largest number of words that you can recite or, in the case of music, notes that you can play, without error, almost immediately, three times in a row, without looking at the text*. Further, when you are able to process a sound bite in this way, it is considered, in a preliminary and very qualified sense, "learned." We will clarify this concept later on but let's not slow down yet.

You will notice that we have refined our definition once more in order to make it operational. Now we call it a proper sound bite if the amount of material can be grasped at some criterion level immediately, while being of sufficient length to possess the essential quality of over-lap-ability.

Here is that first sentence once again:

Even those musicians who agree that a fear of memory slips is the chief cause of nervousness would still defend the virtues of playing from memory.

If we were to consider the first word in this sentence, "Even," as our first bite, we see that it readily satisfies the first principle or require-ment. That is, we can immediately "replay" this information three times in a row without error and without looking at the page. We can, as it were, seize "**Even**," memorize it, and put it away without a second glance. But, of course, you probably noticed right away that it did not satisfy the second principle, that of overlap-ability. And more impor-tantly, why bother with one word when you could absorb half a dozen with little additional effort. Aside from the fact that in Cooke's terms we have no material for splinting, it has the disadvantage of not being challenging, thus of much interest to, the memorizer.

I think that it is important to point out here that, if we were discussing a stave of music instead of this page of text, correctness would mean to play flawlessly in all regards the correct notes in the correct time and rhythm, and, if you like, with some minimal attention paid to dynamics (louds and softs). Having made this important clarification, we will resume our discussion returning to the text of the sample sentence, "Even those musicians," etc., as the basis for our illustration.

Let us try some different lengths for that first bite. How about, "**Even those musicians who agree...**"? Can you read that phrase, close your eyes, and say it three times in a row without making a mistake? Since this gave most of you no trouble, you might choose this sequence as your first bite—which now that we are getting serious, we will call *A*. If you wanted to make it a tad longer, you could try "**Even those musicians who agree that a fear...**" That might be the right length for you. The way to find out is to close your eyes and do the threes test. Remember the guideline: it must be long enough to have linking capaci-ty but short enough to be committed to memory right now.

For purposes of this illustration, however, and because, as an old guy, I have trouble remembering whether I ate breakfast this morning, we shall choose the prior choice: **"Even those musicians who agree..."** You have, at least for the moment, memorized this if you can say it three times in a row without a stumble. Now you are ready to move onto the second bite which we shall call *B*. B will consist of a small portion of A, the small portion acting as connective tissue, the so-called splinting matter, and some new material long enough to qualify B for respectable bite sizeness. Let us assign to B just enough of A, let us say the last two words, **"who agree,"** to provide a splint or intro to the rest of B. This will keep B associated with the rest of A while introducing A to the rest of B. The full B, then, might consist of the words *"who agree* **that a fear of memory slips.."** Now say B three times consecutively correct without looking at the page and, for the moment, "forgetting" A, or at least not focusing on A.

If it was not easily done, you have been warned by your nervous system that this was an overly ambitious sound bite for you, and that you must excise some information—a word or two—from the end of B. However, if you have passed the criterion test, if you have said the B segment three times consecutively correctly, you are ready to chain A and B together. You will do that, of course, by beginning with A and connecting it to B—the splint material, **"who agree,"** providing a natural bridge, or as the boys in the psych labs would say, an associative bond. You should now be able to say the whole of AB, **"Even those musicians** *who agree* **that a fear of memory slips,"** without breaking a sweat. The acid test is the same. Can you do it three times in a row free of error? This should not take (my readers) very long, but if it does, that means that the individual sound bites, A or B, were a trifle too long—that you, too, may be having trouble with breakfast memories—not only for grasping A and B separately but, more importantly, for anticipating their combined and somewhat more taxing length as the AB dyad.

OK, gang. Time to take a tedium break. Give yourself five or ten minutes to do something fun and meet me back here for the rest of the story.

*****

...more taxing length as the AB dyad.

But if you have chosen skillfully, which you unquestionably will after a few trials, and have accomplished the AB chaining with very little effort—remember from a previous "lesson" that your goals must be easily attainable—then it is time to move onto sound bite C. At this point, you're probably sure you know where I'm going, but go with me anyway. You might be surprised.

Let us take as C, the words **"of memory slips is the chief cause,"** and apply the usual test. Note that **"of memory slips,"** the first three words of C, are also the last three words of B and thus serve as connective tissue between B and C. If this went easily enough, it is time to couple B with C with the overlap words acting again as splint or associative glue: **"who agree that a fear** *of memory slips* **is the chief cause."** Well, you say, what is the big deal? Your method and almost every one else's seem the same to me. I will pause while you think that one over. The more discerning of you have already got something important spotted and I will be patient with the rest.

Here it is then: In the second coupling operation the dyadic pair BC was not hooked on A, which for the moment has been ignored. We had already "learned," at least for these purposes and for the moment, that unit, (AB), and we are well on our way, as ordained by the Keep Going principle, to focusing on BC. And we never do hook the three together, at least not in these early stages! We go on to CD, then DE, EF, etc., until the end of the page.

With the tried and true way of addressing this material, we would have picked up A when working with B and C, and would, therefore, be focusing on A for the third time as we looked at C for the first. While this particular instance doesn't seem overly serious, it becomes a different story when we reach the Zth case. If we followed the usual "logic" of keeping everything together, with the continuous checking inherent in such an approach, we would be focusing at A for the 26th time while looking at Z for the first. With the Seize, Overlap and Keep Going method we avoid this pitfall by familiarizing ourselves with all of the information on the page with the same measure of attentiveness. Incidentally, with the time thus saved, the total structure can be gone over many more iterations, thus strengthening its place evenly in our hearts and minds.

But how will we know that we truly have ABC or ABCD or ABCDE learned if we don't go back and check. The answer is, you won't know, and you probably don't have these combinations "together." Not yet. But something has happened in your nervous system that will pleasantly surprise you later on. The key here is to trust that something meaningful *has* happened to you with regard to AB or BC or MN and to just keep going in like fashion until you get to the end of a much larger unit, which for you at this point may be a page of music. Later on, the size of the overall chunk to be memorized at one gulp, so to speak, will be increased to three or four pages or possibly even larger. Going forward "in like fashion" means never going back and checking how much you have learned—the so-called "Keep Going" principle—whether it is CD and then DE and then EF and so on. When you get to the end of the page you will have, by my reckoning, "learned" or "memorized," *if only momentarily*, every set of couplets or dyads on the page, each with a splint holding them together. Have you memorized the whole page? Well, if you are of normal intelligence, certainly not. Will you be able to recall *any* of these pairings? Perhaps. Has anything at all happened? You bet. How will you know that something has happened?

The way to measure the gains or, perhaps more properly, the savings, in this pairing of easily digested sound bites, is to time the first trial, or any trial, through and to do the same for succeeding iterations. Because so little seems to happen from these apparently transitory linkages, you will be most pleasantly surprised at the timed differences between trials and the consistency with which this process advances. Repeat these steps X number of times—the X allows for individual variation of memorizers and materials—and you will commit this page to memory far more quickly than you would have guessed possible. And, if you will permit a mystical transposition back to the world of sheet music, you will have focused on every note and phrase evenhandedly. Now, with your entire body in support of where your hands join the keyboard, freed from the constraints of the page, you are ready to take on the challenges before and below you.

Is it fun to do it this way? Only if you are into factory piece work. However, I must say, the experience of "capturing" a fine musical composition so early in the hunt, to work on at your leisure with the "hard" part already done, is both gratifying and functional.

As Promised: Another Way

What I have essentially done is present the extremes. On the one hand, we have the usual method of memorizing, the adding on of increments always keeping the total picture in the frame: A, AB, ABC, ABCDE, ABCDEF, etc., which I have characterized as psychologically reassuring but hopelessly inefficient. This method generally goes along with having played through the piece a fairly large number of times, thus giving the student some rote feelings about where his hands will be going, and some musical clues—since he has heard the piece a great deal—as to what he is trying to retain. On the plus side, both of these characteristics, the rote feelings and the aural memories, are certainly aids to memorizing and most assuredly take some of the assembly line character out of the process. Having played through the piece a number of times while attempting to master its technical and conceptual challenges, you are becoming old friends. When it is finally time to be weaned from the score, if you haven't learned to hate the damned thing (as does happen occasionally, even with old friends), you have more to pin your memories on.

The reason I had argued against this approach earlier, despite its evident advantages, is that it takes some time before these impressions take up serious and committed residence in your memory. The longer it takes, of course, the longer your head must swivel dysfunctionally between the music rack and the keyboard.

The other extreme, of course, is the one presented in some detail in this chapter—my entry in the memorization derby—which I believe to be a model of efficiency although clearly lacking in the amenities of humanity.

The answer, of course, and I'm sure you are tapping your fingers waiting for me to catch up, is to combine elements of these extremes into a mix that is right for you. From the more usual approach, you can play the piece for a while but not so long that it borders on conventional irrationality, rather just enough times to explore the composer's intentions and what you are wanting to express. This picking up of ideas and meaning, neurological and spiritual, can then be converted into the dyadic sound bites somewhat more quickly, and certainly more comfortably, than the exclusive use of the "Seize" system in its more sterile state.

What you are bringing to the traditional approach, then, is an anti-dote to the senseless returning of the carriage back to the beginning of the line every time you add some information, which now can be governed entirely by your need to balance meaningfulness with efficiency. Only then do you begin the grunt work of putting the sound bites together.

And, so you see, it all comes down, as it should, to doing what is best for you. If you want to master the piece quickly and you don't care how you get there, you use the factory (my) approach. If being more leisurely is your style, pleasure is a large item in your life, and efficiency doesn't mean all that much, than you will take another path. Neither course is superior! But there is a middle ground!!

And while you are thinking that one over, let us go on to the next chapter where the development of a practical technique is explored. You will find that how you approach the learning of the notes will affect the way you will want to memorize and vice versa.

Before you turn this page, however, a word of caution. If you are a person who is unduly afraid of making mistakes, you may need some encouragement before taking up the next chapter. The strategy presented there for acquiring a solid technique is based on learning how to generate errors systematically—with a formula devilishly devised for this purpose—and then responding appropriately to the controlled mess that you've made. If you do not mind making mistakes, even making them somehow "on purpose," you will have no problem adopting this point of view. If, on the other hand, this sounds forbidding, do not worry, as I shall teach you exactly what to do. You're traveling with one of the great mistake makers of our time.

And, if you are still concerned about making mistakes after that, just be grateful that William S. Newman is not your teacher. Because straw men are fun, I have included in the next chapter his unthinkable Iron Maiden approach which embodies his less than Christian attitude towards the making of errors.

Practice

Three to Get Ready

There are people, however, who think they may achieve great ends by doing this; up to an advanced age, for many hours daily, they practice mechanical exercises. That is as reasonable as trying to recite the alphabet faster and faster every day. Find a better use for your time - Robert Schumann[12]

Technique is the practice of making your fingers go where you want them to and then allowing them to go where they "like" -
The Platespinner

For many years, now, in the halls of musical ivy, perhaps forever, the teaching of technique has been based largely on the practicing of scales, arpeggios (broken chords), and books and books of musically trivial exercises—Hanon, Czerny, etc. The exhaustive exploration of this so-called vocabulary of the keyboard is championed as providing a broad-based foundation for meeting the endless technical challenges appearing in the piano literature. So persuaded are some teachers of the validity of this approach that they will not encourage the student to play much in the way of repertoire until this foundation has been unmistakably demonstrated. Consider that one of the integral parts of the examination process for ascending the grade levels in these austere settings is the proficient articulation of all the scales known to the occidental mind. And, of course, most teachers schooled in this monastic approach will dutifully pass the gospel on to their students, never questioning their practicality or effectiveness for individuals who have neither the time nor the interest for this labor-intensive study of the musical alphabet.

And while these activities may seem a reasonable step in the training of hand coordination and finger independence, there is little evidence that they facilitate, in a cost-effective manner, the student's ability to play bona fide compositions from the literature. Beyond giving the aspiring player a sense that she is diligently working within a structured framework sanctified by tradition, the exercises appear, in a relative sense, to accomplish little. And the time lost, when precious, meaningful repertoire could be learned—and real technical problems, from real and admired works of art, worked on—is disheartening and irreplaceable.

Interestingly, my impression is that students willing to pay the scale prices do generally achieve a higher degree of technical proficiency on their instruments. If true, it would seem a powerful vindication for these determined treks across the keyboard. But as any logician will quickly point out, the fact that two things are closely associated does not, by any stretch, mean that one is responsible for the other. And, in fact, rather than a causal relationship, what we probably are observing in this instance are different expressions of the same powerful drive for achievement. Thus, any student, so driven to excel and to please that he or she is willing to risk braindeath from excessive exposure to the musician's version of Latin Studies, undoubtedly finds time to exercise more direct, efficient and salutary kinds of practice.

On the other hand, a positive correlation certainly does not disprove causation, and it is at least possible that this kind of controlled and disciplined study, this traversing the broad scalar landscape with its multi-hued and variegated patterns, may actually be helpful in the development of an impressive technique.....

Naaaaaa.

To begin with, a really important consideration, in the examination of most technical studies, is that what you are practicing, such as the running of scales, is not very meaningful in musical terms, and the longer you practice these, the less meaning they seem to acquire—an unappetizing cumulative effect. One day you realize that these notes were only chosen to divide up the scale with some sense of democracy and/or to get your fingers from one end of the key, or keyboard, to the other. In other words, there is nothing "behind" these notes. Thus, practicing its exploration is an intolerable violation of the principle that most of what you do at the keyboard should be rewarding in a fairly immediate manner.

This would be a good time to quote Abby Whiteside who, you will learn later on, is a sworn adherent to the critical nature of rhythm and, therefore, the joy of swinging:

Czerny and Hanon [oft used collections of exercises for the terminally traditional] should be completely discarded on the sole basis that they are not sufficiently stimulating musically to further music-making. There is no time to waste on dull literature, for the mechanism can be coordinated expertly only when there is excitement and intensity of desire for accomplishment in the practice period.[32]

For most of Pischna, Hanon, and the like, there is really little excuse. In fact, a kind of psychological lethargy accounts for the great loyalty to their deadly monotonous compilation. The teacher has almost no explaining to do, the student has very little note reading to worry him, and the mind is free to wander into subjects far removed while the required practice minutes tick by.[23]

Now I suppose that I could live without profound meaning, or in Whiteside's words, "excitement and intensity," for a while, if it could be demonstrated that it was practiced for some higher good, that is, if the patterns in the exercises could readily be translated into musical output in the pieces in which I am currently working. I would even settle for that translation into pieces that I would *someday* play. But rarely will a scale or an exercise pattern be found in the same configuration and/or level of difficulty in compositions from the repertory. As William Newman puts it:

The vital point, however, is that the practice of a Czerny study leads mainly to the perfection of that Czerny study rather than to Beethoven or Chopin or composers in general. The practice of Czerny can help Beethoven only when an identical passage occurs in both [Essentially never].[23]

To be sure, there is *some* meaning sacrificed (or, at least joy delayed) in my own system as I practice the notes of a passage prior to exploring its expressive possibilities. But even while I am temporarily ignoring, as best I am able, the meaning of the notes that I am practicing, I still know the meaning is there. Not even while operating in my most insensitive and disciplined mode can I be entirely free of its esthetic siren. No matter how mechanically I practice a Chopin Etude, I am still arrested by its beauty, impressed by its balance and ingenuity, and continuously reminded of the profound chasm between it and the most poetically played Czerny exercise.

The runs in the rapid section of Chopin's *Waltz in C# Minor* appear, to my knowledge, only that one time in the literature; likewise his left hand figure in the *Revolutionary Etude*; also the octaves that run in contrary motion reaching a climax in the *Fantasie*.* While thousands of scales and exercises presented for general flexing of the fingers might help by some small measure, a fraction of the time invested in these unique passages, head on, will complete the mission more effectively and with greater satisfaction in the process. Further, since you are using the source material of this composer, the coordination acquired will correspond more closely to his other compositions than exercises fashioned by outside pretenders.

Finally, let us for the sake of argument accept that these exercises and scales do contribute something to the armamentarium of the classical musician. It becomes a matter of budgeting. Musicians who do this for a performance career have had to practice six to ten hours a day for many, many years. They may put an hour or two a day into this kind of activity—scales and general exercises—which they can possibly afford, but that hour or two probably represents our total time available for learning new pieces, working on technique, learning new pieces, practicing sight-reading, and learning new pieces.

For if you are going to have even a modest repertoire, you must spend your time working directly on its inception into your plate life, else these scales and exercises, this so-called foundation, will elbow the dynamic and desired compositions from your grasp. This does not mean

---

* "One learns only what he practices. Each technical feat must be learned separately. Technique does not generalize. The most that can happen in general is that the pianist will acquire enough specific experiences to enable him to meet almost whatever confronts him."[23]

that you can afford to slight technique; only that you must derive the most economic results from your efforts. The fact is, there is no better place to look towards the acquisition of a fully functional pianistic fluency than that which appears challengingly on the pages of the glorious compositions you have chosen to study. It does not take an imagination. It does not take poring through the musician's version of Omne Galle Est Tres Partes Dividatum. It is there before you.

As is William Newman:

Newman's Folly
or
Perfect Does Not a Practice Make

Since I wrote the last chapter I've had time to reconsider my harsh characterization of William Newman and his strange views on the subject of making errors. I've decided to withdraw the Iron Maiden label substituting instead the model of The Pit and the Pendulum. He does, after all, give the student a frightening choice.

The Pit

If you choose the pit(s), you commit to playing the piece *without making any errors*. Instead of a philosophy of practice makes perfect, Newman would have you play perfectly from the gitgo and hold the rudder implausibly steady. (Now this is serious, mind you, so consider what this noted musician has had to say on the subject. He was, after all, a highly regarded piano pedagogue in his day, and, indeed, I have used his excellent book as source material favorably throughout this work. Generally I find his approach to be sane and reasonable, his writing compelling. On the subject of errors, however..."without making any errors?" *Come on Dr. Newman!*). One does this mind-boggling feat, this mandated perfection, by *anticipating* one's errors before they are executed. Of course, to pull this thing off it is necessary to go at a very slooooow temmmmpo. This is particularly true for the beginner who must deal with watching the page, keeping track of where his or her hands are *and* trying to keep strict time in the bargain. Then the student is encouraged to slooooowly increase the tempo always with the same unyielding principle firmly in mind: Make no mistake!

I'll just bet you think I am exaggerating the good professor's position. Here then are his very words:

> But, the student will argue, accidents are accidents, so what can I do? And the answer? You can do a great deal if you set your mind to it. Mainly you can catch yourself before you make the mistake, just as you would if you found yourself about to walk off a cliff or to run down a pedestrian. The fact must be granted, however, that catching oneself or anticipating the mistake in advance can be very difficult. The student who has fallen into the mistake habit is usually the type whom the momentum of the rhythm leads around by the nose. Once he is on the verge of a mistake, the rhythmic drive pushes him over, and he realizes his error too late. Too late, because even going back to correct the mistake does little toward counteracting the muscular coordination that has been practiced. The cure for this habit often takes patience and time. First, the student must establish as his motto the words *Hesitate rather than err.*[23]

The logic is, in fact, first rate. Those of you with orderly minds will applaud an approach which does not allow for the formation of bad habits. If you never play wrong notes in practice, you should be wonderfully prepared for the real thing. Or so the argument goes.

I couldn't help wondering whether this approach by Newman was representative of how he lived his life? Did he, for example, drive to the market 15 miles an hour though empty streets? When he spoke to the clerk, did he rehearse each phrase before speaking? When he went to bed with his wife, did he....? If this approach wouldn't cause impotence, nothing would. And an impotent pianist, one who cannot make a mistake, must play with an absence of passion.

Consider the baby once more as he approaches free speech. The "method of choice" is trial and error. It is through the making of errors that the baby, or any of us learning practically anything, have the opportunity to learn the right connections. It is only after choices have been compared that we have the opportunity to learn "right from wrong." If the baby had to make only right choices before taking up speech, he or she would have to put off this learning experience for a disquieting period of time. Indeed, in terms of learning, babbling, as metaphor, may be our most important strategy.

And what about flow? And joy? Where's the spontaneity? No doubt about it. Newman's approach sounds like a killer—particularly in terms of bringing you back for more—and worse, it sounds exactly wrong efficiency wise. Before we get into that, let us not forget the pendulum. Remember, Newman gave us a choice.

A Non-Swinging Pendulum

Instead of, or perhaps in addition to, not making mistakes as a first line of defense, Newman suggests an horrific alternative for reducing their occurrence, to wit, begin the entire piece over *each time an error is made*. Again in the words of the wary Dr. Newman:

> Second, a corrective should be instituted, a corrective more painful to the student than the disturbance caused by his mistakes. One telling corrective is to begin a piece and start over every time the slightest slip of any sort occurs, even the kind that is truly a human error. After one gets almost to the end several times, and if the patience of student and teacher are not yet exhausted, the desire to get through piece will usually overcome the momentum factor and bring home the value of hesitating rather than erring.[23]

This idea is so preposterous that I shall simply ask you to join me in the next paragraph without so much as a backward glance.

Why have I gone on so about Newman's approach? Well, I thought it a most convenient way to introduce that most important element in learning to play the notes of a musical composition, namely, how to respond to the making of mistakes. I picked Newman's approach, frankly, because it seemed an easy target, a perfect straw man's choice. At least he did make an effort, in print, to erect a rational defense against the possibilities of error. It may be a flawed system but he gave us something to think about, and respond to. And curiously enough, precious little else about this important subject appears in the literature of piano instruction.

In fact, I have pored through many volumes of music instructions—including those residing on most of the library shelves of the English speaking world—and they all seemed to share one glaring defect. There are essentially no discussions on how a student should react, in precise terms, when he or she does the inevitable and plays a wrong note, or a hundred wrong notes. Oh, they may say that he should work on the problem area until it is resolved(?), or like Newman, play slowly enough to avoid errors altogether. But as far as a systematic regimen that will not have the student scrambling for the most effective response, given all the forces in play—the difficulty factor, the number of pieces that need to be covered, the amount of time at his disposal on this day—there is next to nothing.

I take that back. There is one rather notable exception. Curiously, it did not come from the pen of a professional but steaming off the pages of *Playing the Piano for Pleasure* by Charles Cooke. And passion may have gotten the best of Charles (I'll explain shortly). However, let us reserve judgment on the efficiency of his approach and simply enjoy the feelings expressed in this memorable and impassioned passage which, in truth, had a profound effect on this writer:

Recognition of the value of working especially hard on difficult passages is no new idea in piano teaching: it is one of the oldest and soundest ideas. But my approach to this factor in piano study is perhaps unique. For I don't approach it with emphasis, or stress, or insistence. I approach it with fanaticism, with mania! I am now looking you straight in the eye and I am speaking slowly and rather loudly: I believe in marking off, in every piece that we study, all passages that we find especially difficult, and then practicing these passages patiently, concentratedly, intelligently, relentlessly—until we have battered them down, knocked them out, surmounted them, dominated them, conquered them until we have transformed them, thoroughly and permanently, from the weakest into the strongest passages in the piece.[6]

He deserves much credit not only for having given this issue a great deal of thought, but for the forceful manner in which he makes his case. He describes his determination to cure the problems of a new piece by playing the various difficulties, which he labels fractures, hundreds of times in advance of learning the piece as a whole. He set me on the right path, or so I like to think, by his mostly logical thinking and his persuasive style. I owe him a lot. But not everything. I will come back and offer a loving critique (this straw man is slightly more difficult to knock off balance than the one stuffed by Newman) of his approach. But before I do that, let's talk more about the "separation of musical powers."

You'll recall in the chapter called "Structure," I confessed that working on the technical difficulties of a piece prior to working on its musical expression was, for me, a more comfortable approach, and, I believe, a more logical one. Attempting to be fair, I presented arguments for following the opposing and more traditional path, that is, for an integrated approach, one which suggests that technical development and musical interpretation move forward as one. This unfriendly argument, you may remember, seemed unassailable, yet, stubbornly, I have resisted and gone my own way.

The reason I shall now retrace this ground is that I am going to share with you practice methods based on this separatist philosophy. And before I can ask your serious consideration of this approach, I need to convey what I like to think of as its logical underpinnings. I hope to persuade you that it is not only all right to practice a great work mechanically with callous indifference to the meaning of the piece, but that it is in the very service of musical expressivity that this approach is vigorously championed.

Here are three reasons that I would offer as support for the divide and conquer approach:

(1) The first has to do with not wanting to be bogged down by technical problems while attempting to explore the spiritual connection one has with a piece of music. If your mind is distracted by the problems presented just getting the right notes sounded, the amount of energy left for attending to the essence of a work becomes drastically curtailed. There must come a time when we focus only on this essence unimpeded by such pedestrian matters as the turn of a musical ornament.

Any musician worthy of his artistic stripe knows that more than technique is required for the revelation of a composition's secrets. Except for those sleight of hand artists reveling in the demonstration of their own virtuosity, technical fluency is *not* the end of the game. Without question, the highest achievement for the artist/musician is that, even as he plays compositions of extraordinary difficulty, his listeners are transported by the poetry of his reading. When you find yourself focused on the sweep of the story, you are in the company of an artist who has rendered the usual means of communication "senseless," having gone straight from his heart to yours. If, on the other hand, you find yourself bowled over by an astonishing display of manual dexterity, you may have been taken in by a musician failing his most sacred trust.

When I separate the practice of technique from the exploration of esthetic values, I am determined that someday these means will not be noticed, that they will serve, not drive my efforts to make music. Further, and most importantly, a technique that will serve my fondest wishes is one that allows me to play in the moment, to romp, to capture the feeling of unencumbered spontaneity.

(2) The second factor, in fact, has to do with this joy of spontaneity, with giving fresh, involved readings of the materials *every* time you return to "play with" a composition. The essence of this approach is articulated by two extraordinarily accomplished performers:

I truly believe that our spontaneity comes from practice -
Billy Jean King

Only after long acquaintance with a work can ones playing acquire a fresh spontaneous quality, as if one were playing it for the first time - Leon Fleisher

These two consummate performers have reached the pinnacle of artistry and competence in their respective fields. Both agree that work, practice, repetition are key ingredients leading, somewhat surprisingly, to the desired appearance, perhaps even reality, of spontaneity.

Moreover, there are a number of circumstances which argue, almost demand, a greater sense of freedom in the music performance. We are not machines able to reproduce the notes precisely as we have practiced. There are our ever changing psychological states. There are our ever changing physical states. Even the instrument is often not the same even when it is. Always, then, you will have to react to the instrument, to the emotions of the moment, to the reactions of your listeners. Always, then, you will be forced—for that is the liability and the beauty of live performance—to respond to what is, to be centered in this present time, in short, to re-create, not replicate.

Thus, if the classical musician achieves readings frozen in time, burnished musical etchings, requiring little thought or listening to by the player, what could be the point of the live performance? With the jazz musician of honest intentions, the music will never sound this way again, it continually being "rewritten" from one performance to another. But the classical performer, despite the inherent restrictions,* must strive for some likeness to spontaneity, perhaps even more so because of the very constraints imposed upon his music making: to begin with, the notes all specified, then a mandated loyalty to the dictates of his master's voice and, when applicable, having to blend with other members of an ensemble.

Remember the challenge facing actors in a play. Everyone knows the lines being spoken are not owned by the person bringing them to life, but it's all over when the audience is reminded of this fact. Only when an actor appears to be expressing ideas from within—when acting seems invisible—can the audience be moved along a dramatic journey. For the actor, *this* is virtuosity; and so it is for the musician. If, in the classical musician's performance, the music is not actually being created, then neither are the actor's words.

(3) Finally, both elements of the learning of a master work are too important to slight. Each demands and should receive your fullest attention when they are on the center stage of your imagination.

Practicing for technique and playing musically are operationally at sixes and sevens with one another. Conscientious involvement in the one

---

* At one time, however, the classical musician was much closer to the jazz musician on this dimension, improvisation being a highly valued asset.

works seriously against the other. Everyone agrees that to acquire technical mastery of a composition we need to concentrate on the more difficult passages, even making exercises of them. But while we are in the midst of listening to music profound and moving, it is not easy to make pit stops for minor repairs. And, if we get caught up by the aesthetic siren luring us into the sweep of a composition, we will have a devil of a time getting the notes accurately into the musculature. We know that this passage needs work but it is so tempting to follow the phrase to its conclusion and not stop for such pedestrian activities.

But how, in the short run, can pausing for necessary repairs serve the musical dramatist? Every time one stops to work on a sticking point, it is an impudent intrusion into the expressive mode. Too, if you allow every dropped note to interrupt the thrust of the momentum, you will not have the necessary experiences of letting go musically. As no one giving a recital would dream of correcting an error in performance, it is necessary to practice this mind set, too, this letting go behavior. It is every bit as important as the hours given over to working on the physical delivery of the notes.

In sum, if you are determined to clean up your technical act, your expressive side will rail against the constraints of the detail work, while when you are trying to be the poet, the mistakes will nag upon your technical conscience. These effects will occur if you insist on blurring the lines between these two operations bringing them too closely into the same work area. Thus, separate but equal must be the watchword...and attended to with the greatest vigilance.

There is one more united front argument advanced by the bad guys, with, it must be said, a rather compelling ring to it. "Since you use one muscular attitude to play mechanically and another to play with feeling, an excess in either direction will always yield undesirable results. You must, therefore, strike a balance between emotional involvement and critical objectivity."[2] I certainly concur that the playing of a piece mechanically does have a different feel, both psychologically and kinesthetically, from the touch one employs when attempting an expressive reading. Further, when you practice mechanically, and then later switch into musical mode, certain adjustments will have to be made.

But make them you will! You are not a robot and this kind of modification comes quite easily when the noted habit structure becomes a solid part of your being. Actually, what happens to me is that the shift from practicing mechanically into a mode more musical is nearly an unconscious one. I continue to work on technique, gaining accuracy and, without thinking about it, the music begins to sound better. And as I have practiced the piece for months or longer, the difficult places become less taxing, less interruptive of the flow. Again, automatically, not because I will it so, the piece is being played, imperceptibly over time, in a more musical manner.

The fact that it happens almost out of my control seems curiously important to me. The music is not worked on self-consciously. The phrase is not sculpted with an idea as to how it will sound but simply because it begins to go in my direction, as though my inner voices are leading the way. In my idealized scheme, you don't really make music, you become the music. Musicality, when on a regimen of getting the notes right and on time, steals silently in the back door, almost unnoticed.

But that is way ahead of the story. We are going back to the beginning. We are going to divide and conquer. First things first and every other cliche I can muster to take you on the righteous (Oh, Lord) path to The System.

The System

...the student, resourceful and thorough enough to create the proper corrective exercise out of each technical deficiency that shows up in the actual music he plays, will never need to bother with other exercises. [23]

This afternoon Liszt explained to Valerie how he proceeds in assimilating a new piece. First of all he makes a thorough examination of the music and plays it slowly a few times in order to eliminate any possible reading mistakes. The second time he pays stricter attention to the values, the rests, the tempi. Still another time he concentrates on the dynamics, the fortes, pianos, crescendos, sforzandos, all the shadings indicated by the composer. [12]

Step right up folks. What I've got here is a systematic remedy for what ails your fractures without making a hospital case out of it. This portion of the practice regimen begins and ends with technique. Only when you are finished applying its principles to a composition are you ready to make music. First you must build the technical superstructure (with the strength of a house); then you move in applying your personal "touch" (giving it the warmth of a home).

The first and probably most useful thing about using this system is that it virtually decides for you how to apportion your time on each piece that you practice. The design intention is to have you devote approximately ninety percent of your practice to the elements of a composition that you cannot play, or play with difficulty, and ten percent, to the sections that you are on good terms with. And, when you are working properly, this will happen "automatically." Actually, if the percentages aren't quite right, if, for example, you think spending 10 percent on those things that you can already play is too wasteful, this approach lends itself to an almost instantaneous course correction. By a simple adjustment, to be described shortly, the time proportion can be shifted one way or another without missing a beat or unduly disturbing your thought processes. Already more than implied in the above description is the second important benefit of this approach. It actually takes most of the thinking out of the practice sessions. For example, it not only "decides" where you spend your time, but precisely how to respond to the errors that you generate. The importance of taking excessive thinking out of this experience cannot be overstated. The mind is a terrible thing to waste (on a practice session). There is simply too much to do!

Third, although they are relatively independent of one another, the approach to learning technique is consistent with that used for memorizing. The advantage to this congruency is that they are overlapping functions with just one set of instructions. Those of you who have tried different kinds of software for your computer will realize the advantage of this management scheme.

And finally, this approach lets you know, with remarkable precision, what tempo you should be setting for the pieces you are working on. How it does this, and the other advantages of this system, will be made clear in the paragraphs to come. But for now, let us pause and learn how to make mistakes correctly.

The "right" way to produce errors that you can live with is to practice at a tempo that allows the maintenance of a regular beat. This qualification is critical to the success of the program. Without the enforced regimen of a strict beat you will not have available the strongest tool possible for isolating the areas that require serious and protracted study. Of course, when you are just beginning a piece, and if you are new at this game, the tempo that fits this guideline might be incredibly slow—slow to Newmanish proportions; but not quite. Remember, with Dr. Newman, the object was to *avoid* making errors. That is emphatically not the case here. What you are trying to discover, at this stage of your relationship with this particular composition, is the speed at which you are able to play about ninety percent of the notes as laid down by the manuscript.

Incidentally, please don't worry about the supposed precision of this number. It is simply an attempt to convey a reasonable proportion to strive for at some point in your development. No scientific measurements should be taken nor concern about how close you are coming to this "ideal," and somewhat arbitrary, setting. Perhaps at your stage of development, particularly if you are just starting out on this musical endeavor, a setting of seventy percent right vs. thirty percent wrong would be more appropriate or maybe even 50/50. Do what seems right for you, but eventually, I would think, you will want to approach the 90/10 split. Remember, the overriding principle of this approach is to bring to the surface, in a systematic fashion, the most difficult passages of a composition whether you are working at the ten, thirty, or fifty percent levels.

Although the tempo may have to be extremely slow, do not use a metronome. We're talking free will here, taking responsibility, and getting you used to playing with time. If you have to, count multiple beats to each quarter note. So, for example, if there are four beats to a measure, where you would ordinarily count to four and begin over again at the next measure, instead, count to 16 at the same speed, within that measure, giving each beat four counts, effectively slowing the speed to one fourth of its usual velocity.* In other words, do anything you can,

* A quarter note is a note that takes up one fourth of the time in a 4/4 measure. There are, then, four beats in a measure and the quarter note gets one of these.

no matter how unconventional, to render the beat inflexible and within your ability to stay at a given tempo. Remember, the beat is your best friend and chief error detector. Anything that you cannot play strictly in time, and accurately, of course, is deemed an error. If you do not keep a strict beat you will not know for sure whether the unscheduled pause you made in the striking of a note prevented you from making an on-time error. (I know, but I shall be kind.)

I have implied that you may have to play incredibly slowly, but only if that is what is required to keep afloat the proper proportion (90/10). If, on the other hand, you find that you can cruise at a reasonable clip without missing the required number of notes, i.e. ten percent, you may have to pick up the tempo a bit. In either case you are striving to make the composition conform to your agenda, to wit, to practice on the difficult portions most of the time with very little left over for those portions that you can, in some sense, already play.

OK. You have set the tempo that your educated guess tells you will give you the proper proportion of errors to correctly played material. Your hoping that 9 of 10 notes or 9 out of 10 measures will be played flawlessly. (Actually, you are more than hoping; after all, you're still in charge here.) If you see that you are making too many errors, you will slow down. If not enough of these warning signs, you crank it up. What you want to insure, at this early stage of interaction with these notes, is that you do not play the piece without error!

Clearly there is a delicate balance to be struck, with the fulcrum of the balance always shifting towards a quickening of the pace. As you begin to master the difficulties of a piece, you will need to increase the tempo in order to achieve the right proportion of right to wrong notes played. Ultimately, through this process, you will reach the tempo that seems right for performance. No need to go faster, at that point, even if all errors have been accounted for. What you gain in effectiveness by speeding past the desired tempo is definitely outweighed by the cavalier use of time, thus the neglect of further repertoire. By the way, this process can take hours, weeks, months, even years depending on your musical appetite, that is, how many plates you've got vying for your attention.

When in this technical learning mode, you are forever attempting to strike a comfortable balance between variations of tempo. Each deviation leads, potentially, to an error of some import. The first comes from playing too fast, the obvious result of which is the production of too many mistakes. Since, by fiat, you have to stop to work on each miscue, you will find yourself working on materials that were really not all that difficult and would have survived the cut at a more modest speed. As noted, this is worse than not making any mistakes at all. It does not sufficiently differentiate difficult passages from relatively more compliant ones. The waste of time of such an approach must be clear.

The second error is brought about by playing too slowly. At this reduced pace, you will make too few errors for the discriminating player. You will then be addressing all of the material evenhandedly with no shading towards the more difficult and needy passages—passages would have been forced out into the open at a more appropriate tempo setting.

Actually, there is more to say about this latter option. In some ways, it really is all right to practice more slowly than would be natural. Often you will make the transition to a faster tempo more readily with a piece secured at a slower pace. The problem again is not that it is a bad idea—particularly on really difficult passages—but that you are spending so much time on other, possibly more elementary, material that would have been a cakewalk even at some advanced tempo. It really all comes down to whether you can afford this luxury and, once again, how many pieces you would like to get to before quitting time.

Practicing slowly is particularly important when technical difficulties do not seem to give way at "normal" tempos, when the problemed area is, in some sense, seemingly beyond the capacity of that person at that time. In fact, many pianists and pedagogues argue that the only way to conquer some technical difficulties, particularly those that call for great speed, is to practice these pieces or passages at an extraordinarily slow tempo. The argument is that once you have locked these into the correct patterns at a very slow pace, you can, by a display of grit, tenacity, patience and trust, gradually bring them to the appropriate tempo markings.

As is always the case, not everyone would agree:

Is slow practice always a virtue? Does slow practice further accuracy in a fast tempo? "By no means! Quite the reverse. Slow practice can establish habits which are completely unrelated to the coordination demanded for speed.[32]

"Try it up to tempo", I suggested, "but be prepared to make mistakes. At all costs, let yourself be carried away by its exuberance."..."practicing slowly exclusively will not necessarily enable you to play fast."[2]

Which all goes to prove that if there is a possible view on a subject, someone, somewhere will hold that view and defend it well—and, they may be right!

Curiously enough, slow practice may be more important *after* you have learned the piece to a reasonably advanced level—in other words, when you are ready to concentrate on interpretation—rather than when you are working on problems of technique. At a slower tempo you have an easier time hearing what is being "said," more time to react to the beauty possessed and sometimes hidden in these works. I have been struck by how creative many jazz musicians are at slower tempi where they have time to develop their ideas. In the less kind (quicker) tempos, they must rely more on cliches or passages they have rehearsed for just those harried occasions.

The final note on slow playing I give to Egon Petri. It seems to be consistent with the slowness/reflective playing hypothesis tendered above. "Slow practice does not guarantee concentration, but concentration—on problems to be solved—necessitates slow playing."

Well, our digression was pretty slow going, itself, so here's a brief recap. Play each piece at the speed (unvarying) that will turn up mostly right notes—arguably at about the ninety percent level. Prepare to work on the errors generated each time they happen. Remember that an error is any note or rest that is not played precisely when, and as, it was meant to be.

It is so easy to say "Gosh, I really can play that, I just wasn't concentrating," or, "That was such a small slip. Give me a break." This is dangerous business. Much better to be safe and to apply the correction body fluid each and every bollixed time, without thought, fixing the amended habit in dendritic stone.

Now that you understand part one, the play of the game, you are ready for part two—what to do with those mistakes that you have cleverly generated by doing the right(!) thing. You must now convert that ten percent of the piece, the errors, into ninety percent of the time spent practicing, leaving the remainder for merely brushing by those things you do now successfully with so little effort. What I have chosen to do, because it seems to bring about the right proportion fairly reliably, is to practice any missed passage until I can execute it three times in a row without error.

You may wonder how I continue to settle on the number three. Easy. Two times *wasn't nearly enough*, the chances of getting a passage right twice in a row falling more frequently within the range of a lucky occurrence; and four times *was too many by far*, evoking a number of neurotic symptoms. Thus, in this highly scientific manner, the number three was arrived at. I'm sure you remember its use in the memory approach and see that while you are memorizing, particularly if you are able to manage a steady beat, you are unavoidably working on technique.

To recap the most important point, remember that each error must be given the full treatment. You muft not — oops. You must not let yourself off the hook for any reason. You must not let yourself off the hook for any reason. You must not let yourself off the hook for any reason.

Now the question is, what exactly is it that you practice when you make a mistake, and at what tempo? In the first place, when you are practicing the offending passage, it must somehow relate to the rest of the piece. For this you need a small bridge, i.e., a very few notes, that takes you into the problemed area, and a like connection taking you back into the piece proper. This connective tissue must be chosen with care always leaning towards less rather than more. The more of this bridging-the-gap material that you pick up, the less efficient your practice will be. First of all, you are playing more notes each trial, even if they are easy ones, and when you multiply that by the times that you may have to go over this passage, it begins to accumulate into serious clock time. The second is more troublesome. You are playing more notes, even if they are the same easy ones, and you therefore provide more target material for making mistakes. Each mistake, no matter where it is found, no matter how simple the material, says go back to go and do the threes number. Since this already may have been a very difficult passage, lengthening it this way makes you vulnerable to staying up past your bed time.

Now you might ask why this regimen of three in a row correctly executed would have you practicing the trouble spots at least 90 percent of the time. Actually, if the passage is truly difficult, achieving three correctly played iterations in a row could take hundreds of trials, placing your time distribution closer to 99/1.

Having said that, it really shouldn't be allowed to reach this top-heavy proportion. If it takes this long or involves this number of trials, you should drastically reduce the speed of its practice, living to take up the challenge another day.

In the event that it is possible to work on errant measures at the same tempo assigned to the practicing of the overall piece, the remedial work will be reasonably brief. But if you have to slow the wounded passage down some, perhaps even a great deal—a much more likely scenario—so that you will not be stranded there forever, then that is what you must do. There are, you will remember, other considerations, such as the rest of the piece, the rest of the plates spinning jealously about, and the rest of your life.

Now let us review and see if this approach, at least in terms of appearances, seems likely to live up to expectations. The first benefit promised is an assurance that it will distribute your time in an efficient manner. Of course, this will take consistent cooperation on your part. If you can stick to a disciplined regimen of a strict tempo while showing an absolute intolerance for miscues—that is, by taking proper measures to remedy the problem areas without exception—it is practically self-evident that you will achieve a high level of success in terms of time management.

Incidentally, even though you may conquer the most problematic passages of a composition, others—perhaps once well-played sections—will occasionally float to the top of the error barrel and have to be dealt with accordingly. Some technical problems will appear only during certain phases of the moon or be kicked off by your own biorhythms, and other scientific reasons, and the beauty of the system is that you are there waiting for this to happen, the number three scoop on the ready—

with no need to devise an original response nor bemoan your lack of progress.

The second point promised that it would take the thinking out of your practice sessions. Let's see. When you make a mistake you automatically work on it in a prescribed manner. You won't need to wonder how many times you are going to go over the material. It is always the same. You are striving for a given criterion level and that is all there is to that. As far as tempo, the fourth item promised, is concerned, your ears and fingers will tell you whether you are going too fast or too slowly by the proportion of mistakes that you are making. So you see, there are no decisions left to be made, not, at any rate, at the time-consuming high level areas of consciousness.

Finally, the last point, number three in the original list, is that it dovetails with the memorization approach. I'm sure you spotted that immediately. In fact, if you memorize from the very beginning, they merge into one system with complementary goals.

This would be a good place to compare The System with other approaches to mistake making (or fixing). Unfortunately, as previously noted, there is little in the literature with which to make such a comparison. I had hoped for a body of information to review, either in the journals of musicians, which journals are, as you might expect, woefully short on scientific examination; or those of psychologists, which, surprisingly, have not found it useful to focus directly on the learning of a musical instrument. Now, there are most assuredly principles of learning in the field of psychology that would apply to this practice, but no one, to my knowledge, has taken these and made them applicable, that is, customized them to bridge the gap between the printed score and its manual execution. Musicians, lovely and enterprising as they are, need this kind of help.

Of course we do have the approaches of Newman and Cooke. And, in fact, despite my harsh words about Newman's approach, both of these men have made fine contributions. As noted, they at least committed their strategies to print form. And both were *nearly* able to convey important principles of practice regarding this subject of making, or not making, errors.

In the case of Newman, I must confess it was because I wanted a worthy adversary to play off that I took his teachings so literally. (Probably nobody should be held to such rigor, particularly a musician.) Not making mistakes *is* a reasonable goal if not pushed to inflexible proportions, and working towards that end is certainly a necessary attribute for successful learning. It is both a matter of degree and the level of self-consciousness with which I am concerned. Too, slowing down the pace of practice is a requirement for achieving this goal in any system.

As you can see, elements of this strategy are contained in my own, to wit, that I would have the student not make *many* mistakes—instead of the impossible any—and the student, in most cases, would have to slow the speed of play to achieve the proper proportion between correctly played notes and those not so happily come by—whether at the ten percent or fifty percent level.

The Whole Versus the Sum of Its Difficult Parts

In Newman's world of practice, one always hears the piece played from beginning to end—its integrity never in question. Not so for Charles Cooke. He is so determined to convert the difficult portions to friendly behaviors that he would ignore all else until completion of those disciplined rounds. It certainly reminds one of assembly line work at an efficiency-minded Detroit auto plant. This is not necessarily a criticism. Putting together cars, with specialists for each sub-assembly, has been honed to an industrial art. There is nothing wrong, in physico-mechanical terms, with having the parts worked on separately, or, in Cooke's scheme, for having the offending measures reshaped until models of perfection. It is merely (and outrageously) that the craftsperson's feel for the overall product has been radically diminished. Using Cooke's approach, the playing through of a piece is not encouraged until all fractures have actually become the most reliable portions of one's musical anatomy.

When I am less the critic, both Newman's and Cooke's approach seem more reasonable, at least as far as they go (apparently, I cannot help myself). And although I didn't "know" Newman at the time, elements of both systems are incorporated in my own. Newman's contribution has been noted above. Cooke's maniacal approach to technical fluency is certainly apparent in my determination to repair every mishap along the way to a fixed number of repetitions no matter the "accidental" nature of its occurrence. Of course there is this difference: in my system when a criterion number is reached (usually the reliable three in a row without error), the student may leave well enough alone, at least for this go around. In addition, the problematic passage is always considered as being part of the flow of the piece and is not "repaired" until a mishap actually occurs (if it occurs!) on each iteration. In other words the trouble spot is never predicted. You must err before you are put through your paces, original sin not being a part of this program.

Cooke's assigning of the most difficult passages in a piece, the fabled fractures, and practicing them beforehand is reasonable as far as it goes and as far as it is possible. But whereas you might be able to pick out obvious difficulties prior to a hands-on checkup, there may be other traps not willing to show themselves on such cursory inspection. It may depend on your level of concentration, your confidence that day, the state of the economy, the vagaries of chaos, the tempi (most decidedly), and a host of other factors. Bringing the piece up to speed will undoubtedly uncover many more deficiencies not spotted in the early going, which, more than likely, was approached with more caution. Using this system will help place your attention automatically on those sections that need help *that day*, always keeping the flow and the integrity of the piece in your peripheral "vision." As noted, it also allows you to hear the composition from more or less beginning to end, even while putting it through this somewhat distracting fence-mending process.

Practice

From Carpenter to Poet

Well, that's the black and the white of it. Now it is time to probe still deeper, to answer additional questions that may occur to you while exploring the basic tenets of this ruthless road to technical proficiency. These ancillary issues could be considered refinements possessing only diminishing returns for your efforts, but I would argue that how they are handled could have important consequences for your progress.

The Pause That Refreshes

For example, I have suggested the number of times that a troublesome spot should be practiced (until three wins in a row), but have not talked about the interval between the iterations of those practiced measures. Typically, if it is truly a difficult section, you will play it many times over before completing three error-free samples one after another. Thus you will face the interval *between* trials many times. And although this may sound like we're going a bit far in the subtlety (read, nitpicky) department, I think the handling of this stopping place must be thoughtfully addressed.

My suggestion, in general terms, is that this interval be in the form of a slight but definite pause, at least a beat, perhaps two; that it not be treated in the same way as a normal run-through of the piece—which only sounds sensible, I'm sure. But the temptation to complete, with dispatch, the round of three is compelling and thus must be resisted, particularly if it is going in a pell mell and unreflective fashion. This is true even though you know that the sooner you get this "job lot" done the sooner can you proceed with the rest of the piece, the sooner can you get through the platespinning cycle. This brief pause, after each trial of the correcting process, is of critical importance. It allows your nervous system to capture, savor, reflect (albeit, unconsciously) on what has just happened, on what kinesthetic feelings were produced by this sequence of correctly played notes, rather than confounding these feelings by the rapid pressing forward (or backwards) to the notes that started the problem area in the first place.

A pause can serve another equally important function. Mistakes are often made in physically taxing passages, passages that can bring on fatigue in the muscles being utilized. If this passage is one, rushing into the next trial of the hoped-for triad can confound the technical problem with the products of fatigue. It can be likened to carrying a reasonably liftable object with the object becoming "heavier" over time. Thus, you might be able to play a physically taxing passage quite nicely for a run of two, but be brought down on the third by the acid within. Again, a pause of a beat or two, in the intervals between trials, may give your body chemistry the recovery needed to add the necessary third success.

Just a Little Bit

If you have been raised properly, you were taught to leave things (people, institutions, buildings, the Earth) better off than you found them, certainly no worse. In this context, one question that may well occur to you is how perfectly correct should an imperfect, or corrected, passage be before moving on. That is, how correct is correct? It may seem that this has already been tiresomely answered: three error free trials in a row! What could be more straightforward? But, you may remember, we have already discussed an exception: a passage can be so difficult that it must be dramatically slowed to reach the criterion before nightfall. Having played it three times correctly at a slow tempo certainly does not qualify it as performance ready at a more accelerated pace. Again a proper balance must be struck between difficulties worked on and number of plates that you want to keep spinning. If the number of pieces you are working on is reasonably large and your patience in good working order, then you will be tolerant of slow, incremental progress (or—just a little bit!).

Even slow practice may not be sufficient to coerce an unyielding passage into an improved state, in which case you must then separate your hands and try to do this passage three times correctly for each hand alone. When you can do this easily, you may see if it is now possible to put your hands back together with more luck. It is important, however, if this is not easily accomplished, that you return to the separate hands mode and practice the difficult section religiously before continuing with the rest of the piece that day, and, most importantly, not to worry about putting your hands together until the problem is first mastered, even overlearned, in this separated fashion.

The lesson of these examples is that you should drop back to what you can do successfully as the last impression of your experience with a problemed passage. To have tried to put the hands together, or to have practiced too rapidly, as your last experience, when either of these conditions was beyond your present capacity, will leave bad neural traces for your next go round and an even worse level of confidence. To put it more positively, you want to leave each passage, as you return to the piece proper, with good memories and good feelings of what you can do, not what you cannot. As a bona fide platespinner you want to set as your most important goal to leave each section and each piece *just a little bit* better off than when you started that day. Remember, it is the consistent increase in the spin imparted, even if the increments are of a quite modest nature, perhaps most assuredly then, that will keep you coming back for more.

Slow Down at the OK Chorale

After you have been practicing a piece for a time, you will come to know—in its now familiar terrain—where the difficulties lie, and will have a sense of how well you will fare on these passages even before playing them. In some cases an uncomfortable level of anxiety may develop over certain unfriendly sections. So, for example, if passage X has consistently given you trouble, you know it is lying in wait as you draw close to its treacherous neighborhood. You have several choices as you anticipate this showdown. (Of course, if you are really concentrating, none of this will occur, but I know most of you are human and will fall prey to this distraction on occasion.)

One option, given that a section is substantially more difficult than the rest of the piece, is to play this section at a reduced tempo *before* you make the error (an exception to my dogmatic-keep-up-the-good-fight never-slow-the-tempo precept) so that the experience of passing this way is not yet again an accident waiting to happen. You can even practice this section as though you had made an error before moving on—which having slowed down actually qualifies for—repeating this process until confidence finally carries you through this neck of the woods at a more lively pace.

The other two choices that occur are more connected to dealing with the mind—or at least Gallwey's Self 1—in its interminable attempts to undermine the body. If you have been repeatedly knocked off balance by a passage that you are about to play, it might help to remind yourself that this is simply another challenge that you are going to meet, and to welcome it with open arms for the opportunity of rising to these kinds of challenges. If that doesn't work (and nobody in his right mind would think it likely), you will be happy to learn that when the kinesthetic feelings are sufficiently grooved for this passage, when you have practiced it to a fare-thee-well, the body computer will absorb the mind's cheap shots at ending the party.

I must admit to a small measure of ambivalence about discussing this next with you. In general, I believe that for the first several years of practicing, you need to follow The System to the letter of wal silograM eht. Fooling with the three in a row principle can lead to sloppy habits, and in at least several instances has resulted in pronounced alcohol abuse.

But if you can assure me that you will be prudent, I shall suggest that if a piece has been played many times over, and you make a mistake where you have rarely done so before, you might reduce the mending procedure to playing the passage only twice in a row correctly (ooh, I hate doing this) while making a mental note to see what happens in this same passage the next time around.

The other side of this devalued coin is that if you have played a piece for a very long time, yet a passage will not comply to your studied demands, you up the ante to a killer four or five correct plays in a row. All I can say, as a cautionary reminder, is that the other plates spinning may not take this sort of thing standing up.

It is time to bring in pedalling since it is important, in an odd sense, to the practice regimen. I confess that I have not discussed this subject before because it is something I know so little about. When I hear that whole tomes have been written on its use, I am nearly intimidated by what I must be missing. On the other hand, since I am reasonably content with getting the sounds from the piano that I am striving for, or at least willing to settle on, I have never been motivated towards its serious study. At the risk of sounding terribly arrogant (or, more likely, insensitive), it just doesn't seem that complicated. However, to be fair, you may want to research this further. I certainly could be missing out on something worthwhile, a something which might well add an important dimension to your play.

The pedal on the far right, of course, is the one that most of us will use much of the time, and shortly I will discuss how it doesn't fit in to my practice approach at this point. The pedal on the left is used to keep the instrument on the quiet side. The middle pedal, when there is one that works, is used for sustaining some notes while leaving you to move around on other non-sustained notes—usually in the higher registers—with these latter, then, less capable of blurring the original notes being held. If you didn't understand the use of this last pedal, not to worry. Most people don't, and it will not be a factor in your life for some time to come.

To return to more common concerns, the pedal to the right, known as the sustaining or "loud" pedal, lifts the damper and allows the strings to keep vibrating until they run out of energy. Although this pedal does not really increase the sound of any particular note being struck, it can increase the volume by adding the strength of other notes sounded to the original strings still in motion. This pedal's most important uses have to do with connectivity and with fleshing out harmonies. In the first instance, the notes can be connected by this pedal's effects when the fingers cannot easily do the job, or augmenting them when the fingers are up to it, giving the line a more singing quality. In the second, the pedal allows sounds to merge that appear pleasing to the ear—combinations of notes, or chords, not in conflict (dissonant) with each other. Of course, with changing times the pedal has had an increased functionality, and consonance, i.e., being in harmony, is not always the desired end. But for the present discussion, we have more than enough to consider.

Again, this is not the place to go into the artful use of this tool—even if I were expert in that use—but only to caution against its involvement during most of your practice, particularly when striving for technical gains. It is another layer of coordination to worry about as you seek to read from the page (or struggle with the memory thing), play the right notes with both hands, and act as vigilant cop on the apprehension and disposition of errors.

More importantly, pedalling causes a certain amount of hearing loss. No, no the rock concert kind; this auditory deficit refers to an inability to separate the gold from the dross (errors committed) due to the overlapping, thus blurring, of the tones put in motion. If the conditions under which you are listening for technical mishaps are camouflaged by the effects of a clamped down pedal, you will be navigating at a sound disadvantage.

Additionally, practicing with the pedal seems to nudge most of us into a more musical mode. While this may not seem like a serious disadvantage, it can work against a proper vigilance for things gone awry. This general thinking, of course, has already been explored earlier in the chapter, but it is with the use of the pedal that it becomes most problematical. It is when you are using the pedal to make your best musical impression, even on your own person, that you are most likely to forgive yourself errors. It is the sweetened and befogged harmonies that are most resistant to interruption in the flow of a great masterwork. It is an elixir to be held off for the days when you are stronger. For now, in the early stages of mastering a composition, keep your foot planted squarely on the floor and full speed ahead.

Not So Odd(s) and Ends

There are three more principles that I would like to share with you. Since they seem less complex in their operation, their discussion will be relatively brief. However, the brevity of these remarks and the apparent simplicity of the concepts should not be taken as a measure of their contribution. Each of us has a different way of approaching this complex endeavor of music making, and one of my odds and ends might be central to your scheme of things (and vice versa).

Really Do It

The first has to do with the physical pressure that you apply to the notes as you practice in this so-called technical mode. Since I preach the separation of technical acquisition from the "playing of music," you are urged not to concern yourself with differential pressure in your play. You will not, in this mode, be striving to make some notes louder or softer in order to bring out a melody line or to round out some phrase. To the contrary, all notes will be considered equal. I propose that you practice *each* key stroke firmly, erring on the side of too much rather than too little force. To be clear, I am not suggesting that you play unnecessarily loudly, nor that you raise your hands from the keyboard for forceful delivery, only that the notes be struck with solidity and clarity.

The reasons for this relatively heavy-handed approach are severalfold. Practicing in this way underlines the separation of the practice mode from musical expressivity, finessing the potential distraction of poetic musing and allowing you to be more nearly attuned to your kinesthetic sensations. The second reason builds on the first. It seems that the uniformly firm pressure reinforces the sensory impressions being stored, thus facilitating the memorization process. Finally, pressing each note firmly, as though you mean it, makes it less likely that you will forgive yourself the tiniest of miscues. With each wrong note raising an awful clangor, one simply cannot turn the other ear.

Not to Be Ashamed of the Beat

We've just said that, in terms of force of delivery, all notes should be treated as equals. The fact is, some notes need to be treated more equally than others, especially in the early stages of learning a composition. These are notes that fall on the beat, or every other beat, or on some multiple of these, that is, notes that emphasize the meter of a piece. In other words, even if the piece really isn't about rhythm, rather, one that impresses more with soaring melodies, interesting phrasing or lush harmonic effects, it is advised to give the piece a rhythmic punch in the early stages of practice. (Whiteside would turn in her grave to hear that all pieces are not about rhythm, but I think you know what I mean—it *is* a matter of emphasis.) I would have you punch those beats with vigor even though it offends your aesthetic sensibilities. You won't be trapped by this habit when it comes time for serious interpretation. If an exaggerated rhythmic impulse is not in the best interest of the piece, you will be able to modify your behavior no matter how overlearned it may be. Trust me, this is one of those sublime places in life where you really are in charge.

The effects of stressing the beat or rhythmic impulse are severalfold. First of all, consciously emphasizing these minor milestones puts you in touch with how this music is organized over time. If this seems particularly effective in the delivery of this piece, you will keep it on board. If not, you will, as above, simply soften its contours. Secondly, in the beginning stages it serves as an organizing function for both memory and performance, particularly in the difficult passages. Again, it is like the learning of a telephone number where you separate the numbers into small groups to facilitate the memorizing process.

Rushing Roulette

It turns out that many errors are caused not so much by the difficulty with the notes at the scene of the crime as by what led up to the misplay of those notes. This is a principle that I have known for some time having been taught it in the early years of my learning how to play. But I paid it little heed, and it is only recently that I have come to rely on its consideration more and more. In fact, I've come to see this approach as the most effective aid in working on a recalcitrant difficulty, particularly when it does not seem to yield to the normal procedures described in the body of this chapter. And it is very easy to pass over, as I did for so many years, and not know what is contributing so subtly to a problemed passage.

Once again a sports metaphor seems suitable. Perhaps you have seen a short stop who has just mishandled a ball because he seemed to be ahead of himself. Often you will hear the sportscaster describe the player as having tried to throw the ball before he caught it. Exactly. That is precisely what happens in many failures of coordination. The athlete is anticipating the end of the sequence—possibly the most difficult part, the hurried throw to first base—and, while the characteristic of anticipation is generally an asset, the outcome can only be as effective as the preparation that precedes it. Clearly if the ball has not been properly handled in the first place, the throw will never be effectively (air)borne. Breakdown in execution, then, is caused by this rushing behavior preceding the more obvious problem.

Something very much like this can occur with a difficult instrumental passage, particularly one that has repeatedly gone badly. As you approach the scene of the (usual) accident, your thoughts will tend to focus, then arms and hands strain, even accelerate, toward the point of greatest difficulty thus unconsciously slighting those notes encountered on the way. And if these latter are not executed with great surety, the notes following will most certainly fail.

The cure for this problem is obvious but difficult to keep in mind—one so wants to address the major event in this sequence, the obvious miscue. The problematical passage may be helped extraordinarily, however, if the area just preceding this difficulty is practiced with great diligence. At such junctures these preceding notes must provide a base as secure as bedrock. The way to implement this most effectively is to practice the preceding notes in absolute strict time right up to the edge of the manifest problem. Then, stop abruptly and let the feeling of these preparatory notes "sink" in. Do this at least three error free times in a row each time that you come to this problematical passage. The number of times that this either fixes the original problem or makes it less ornery is astonishing, especially when you consider the lack of interaction with the villain of the piece.

At Last...Dessert

To play a whole piece of music, one has to play the whole piece ...spend extra time on the hardest bits. But at some point, if I am going to play the piece with other people, or in a performance, I have to stop working on the bits and begin to play it as a whole.

This chapter has been devoted to increasing your technical fluency. Until now it has been a series of steps designed to get the patterns of a piece of music so firmly entrenched that you would have a difficult time not executing them properly. The explicit intention has been to free you of any technical and psychological limitations that would deprive you of your creative freedom. With the freedom won, however, comes a profound responsibility: to tell the story in your own way. It all, finally, comes down to that.

Sing, Dennis!

Dennis Day was a regular on the Jack Benny show when a few of you were young. Dennis would appear in the midst of a scene, engage Benny in some rather off kilter dialogue and, in the process, make Jack a little crazy. The purpose of this interaction was to bring Jack to ending the non-sequiturs, which Dennis had in long supply, with the unforgettable, "Sing, Dennis!" It was a good-natured expression of exasperation signalling the comedy over and the introduction of some lovely ballad by this popular Irish tenor. We, of course, had all been properly prepared. We had heard it hundreds of times before. We even formed the words. Sing, Dennis!

After you have been through the rigors of The System, the refinements, the pressing firmly, and the rest of the strictures channeling your activity into an efficient, even pleasurable, but curiously unmusical experience, it is time to sing _____ (Your first name here!). It is time to let go of controlling the notes—and yourself. It is time to suspend concern about your technical uncertainties—your only charge now: to explore the beauty that removing of these chains will allow. *For when it is time to be with the music there is time for nothing else*—what came before as useless as the babbling sounds to the baby grown older. Now that the pieces are more nearly yours, it is time to bring your soul into play. Your heart should be free to be with the sounds you are making as your hands follow the grooved determination you have prepared them for.

However, in this new mode you may falter, playing notes not intended. After all, this is a new experience, with a new mind set, related to, but certainly different from, all that has gone before. In this unloosed condition, don't worry about reversing all of the good work you've invested. Up until now what you thought about was getting those notes on time and in their rightful places. Now you are on a different level, one that requires feeling the sounds and responding in kind. In this new place, with this new "distraction," the notes will not always be there when you call. If you have prepared (and prepared, and prepared), however, you will have technical capital to spend; and it is now, finally, all right to expend this reserve on a feeling spree. This kind of mind set takes as much practice, and is certainly as important, as the physical mastery of the notes.

When is it time to leave the security and the confines of technical practice, to let your sensitivity to sounds take over as prime mover? This too will take practice. At first you will be impatient and take a few headers. It is not terminal. If you were not yet ready—you may have made a premature withdrawal on your technical investment—you will get the message. You simply return to the practice mode that got you to this point, hop back on the saddleless stool, and return to the joy of replenishing, then increasing, your technical capital. It is not like you are starting over. You are simply strengthening patterns and reinforcing rhythms that were nearly yours. With experience you will become more expert on when to make this move, i.e., when it is time to trade in the chains of technical restraint for the freedom of musical exploration.

Of course the above is somewhat simplified for this presentation. The truth is that once I feel ready to try my musical wings, I still do the technical number a proportion of the time. It is more or less a weaning process, with several trials of mechanics preceding the trying of wings, the proportion slowly shifting to a state where very few mechanical brush-ups are needed and more trials free of disciplinary measures, the rule.

When you have arrived more securely to the aesthetic mode, anything goes, as long as you are thinking about how to make this music sound *most pleasing to you*. You have worked hard to erect a structure within which to dream. Now it must be inhabited by your most real person, not one who (musically) impersonates others. Of course, this is much easier said than done. Just as being true to your self in any walk of life—particularly if your personal drummer insists on offbeat rhythms—is difficult to maintain.

And, grand heresy of them all, only now, *after* meeting the technical challenges as best I am able, *after* looking within to see what I really feel about this music in my most naive and trusting state, will I consider the myriad stage directions of the composer and his followers—editors and famous players kinds of folks. Usually his ideas are compelling—depending on the edition, depending on the composer. When they are in conflict with mine, I devote serious study to his "reasoning." Often he wins me over but certainly not always. When, in other passages, we have "agreed," it is a nice thing, and on that composition my work is nearly completed.

If you've thought me arrogant before, I'm sure the above has cinched the case. But for me, the process of working through the raw materials "undirected" for a time, even a long time, allows me to grasp what I can bring to these pieces different from all others. Otherwise I am too easily influenced by what they would have me do. And I would then be like Allport's "all other men." I think that is wrong for me. I think that is wrong for you.

After that I simply play through the piece over and over again, without much conscious (read analytical and objective) thought, listening as best I am able to the story being told. The next time I convey this same story, a new idea may occur which I can add to the tale but only if spontaneously come by. The contrived stage business has no place here, only those things that come wafting up from your soulful storehouse—a recounting of this story through your special prism. If you were to read this last sentence over and over again, you would begin to develop a way of reading that seemed best for delivering the message that it possesses. How you would group the words, how you stress certain syllables, where you would insert a pause, would change over time and coalesce into a reading that was right for you. You might even be able to make the listener oblivious to that sentence's length and awkward construction. That, it seems to me, is all there is to playing a musical composition. I'm sorry if there is a bunch I am missing but it doesn't seem any more or less than that.

And One More Thing

Before ending this discussion on your newly won freedom for musical expression, I am going to challenge a highly questionable assumption—nearly universally held in the halls of musical academia—concerning the importance of analysis in the interpretation of musical art (or, indeed, any art). This assumption suggests that the understanding of the grammar and structure of a musical composition is of utmost importance, even essential, to the interpretive process, that by holding up a composition to rigorous analytic inspection you will achieve a more faithful and persuasive rendering of the composer's intentions.

With a bravado appropriate to the untutored, I shout, "Nonsense!" Analyzing an object of art to better capture its essence is not only rubbish, it is aesthetically dangerous. Putting a musical composition through the paces of a detailed examination brings us no closer to illuminating its heartbeat or its power to move, uplift, or change us. The danger of being involved in such an exercise, moreover, lies in distracting us from the intended emotional impact of the experience, itself.

For the secret of a masterpiece is not contained in its elements, not even in the sum of those elements; to this end one must look beyond such rational investigation. Further, to practice a reductionism of this kind is to invite incautiously the listener/performer behind the scenes, diminishing the desired and wondrous naivete of his emotional response. The moment that one discovers Frank Morgan working the levers of the great Oz, or how the lady sawed in half remains whole, something wonderful and important is lost. To know the cellular construction of a rose contributes not a whit to the receiver of this love message. A description of the chemical makeup of the atmosphere during a glorious sunset can only be rudely distracting. Far better the sheer joy of wide-eyed wonder to carry us deliciously among life's unexpected treasures.

The art of interpretive performance should be approached in a childlike manner and, as far as intellectual preparation is concerned, with utmost restraint. To communicate his or her own sense of naive appreciation is the highest charge one can ask of the performer, one which, indeed, will have the greatest impact on his audience. To overly involve the analytic mind complicates the process unduly, straightjackets the spontaneity of both the performer and his listeners, and generally detracts from the awesome power of this experience.

The intellectualization of art is clearly a person's heroic attempt to comprehend with his mind what he absorbs with his spirit. To love and appreciate beauty, one must take it on its own terms, to receive it wholeheartedly, as it were, not impose arbitrary rules as admission to our souls.

Before the reader concludes that I am for disconnecting our glorious capacity for intellectual achievement in favor of simply and blindly proceeding on instinct, let me say that, while I will partially plead guilty to this charge, and believe it to be the better error, it is closer to say I would counteract the powerful and bloodless tendencies of over-intellectualism. In reality, as with all things, a certain balance is needed. In the case of the interpretation of musical art, for example, the intellect is a handy and necessary manager for weighing the importance of the thematic material, for being receptive to the thrust of its language, its phrasing, its climaxes, its final direction.

Perhaps an analogy to a communication form closer to home would be of some help. When one gives a speech, it is of little consequence for the speaker—beyond remaining within accepted usage—to understand the rules of grammatical construction in play. A self-conscious parsing, in order to make a moving and credible presentation, would be a disagreeable intrusion into the finest of speeches even in the preparation of its delivery.

Bringing into play the ideas of Zen teachings, Seymour Bernstein elegantly expresses this point of view:

> Your initial response to music occurs without intellectual analysis. Gifted children, for example, often project deep musical feeling without being aware of musical structure or historical facts. It is this kind of innocence from which adults can learn. Therefore, in practicing, avoid an excess of analysis and allow the music to reveal its own beauty—a beauty that is answered by something deep within you...A Zen philosopher put it this way: "If you would paint a chrysanthemum, look at one for ten years until you become one!"... Great artists succeed in establishing a close identification with the music they perform. It is this capacity that sets them apart from other performers.[2]

And I would add, to establish this close identification with a piece of music, you must love it for reasons that are deeply personal to you.

And as you would not analyze a loved one, unless you are very foolish, indeed, you subject a Chopin prelude to this form of scrutiny at the peril of losing something very important in the bargain.

Accepting a Brahms intermezzo, without "knowing" the source of its magic, may be likened to accepting the beauty and uniqueness of our fellow human beings. Just as the Freudian would reduce each of us to the sum total of our (early) experiences glaringly, if falsely illuminated by the analytic process, the performer, who brings analysis to bear on a piece by Brahms, better have an abundance of the humanitarian spirit lest he gain the notes but lose the music.

That many great artists (probably most) do indulge in this act of intellectual examination does not shake my feelings at all. It has, after all, been inculcated in their training, a product of scholarly tradition. It does demonstrate, however, the remarkable strength of a composition to withstand such insults to its mysteries, and the triumph of the human spirit to rise above this objective and tawdry process. The capacity to make great music survives, then, not because of such intellectual probing but despite its best efforts.

I shall end on an annotation of Keat's *Ode to a Grecian Urn*. Ending on this note is my way of suggesting that all of the disciplined and reinforced principles presented, while essential to getting you there, are only as good as the poetry that ends the story.

Beauty is truth,   (Be true to your own voice)
Truth beauty,   (If you are, it will be right)
That is all
Ye know on earth,   (That's really your only choice)
And all ye need to know.   (And that's just fine)

Performance
Setting the Stage

Stage fright is a revolt of the entire body against a situation which resembles a trip to the gallows. And, as in the case of genuine executions, there is little that rehearsing can do to make one eager to appear as the main attraction - Frank Wilson

Just recently, as a happy by-product of doing research on musical latebloomers, I was invited to a small musicale where early and late bloomers alike would perform. After a planned interval of social pleasantries, each person would play the piano (the majority), the flute or guitar, or act out a scene in a play. Since everyone else was to do something, I suggested that I could join in by reading an excerpt from the book that you and I are sharing at this moment. Hoping it would be relevant to those facing the trials of performance, I proposed reading from the chapter on concentration.

Since I had never done anything approaching such madness before, I have no idea what prompted my offer. I looked forward to it with increasing apprehension; with luck a severe storm would scuttle the whole affair. In hiding for nearly six months working on this project, I had shared none of the writings excepting with Ann whose objectivity, thank God, is suspect. This would be the first report from those unrelated others out there as to whether I had anything of moment to share. Would they like what I had written? Would my reading do justice to the message? By practicing instead of eating and sleeping, I was able to reduce my anxiety to a fever pitch. The more important question, however, would they like what I had written, must await its presentation.

Mine was the last spot on the program. Each person having already played, running the emotional gauntlet so generously provided by this experience. Finally, I took my place on the piano bench and faced the blank expressions (by actual count, nine persons of the stoic persuasion). Would they be (a) gleeful critics? (b) warmhearted friends? (c) manikins from a nether world? It would all happen soon enough.

I read with head inclined well into the pages. *They* would have to come to me. I would not force their attention by a sly seeking of eye contact, by prying loose unfelt courtesy. To count, it had to be genuine, unsolicited, spontaneous.

I began.

The reading went along well enough, I suppose, but the first place of intended humor passed silently by. Oh, ohhhhh! (Keep at it, Margolis, you asked for this.) I ventured further into this unknown region. The second place of hoped for laughter was acknowledged by pleasant sounds from out there somewhere, followed by others in their rightful places.

That was better. Much better. Calmer, I read more easily, the chasm between us miraculously bridged. With each pleasant sound my tension diminished, the same for my friends (choice b from above). The stranger would not ruin the party, after all.

This was an important event for me in a number of ways. There was first that initial interval of ominous quiet from the audience, followed shortly by the extraordinary pleasure of manifest support and appreciation. Of course, those listening could have waited until the end of the piece and applauded my efforts, even vigorously (which, in fact, they did do), but then, what would I have learned. This after-the-fact courtesy was "mandatory" and rationed out in equal servings for every performance, regardless of the quality of the play. And, I would argue, properly so. But I knew *as I went along*, from moment to engaging moment, whether we were in this together or I had been relegated to the periphery of their floating agendas.

By this welcome interaction, my "performance" was received differently from the others, not because it was in any way superior, but because of the different traditions attached to our various efforts. Afterwards, in the car going home, I got to thinking, and remembering.

Memory #1: With friends like this...

I thought first about a tale of two comedians in Las Vegas some years ago. It begins somewhere near the finish of a rollicking Buddy Hackett performance at the Sahara show room. Although it sounds unlikely, Buddy persuaded his *entire* audience to accompany him up the strip to the Desert Inn for the late show where Jan Murray was "knocking 'em dead." As "incentive," Buddy presented his good time conspirators with instructions to dummy up during Murray's act—"not a sound," says Buddy, "make like a painting." Murray was about to draw a blank to a full house.

Murray describes the event as one of exquisite torture lasting forever—actually, Hackett restrained his charges a modest yet unconscionable twenty minutes—with the flop sweat (Murray was perspiring audibly*) descending from his every pore, his career, from borscht belt to broadway, flashing before his incredulous eyes.

Punch lines followed one another around the mirthless room searching for faces to set into motion, yet found only unsmiling eyes staring back through the haze. Finally, moments before irreversible harm, from the back of the room, a single person's side-mouthed cackle (Buddy's) could be heard, pulling Murray back from the edge.

I considered the experience of the performer of classical music who often must wait for twenty-five minutes—the length of a Brahms concerto, perhaps, or one of the more ambitious Beethoven sonatas—to find whether his listeners have "stayed with" the program. (If you think twenty-five minutes is not a long time, a very long time, there are moments in everyone's life—we have all experienced them—for which there is no adequate measure.) Moreover, in the classical concert the well-trained audience, American style, is going to applaud, almost certainly, even vigorously, all efforts fashioned for its consideration.

Imagine a comedian doing his or act act with these same rules of engagement. The audience, under these absurd guidelines, would share its reactions to the comedian's efforts by laughing at the end of each set. They would respond with whatever goodwill they had stored, i.e., their uncertain delight and surprise, in much the same way as practiced by the classical music crowd.

It is accepted without challenge that applauding or otherwise show-

---

* My appreciation to Woody Allen for undoubtedly giving me permission to use this line.

ing one's feelings during the play of a classical music concert will severely break the concentration of the most focused performer, dramatically limiting his ability to do carry on. A similar argument is offered concerning the protection needed for fellow audience members who, ostensibly, would have their capacities to focus irremediably lost.

Should not the same general argument hold for the comic performer? Would not loud and intermittent laughter break his concentration as well, disrupting the necessary rhythms of his act? But we know the opposite to be true. Once the comic breaks down the emotional reserve of those once so distant, wins their trust, receives their active participation and obvious delight, he has won the game, at least for the while. He has found his way with this audience and can more readily take them on the comedic journey he has charted.

Most stand-up comedians have learned to incorporate these loving sounds adroitly into their presentations, and, in fact, as the Hackett-Murray story illustrates, the *absence* of this reassurance can dramatically alter the comedian's ability to concentrate (except, perhaps, on his own demise). In addition, there is an inestimable advantage that accrues to the comic for embracing the audience as "part of the act." The line by line response provides him with a laboratory-like experience for honing his presentation. Of course, this would be possible in a limited way if no one laughed until the end, but the impact of instantaneous feedback provides a much more powerful tool for these purposes.

In much the same way stage actors enjoy the live performance for the information and sustenance that can echo reassuringly across the great divide. Compared to the night club comic or comedic play, the signals are, of course, more restrained, there being a greater concern with not breaking the concentration of the principles. But it is still an environment rich with clues and far superior to that which the movie performer, for example, can glean from those in "attendance," and stage performers swear by this subtle, sotto voce communication.

I am sure this comparison of the serious classical concert to the comedic performance would be heard by most serious music players as inappropriate if not completely out of touch. But since you are not yet a card-carrying member, I would like you to meet Bernard.

Memory #2: With friends like this, on the other hand...

Bernard. I don't know where you are but you have never left me. We met only once, and then all too briefly, but you have changed everything. There I was, five o'clock in the morning in a church in Baltimore, where the minister had made the church piano available for my practice, when suddenly I was aware of your unrestrained presence. I froze at the mere hint that somebody was listening, especially at that hour.

Of course, practicing is not what it became as soon I sensed you were there. But oblivious to the rules and the state of my nerves, you sang with the intricate melody of Chopin's *Barcarolle,* moved in time to its subtle rhythmic invention (this was not a dance piece...or had I never listened?) all the time with me, encouraging me, sitting next to me, even touching me. *I had never seen you in my life for God's sake!* "Hey man, you can play." "Yeah man, that was niiiice." "Do it, man, do it."

He claimed himself maintenance person for the church but clearly he was something more. My faith in the profane was sorely being tested.

Hey, Bernard! Don't you know the rules? Don't you know when somebody is practicing the pianoforte, when one is poring over the sacred texts of classical music, they are not to be disturbed; why it would be like interrupting another kind of service.* This is not folk music where people are naturally approachable (like folks, you might say); or jazz, that music seeming to rise, even coalesce from the energies of the group—where audience and players alike call out expressions of encouragement, comfort, love and joy *while* the players are giving their all (go man go!, yeah!, right on!, do that thing!, I hear you!). No, Bernard, this is not that kind of thing. This is music to be played, and listened to, by persons of great and studied seriousness.

But, there was something different, so alive, so connected, in the way you listened, the way you absorbed the music, the way you responded to this player. You approached, engaged all my senses, sat down not near me, no much closer than that, in a way that was absolute-

---

* Which church proceedings Bernard doubtless would also illuminate with his zest for the essentials.

ly right, perfectly natural, and you listened. No, I mean *listened*, with mind *and* body. Nothing else existed. When something moved or delighted you, you made sure I knew. "Right on," "Yessss," while touching me in loving punctuation, then moving rhythmically to stay connected.

Instead of being put off or frightened, I knew you were with me, a part of me...and, after all these years, you still are.

This being the unlikeliest of events, I acted quickly. After getting Bernard to swear that he would not disappear (you can't be too careful with an illusion!), I went home and woke Annie, urging her to share in this experience, making sure it was real. If she saw and heard what I've just described, it would be safe, a part of our permanent record. I told my story with the same excitement that I am telling you now. She was immediately transformed from a distant sleeping person to an eager active friend and joined me in this transcendent experience.

Afterwards, I thought about the usual playing of classical music; how arid, how devoid of real life and energy it can be. This, of course, is where we are heading. But it is early. I have one more memory to share. This is the last in the set and will take us directly to the (fourth) wall. You remember the fourth wall, do you not? Well, the Words and Music experience made me understand where to put that wall.

Memory #3: Words and Music, the Sam Hinton Legacy

Actually Words and Music had other spiritual forebears: Karl Haas, Andre Previn, Leonard Bernstein, Billy Taylor, to name just a few. In case you don't know what these people have in common, I will tell you presently. But I was privileged to see Sam Hinton in person, and his manner of performance had a profound impact on how all subsequent performers would present themselves and their art in our (Ann's and my) fantasy world come true known as The Words and Music Book Gallery. Lets go back, before Sam made his entrance on that stage, for some background.

This is one of those tales that begins "Once upon a time." At that storied beginning (1948) MGM made a movie, described by Leonard

Maltin* as a "sappy musical," called *Words and Music*. It concerned the collaboration of composer Richard Rogers and lyricist Lorenz Hart, in which reality did not interfere with the creation of this vehicle for "more stars** than there are in the heavens."***

However,**** I saw the movie as a kid—Maltin was not yet able to dissuade me from seeing it since he hadn't yet gone through the birth thing—and loved it. The title alone conjures up all the lavish, mostly MGM, musicals being made in the thirties, forties, and fifties, wherein the credits it had—just before Ben Nye, "Makeup," or Edith Head, "Costume Design"—"Words by" (say) Yip Harburg and "Music by" (oh) Jerome Kern and even "Words and Music" by the Gershwins. They—these long ago and faraway musicals—seemed to possess everything that was important in life; the most ennobling ways that we communicate and provide joy and merciful escape. I was, after all, a youngster eagerly distracted by fantasy so lovingly created.

And when Ann and I were trying to figure out what to name our bookstore—one we were about to visit upon the city of San Diego; a bookstore that would give great emphasis to the arts; a cultural haven with a piano playing proprietor providing browsing music somewhere in the shadows, practically unnoticed except for the heartfelt sounds that he hoped he could sneak past his self-consciousness—this title crowded out all competitors. The "Words" were the books, of course, and the "Music" was the accompanying browsing music. A nice simple concept, right?

This would be the way I would insinuate myself, elevator music like, into the performing arts. I was not at all prepared for what was to come: the evolution of Words and Music into WORDS And MUSIC. For in the hands of the interior designer and Ann, my otherwise sensitive helpmate, the piano, a reasonably nice, small Baldwin grand, moved in concept and in physical space from somewhere in the background—off to the side, unobtrusive, a place of suitable humility for my

* The otherwise balanced movie critic who puts out the most widely purchased book of reviews each year.

** Here is a sampling from this movie: Mickey Rooney, Judy Garland, Gene Kelley, Mel Torme. How bad could it have been?

*** The MGM "mission" statement.

**** I just love footnotes!

tentative offerings—to the very dangerous center of things. Now the piano and, oh-my-God, the pianist were the dominant visual features in this award-winning* use of space by a retail business. I accepted the role with a mix of feelings shaded by terrified excitement, deciding that after several thousand trials of being "on," I might overcome the dangers of this new position.

But that seemingly insignificant alteration in the original floor plan, the move from off in the wings to center stage—literally, now that a raised construction had been built to showcase the piano in the middle of things—initiated a sequence for which I had to don my scrambling shoes.

Since we now featured a performance area, we invited a fine local guitarist to give our first formal musical evening. Although the book gallery was reasonably large, there was at that point neither space nor chairs available for this purpose. Looking about, we thought seating for twenty-five would make for a comfortable audience. As it turned out, despite this small number who christened our performance series, the concert was a huge success, especially in the aesthetics department: the subdued classical guitar music framed in the artistic setting of our store, the dramatic stage lighting, the beautiful paintings on the wall, and books, wonderful books, everywhere you looked, on gleaming white shelves.

Our small public wanted more. And now, so did we. We moved rapidly in the direction of being a bona fide performance space—still within the context of a book gallery—featuring a diversity of styles geared toward the musical intelligentsia: classical, folk, jazz and Broadway-inspired. We even bought seventy-five more chairs and rear-ranged the furniture. Because of the dramatic setting, many fine musicians were delighted to showcase their talents for small consider-ation. Thus we increased our efforts for musical notoriety in the hope of making an impact on the book-buying community.

One of these fine musicians was Sam Hinton, certainly one of the great folk singers and musicians anywhere, who happened, to our good fortune, to live in nearby La Jolla. Sam was special in many ways, but

* An Orchid Award-winner—a prize awarded by the architects and design people of San Diego—for best interior design for the year 1984.

the first thing I want to share about him is the somewhat atypical format of his presentations. He would organize his music around some important theme, which was articulated with a text, so that the musical performance was broadened into an extraordinarily satisfying integrated presentation of words and music. The wonderful playing and singing of the folk music—Sam was a truly great musician blessed with an enchanting stage presence—bundled together by expository strands of text describing some aspect of the music—perhaps its treatment of farmers, or other important social events—provided a remarkable and meaningful experience for the audience. Here the performer talks to you, along with playing for you; here monologue contrasts with music in much the same satisfying way as silence does with sound; your intellect is treated with equal measure to your thirst for emotional fulfillment.

Of course, while you learned how a folk song, originally sung in rural England, transformed through its adaptation by the farmers of Tennessee, then passed on to the ranch hands in Texas, who etc., you were also getting a glimpse of Sam: his choice of vocabulary, his textual rhythms and allusions, the stories he would tell, his asides, and, most importantly, his manner of being with you.

Before I leave Sam, I must make mention of several other elements of his concerts that set him apart. By this time, perhaps six months into our existence, Words and Music was presenting a variety of performances: classical music recitals, small jazz groups, broadway show revues, some opera and play excerpts, and even excerpts from experimental plays. Unfortunately for the musicians in town, there were too many of them—and many wonderfully talented beyond description—and too few of us—places where they could play. As a result, with judicious selection, we had absolutely smashing performances virtually every time out.

But as fine as these other performers were, there was invariably a difference between their efforts and Sam's, particularly in terms of that most revealing feature of any concert, the audience response. Besides the organizing text described, which he would fashion for each performance, there evolved a quite different relationship between Sam and his audience than exists with most other performers, particularly those playing classical music. Sam treated the audience like friends, as though they were in his home or he in theirs: *Sing along, if you like. Here, let me teach you the words. Why, isn't that a lovely baby. Sure does have a good set of lungs. Hi, Jonesy, you better get to your seat or I'll mark you tardy. What's that you say. The song that I attributed to Mr. Earl Scruggs was really written by Blind Melon. Why, thank you. I sure am glad you were here tonight.*

He was absolutely available before the concert, at intermission, and afterwards. Sam, by turns, would show people how to play exotic instruments, be engaged in a lively discussion on almost any subject, or just spend time browsing in the bookstore, shoulder to shoulder with members of the audience.

Anyway, I have gone on at length because the people who attended these concerts left with a different bearing from those leaving more seriously, if contentedly, from the otherwise splendid presentations by the other performers. There was a smiling softness, a serenity so uniformly worn, one suspected an injection of serum soma from *Brave New World*. If you saw *Singing in The Rain*, you know what I mean.

Was Sam less an artist because he allowed interruptions, made himself available to all comers and shared the spotlight with others? Did he have less to concentrate on, *only* doing folk music, than the other performers? Actually, he had more. Sam, who had a working repertoire of over 1000 songs and played fifteen instruments with consummate skill, gave roughly fifty concerts over a four year span at our gallery and no two of them were even remotely the same, either in terms of choice of songs or "story line" constructed.

I guess if you had to sum up the difference in a word between Sam and the other fine artists appearing on our stage, that word would be accessible—accessible to his person, to his music, to his delightful and informative world view.

Well, I couldn't expect everyone who gave concerts to become over-night Hintons. Sam, in his seventies when he performed his magic at Words and Music, had been crafting his skills since his appearances on the Major Bowes radio show fifty-five years earlier. But, at the very least, every performer could, and certainly should, put serious consideration into their choice of program materials, how they relate to each other, if at all, and to share this preparation with their audiences. An even superior agenda, of course, is starting out with a theme that actually "drives" the evening, that is, becomes a determining motive for materials chosen, which then can also be shared from the stage with great effect.

And in so doing, we would learn not only about the subject of the concert but the subject's presenter. In discussing Gershwin, the performer could not help but reveal facets of his own personality, if only to hear the sound of his voice. But if he has put some good hard thinking into it, we might find out why Gershwin attracted his attention, why certain pieces were chosen over others, even, perhaps, how he would evaluate Gershwin's attempt to utilize elements of jazz within classical forms.

Another important reason for my fascination with this format was the fact that it relieved the sound of whatever instrument was being played—the contrast then being not only in messages delivered but in quality of sound. This was particularly helpful, even, from my point of view, necessary, when only one instrument was featured for performance. Thus, in a piano recital, you have a piano sound for an interval alternating with the sound of the pianist's voice, as he or she gives textual meaning to the musical proceedings, each timbre refreshing and preparing the listener for the other.

Also, you should know that the physical setting at Words and Music was conducive to this kind of discourse. The stage was fairly surrounded by the audience and of close proximity, there being just a few feet between the performer and the first row of audience members.

It was, of course, not the first time I had heard music presented in this manner. Karl Haas has been doing it in brilliant fashion with classical music on Public Radio for thirty-five years. His ability to develop a theme without ever repeating himself over all these years is a matter for disbelief. It might be music written about gift-giving holidays, or music with extremely odd rhythms, or music by left-handed composers. Both words (the text) and music are given substantial airing on Dr. Haas' shows with each contributing equally to a most satisfying, integrated presentation.

Leonard Bernstein had, with the New York Philharmonic, done a similar and highly acclaimed turn with the Young People's Concerts, bringing classical music more within children's reach. Billy Taylor has, from time to time, presented a like format with the subject of jazz piano and pianists, and Andre Previn, with the help of the Pittsburgh Symphony and guest performers, made a series of integrated presentations on public TV Symphony in both the classical and jazz genres.

But Sam Hinton's concerts at Words and Music were the first where I had had a chance to view this kind of presentation in person, in an intimate setting, with the audience having the opportunity to relate actively to the performer on a number of levels. This was a performance with a more meaningful relationship between the audience and performer, each actively reaching across the divide, each contributing, in no small measure, to its outcome.

Thus, Words and Music became a "born again" book gallery. What once had been descriptive (words and music) of live music presented in the milieu of a bookstore—and then, mostly for browsing purposes—now became, retroactively and additionally, a romanticized description of the concert series format, namely, the integration of text and music bundled in lively presentations. I, of course, took credit for having created the store and its interior design for just this purpose—a brilliant concept, I was told, graciously accepting any kudos tossed my way—but, as you have seen, the whole thing sort of just happened, certainly more *to* me than *by* me—from where the piano/stage was placed, to the regularly performed concerts, to Sam Hinton's version of the integrated concert.

Now all concerts at Words and Music utilized this most sensible model, including integrated presentations of classical, folk, jazz, and Broadway show tunes. All performers were asked to embed their musical presentations in the context of an organizing and elucidating text. In the midst of an evening of Chopin music, for example, we might learn how this master composer revolutionized the use of the keyboard; perhaps a folk musician would demonstrate the various musical instruments used for love calls around the world; a jazz artist playing an evening of Thelonious Monk might suggest and defend the thesis that Monk was one of the great composers of the twentieth century; and probably the finest use of the Words and Music stage, a history of the evolution of the Broadway theater—as performed by the all around brilliance of Bill Wright in a facsimile to real theater productions—by the artists whose greatest works had been generated and inspired by that venue. We had evenings of Irving Berlin, George Gershwin, Cole Porter, Stephen Sondheim, and many others, beginning and ending the series, appropriately enough, with concerts on the collaborative efforts of Richard Rogers and Lorenz Hart—which in case you are keeping track, were the subjects of that "legendary movie," *Words and Music.*

These, then, were the memories vying for my attention to the road as I drove home from the musicale. To take you back (well, perhaps you took a break from your reading—I can't always be sure of what you are doing out there, and this has been a long journey down memory lane), I'm speaking of the musicale where I learned once again how important it was to have those ongoing and reassuring strokes, that interaction that lets you know that you are not alone (or as they say in show business, dying) in the performer's role. The first memory, of course, was The Buddy Hatchet (sic) job, then the Saint Bernard mission, and, finally, how Words and Music evolved from an MGM musical into a haven for the mavens of musicology. Of all the jumbled fragments rattling around in my brain, why these memories?

As I reviewed this chain of images, it became clear that all concerned the structure and mores of performance. When I considered the spontaneous laughter and helpful comments that had taken place during the painless* initiation for me as a reader of my work, I had been struck by its interactive character—how this interplay, with its clear signal of approval, had allowed and encouraged me to perform at my best—particularly when contrasted with the other performances in the very same setting. This likewise was the case with Bernard where his uninhibited and positive response to me *during* my playing was reassuring and facilitative.

The Buddy Hackett story, on the other hand, is a vivid illustration of what can happen when the opposite condition is operative—uncertain, absent, or delayed response from audience members during a performance—and serves to dramatize that what happened to Jan Murray, happens on a regular basis to classical music performers, albeit on a less theatrical note.

Finally, the Sam Hinton (Words and Music) story has to do, in an obvious way, with the impact that integrated presentations of the kind described have on audiences. However, less obviously, but of equal im-

---

* As it turned out!

portance, are the effects of that experience on the performer, himself. For not only is the audience entertained more completely, one may say, on more levels, but the performer, due in no small measure to the lessening of his isolated position, has an easier, more civilized time of it.

Again, my special interest in all of this is the structure of performance, that which facilitates the process, that which does not. You might ask what a chapter on performance is doing in a book of this sort. You are not going to be performing soon, certainly not professionally, and perhaps not ever. But, let us consider...

Performing, or perhaps more modestly put, playing for others, does seem an integral part of the story, a compelling motive for the taking up of music, even later in life. It certainly was for me. Maybe it will be on your mind as you practice, or as you see and hear others perform. Certainly, when you learn some pieces you really love, and are justifiably proud of your accomplishments, you will want to share this experience. And sharing it means performance, even if a lower case p. Unfortunately, in my personal experience, and for most others who have gone before you, even the sharing of these efforts with once-trusted friends can be an exceedingly tough sell to your nervous system. Put it in a slightly more formal setting where others will also play, and your body can turn on you with amazing ferocity.

Most of us are all too well aware of this possibility, this astonishing fright when trying to perform. We have had the dreadful experience of shaking uncontrollably as we gave a talk in a classroom, had to say a few words in some neighborhood or PTA meeting, or made a presentation to our business management team. Even for the accomplished, well-traveled performers, who have been this way countless times, the experience can be a series of surprising neurological displays.

You don't even have to wait until showtime. Once you have been through these shocking events, the thought of putting yourself through this experience again, even in some far off future time, has an insidious way of working its effects back into the present. This can lead to the testing of your capacity to perform now by pretending to play for others, putting in the musical dip stick, as it were, noting your progress on this facet of your development. Watching yourself to see whether you come through under pressure is really another form of performance anxiety in which your erstwhile ally, the nervous system, can turn on you even in the privacy of the practice room.

According to a recent survey, our greatest fear is giving a talk in front of a group of people, particularly strangers. To give you an idea of the magnitude of this fear, the second place "winner" was that of dying. (Of course this prompted Jerry Seinfeld to ask, If you were going to a funeral, which role you would seek?) Well, if giving a talk in your native tongue is rated the number one anxiety provoker of all the scary things out there, is it not reasonable to expect that holding forth in a second language, requiring the skills of a sleight of hand artist, would also evoke monumental fright?

And, it takes a number of guises, this evil thing. For one, it can mount an absolutely devastating attack upon your memory. You can try to perform something that you have played hundreds of times "perfectly" only to draw a complete blank when put on the spot. And once experienced it can, and usually does, take on a life of its own. What do you think will happen the next time you consider playing for someone after such a debacle? It is extremely difficult to ignore one's past defeats of this sort, our ability to reflect on such experiences being not much of a virtue or kindness.

A second effect of this condition (called Pianoso Nervoso in the *American Psychiatric Diagnostic Manual for the Pleasantly Gullible*) is that many beginning players find themselves in overdrive, speeding up their play, trying not to take up their listener's valuable time. This too can be a prescription for slipping through the cracks. First, it is difficult to "keep up," causing you to stumble desperately over your own fingers in this senseless one-contestant race. Secondly, although they are every bit as important as the notes actually played, there is a tendency not to give rests, and long notes, the time they deserve. If you do succeed in getting through the notes, then, sometimes that is all that you accomplish, the results being a kind of frenzied mechanical journey through something that means so much more.

As already noted, probably the worst thing that happens as a result of such nervousness, or as it is more seriously known in the concert world, performance anxiety, is that your limbs can begin to shake out of control. You will recognize it immediately. It feels like that talk you gave to the eighth grade class who seemed intent on turning their thumbs down on your heartfelt efforts. And small wonder. Put together a complex task that pushes the upper limits of the body's facility for finely programmed dexterity, mix with a palsied condition of unbridled proportions, and it is a miracle that any of us make it to the finish line.

The playing of music is rewarding on so many levels that it is completely maddening and even more puzzling that this barrier would exist. Why should such a harmless activity involving the sharing of one's personal expression, using a vehicle of unassailable beauty from "his master's* voice" (certainly he wished no harm to come from the playing of his music), be cause for so much angst. One questions one's ability to function under pressure, even one's worth.

And then my thoughts, giving no quarter, take me still further. Why should I question myself so? Is it appropriate for me to respond in this way? For most of us, the initial tendency is to shoulder these reactions as part of our own personal baggage. Thus for your author the decided tendency, particularly early on, was to answer yes—perhaps there *is* something not quite right about the way I am put together. Fortunately, and only after many years of observing these same effects on practically all others, I have learned to resist this unattractive psychobiographical summary.

It is a condition shared by the vast majority of people who play, from amateurs only wanting to share with family and friends, to those incredibly heroic persons performing, so seemingly poised, in the great halls of the concert world. Since this is a virus that attacks virtually all, regardless of station, it clearly deserves consideration in the discussion of learning to play at any level. It is not only another challenge that needs to be addressed, it is possibly the most important one. It ought, therefore, to be approached with the same thoughtfulness given to overcoming hurdles to competent play of any sort.

In fact, without question there needs to be a course (Performance Anxiety 101!) in every conservatory of music, one whose whole focus and explicit aim is to help students get over this frightful deterrent to one's best efforts. It is not enough to say it comes with the territory— and it unquestionably does—but to look into its causes with the avowed purpose of ending its debilitating nonsense. Indeed, if we are betrayed

---

* Whoever: Chopin, Bach, Bartok

by our nervous system, of what value is it that we have worked so industriously to master a glorious composition by Schubert.

Moreover, it is a situation of great complexity. There are so many factors acting in concert (in both senses) that it is a wonder that more players are not paralyzed by their overall effects. (Perhaps they are! It is difficult to assess how many people this affects whom we shall never hear from.) Much of the stress, of course, comes from within, from our own uncertainties as to how we are received when we reveal ourselves in this way. Playing a musical instrument provides a remarkably effective vehicle for the deepest expression of our feelings, thus putting us into a vulnerable position to those whom we trust with this expression.

But from this corner's point of view, at least as much stress in the performance arena comes from external and unnecessary sources, that is, from the way these kinds of experiences are almost invariably structured. If these external sources are not the prime movers, they certainly exacerbate our natural tendencies in that direction. In the pages that follow, while all of the discrete sources of stress that I can muster will be discussed, particular attention will be given to those stress-inducing customs which have become reified by tradition, and for which I have an enormous axe to grind. It is hard to say which are the more responsible—the inner determinants or those assailing us from without—but the confluence of these factors wreak havoc on too many of the undeserving—me and you, for example—and it is time we put an end to it. And as you've heard me say repetitively but with mounting conviction, Anything I Can Do—and we're talking a barely recovering basket case here—You Can Do Better.

Performance
The Demons Within

Now, for the battle. As a plan of attack, I propose that we consider each source of anxiety separately in order to defeat or, at least, diminish its disruptive effects. If we are thoughtful about pinpointing the causes and have a rational approach to restoring the necessary calm, we shall approach music making so much more comfortably. Sharing with others may not be all there is to learning to play, but it certainly provides a wonderful (de)frosting.

And now, here is a list of some of the more important and specific fears that shake the most unflappable when the spotlight is suddenly upon us. There are so many of these wretched possibilities, I'm sure I've not got them all. For example, Seymour Bernstein, in his discussion on this subject, eloquently suggests two aspects of performance anxiety I won't be discussing but which are clearly on target.

The day of performance is for all performers a moment of final reckoning—a confrontation with one's art and with oneself to which others will soon bear witness. Not only does the musician (1) assume responsibility for interpreting works that have influenced the very course of civilization [*wow, heavy!*] but he must also deliver his best (2) within a designated time span—that frozen segment of time wherein not a phrase nor even a single note can be redone [extremely good observation and probably one of the more severe pressures on the performer who unlike the writer, the sculptor, the painter, the architect, and the composer has not the luxury of continuously refining the product note] but must live with whatever happens right now! It would serve no purpose, therefore, to pretend that a performance is anything other than an extraordinary feat of concentration, imagination, endurance, and dexterity. The performing musician, be he amateur or professional, deserves admiration for his ability to cope effectively with the day of his performance, whatever the state of his nerves.[2]

Well said, Mr. Bernstein, but if you, dear reader, can, with success, wrestle with the imposing list that follows, you will be a long way towards effective music making no matter the audience, no matter the weight of the masterworks, no matter the lack of a temporal eraser.

Here, then, is that long list of nervous makers, nine challenges to us all:

(1) Fear of memory loss

(2) Feeling like you are not up to the mechanical demands of the music

(3) Fear of (being seen) falling apart

(4) You're looking at my soul. Does it please you?

(5) Fear of not being considered musical or artistic

(6) General self-consciousness when the spotlight is on you

(7) The weight of responsibility in taking up another's time

(8) Nervousness about being nervous

(9) Isolation and separation

Before I elaborate on the causes and "cures" for performance anxiety, I would like to reprint what the estimable John Holt had to say on the subject. I was so struck by his words that I printed up an oversized version of the following paragraph and put it on the wall that I face when I practice. This way I can not avoid seeing it from time to time, thereby possibly absorbing its wisdom. His version of how to get from here to there is much simpler and more to the point than my tortured reasoning and might be the better path for you. I think he is incredibly wise, and so I delight in sharing this with you.

Once you stand up to play a piece in front of people, you have to finish it. No matter how bad your playing is, or how terrified and ashamed you may feel, you have to go on. If you can't play the piece *through*, however badly, before others, you will never learn to play it well. You can hope that each time you play you will be a little less afraid and will play a little better, and this may prove to be so. But that battle against fear and shame is never completely or finally won; it always takes some will power, some courage, to perform before others, and that is part of the excitement and pleasure.

This great man has an unerring child-like eye for the essentials. It is not happenstance that he has written some of the biggest selling and most sensible books in the field of education. I accept as gospel these truths recorded by St. John with the exception of the punch line, "and that is part of the excitement and pleasure." The continuous battle against demon anxiety is *in no way* a part of the lure of playing for others. I would have urged John to end his statement, "and that is the price you must pay for the privilege of playing these great works of art." You John, of all people, one of the great iconoclasts of our educational time, would not have minded, I am certain, my tampering with your text. And before I forget where we are going...

(1) Fear of memory loss
My God! I've lost my place.

I chose this one for first consideration because I think of it as less serious than some of the others, not to be taken lightly (when it happens it is devastating), but somehow more easily approached, dealt with, and won over.

All of us have had the experience of going blank when trying to remember something we "know" quite well. Moreover, this experience seems to happen more frequently when the pressure is on—like an introduction we suddenly find ourselves making at a party—or even simply anticipating its happening. Even when you feel relatively safe, such as playing for your friends, this possibility exists. You know that memory can be a problem in such a situation (you've been there before), and, regrettably, your very fear seems to make it more likely. Additionally, much learning of instrumental music takes place at a muscular or kinesthetic level. Through repetition, complex patterns are learned which, when sufficiently "burnt" into the synapses, help the player move semi-automatically through the required behaviors. Because of this phenomenon one doesn't have to recall each note consciously but experiences the playing of the piece as though presiding over a chain reaction. It almost happens to you, not by you. The playing of one group of notes reminds you—or your muscles, more nearly—of the next group's whereabouts, and so on, until, aided by this undulating mechanism, the piece has played you to the finish line.

Unfortunately, you are also aware that this is a kind of unconscious mechanism and, as such, not subject to the same sort of management as other types of memories, which knowledge, in and of itself, can be quite disconcerting. You cannot, for instance, easily reproduce these patterns consciously in your imagination but only by the actual use of your hands. If before you are to perform, you check your conscious processes for the notes that you are ready to play, you will find *that* cupboard chillingly bare. Of course, that has always been so, the notes never really having been accommodated in that area of your "vision." Yet it remains a surprising and unwelcome realization each time you absent-mindedly send out a search party for reassurance.

You might wonder why all this fuss about memorizing when a simple remedy would be to keep the score in front of you whenever you perform. In the following quote, included for its historical view, near the end of the paragraph, and italicized for your convenience, is the undeniable argument for memorizing. I must warn you that I am dreadfully dogmatic on this point and have been known to turn on my heels when someone takes the other side.

To judge from various accounts of their performing practices, other great artists before the twentieth century apparently played from memory even though they always appeared on stage with their scores. Small wonder then that audiences, long inured to established traditions, were shocked when Clara Schumann dared to go on stage without a score (she never performed concerti from memory, however—not even the one composed by her husband). It was now 1828 and a new precedent has been set. Clara Schumann demonstrated what was already an accepted fact to all performing artists before her—that a score was quite superfluous since serious performers always memorized their performing repertory as a matter of course. It was not long, though, before Liszt, with his well-known predilection for showmanship, seized the opportunity to turn this new development into a dramatic ritual. He had always thrilled his audiences when he peeled off his white gloves and tossed them lightly into the first few rows. But at one performance he caused a veritable uproar by tossing his score after his gloves. It would take even more than a Liszt, however much he was given to flaunting his remarkable memory in the faces of his critics, to camouflage a truth that has been known to musicians for centuries—namely, that *all performing artists, including Liszt, Clara Schumann, and Mozart before them, are able to listen more intensely and play more fluently when freed from the score.* Even those musicians who agree that a fear of memory slips is the chief cause of nervousness [I don't think so but this is Seymour's time. I'll take mine later on] would still defend the virtues of playing from memory. In any case, it would be many more years before audiences and critics would consider performances from memory as anything more than exercises in showmanship.[2]

Remember my saying that nervousness about memory is one of the more tractable problems in this lineup of fright makers. I submit that adequate preparation will overcome a tendency to forget no matter the pressures. Of course, one could reverse this and say that no matter your preparation and resolve, if the pressure is of sufficient magnitude, it will relieve you of all things in your memory banks. Personally, I prefer my position. If you think this dogmatic, please read the relevant section on memory in the chapter on concentration from which the following lines are excerpted.

Imagine yourself a contestant on a nationwide television quiz show with a million dollars on the line. You are asked to name the capitol of the United States, or to...recall your own name. The point is that no amount of nervousness...could shake those answers from your grasp.

So, in my simple-minded world, adequate preparation is the key to defending against memory loss, and setting a criterion that is stringent to the point of absurdity is the operational definition of adequate preparation.

Also for the more tenacious among you, I have written, as you are painfully aware, an alternative approach to memorizing. Contrary to the conventional wisdom of the musical community, however, it is the strength of the rote memory that must be most assiduously addressed. If that, indeed, proves to be the case, it argues for "feeling" to your bones the patterns of the composition as well as you have memorized the name on your birth certificate.

(2) Feeling like you are not up to the mechanical demands of the music
(a) Fear that you have picked a piece that is beyond you;
(b) Wondering if you have prepared adequately.

The solution to this fear is to pick a piece that is not beyond you and to prepare adequately. Sound a trifle simplistic? Some things in life need to be dealt with in just this fashion.

If you are going to play a piece for someone, choose one that is absurdly within your reach. Do this for the first *several hundred times* that you do this scary thing. This is not the time to be on the cutting edge of your technique or testing your mettle. Much later, maybe. Not now. At this point in your performing "career" the technique of a piece should be absolutely accessible, so second nature that you can limit your thinking (or non-thinking) to the soul of the piece unlocked by the automatic play of the notes.

Only when you have gotten several hundred trials of success under your belt, and have the confidence that playing for someone is well within arm's reach, should you pick a piece with immodest demands. It is infinitely better to follow this cautious plan than to accumulate memories ill-serving you the next time you venture out into that dangerous terrain.

In most cases, your listener isn't going to be concerned with the difficulty factor. In fact, your fondest hope should be that he or she is attuned to the important stuff, the feelings being expressed, the sensitivity that is yours. Far better to play *Chop Sticks* beautifully than a Chopin nocturne like a broken record.

(3) Fear of being seen falling apart

Fear of being vulnerable, of losing control in front of others who will think what they will of us. This is really a nervousness about being nervous, about letting others see how damaged or out of control we really are.

Now we are getting to the heart of the thing, at least on those ideas within that have the potential of reigning* over our parade. This one, of course, has no easy solution it being possibly the key issue to living (closely) with our fellow beings. If you are reasonably trusting, and have been fortunate enough to accrue a measure of positive self-regard, this one won't attack you with so much vigor. However, if you are like me, you will need further reinforcements.

Anything that can take your mind off this crippling distraction is worth considering. Check out my chapter on concentration. Better yet, do read Gallwey's book on *The Inner Game of Tennis*. This should take care of 25 percent of the problem.

More importantly, begin playing for those you already trust, those who know you for the neurotic wretch that you are. Perhaps your teacher is such a person (if he or she is not, then you need to find another teacher), or your significant other (if he or she is not, then you need to etc.), and good friends (etc., etc.). And you need to do this often. One philosophical ploy that will help ever so slightly is to plan to fail a few hundred times as part of the dues process. In other words, you must come to understand that this is what it takes and has been endured by all others before you.

---

* I *know* how to spell rain!

Probably the most helpful strategy is to plan to meet regularly, in a musically-oriented support group, with other individuals huddled in this same scary boat. You will have no difficulty in finding such people as virtually every person who plays lives (and dies) with this problem. This kind of group has been described in a previous chapter but is so valuable for these purposes, and so satisfying for the participants, that I'd like to spend some time here with different aspects of its operation.

To begin with, shoot for getting together every week, or as often as group consensus will allow. The idea is that everyone can play on each occasion, but is free not to, with the same level of group acceptance. This is a critical point: no one should be put in the position of having to play until he or she feels reasonably comfortable, even if that time never comes. Encouraged, yes. Being made to feel a really welcome and involved member, participating in other ways, of course. Having the opportunity to talk about what they are going through as they await their turn, fine. But, mandatory to play on a particular occasion, absolutely not. If you succeed in providing the necessary atmosphere of safety and good fellowship, even the most reluctant will come around, and then you will have trouble dislodging them from the only piano bench in the room.

Two suggested routes for gaining participants: (1) Advertising. If you go this route, I strongly recommend interviewing the respondents and playing in a one-on-one circumstance with each person, at least a couple of times, to make sure that this is someone whose musical and personal attributes will mix well with the other members of the group. Like love and marriage, it is a lot easier to begin a relationship than to do the termination number; and (2) writing local piano teachers who have adult students to find out if they would support such an approach and if they have any students who they feel might be appropriate and interested. By writing first, you can explain in detail how you see this kind of group at work—I have supplied a letter that you can use as a model—and the teacher can be assured that you have thought this through with sensitivity and a caring attitude, and will therefore likely be more receptive.

Clearly, the two essential elements of such an undertaking are the proper selection of group members, and the creation of ground rules that will ensure some measure of success for all involved. As with any social group where interaction is a high priority item, good chemistry is critical to this undertaking. Thus, group members have to be selected with the utmost care. Those chosen should agree to attend religiously, to listen attentively, to offer meaningful support, and to "be there" for the people who warm the piano bench, on any particular occasion. There should be *no critique of any kind* on the performance, the focus being entirely on the emotional impact on the performer of his or her playing for others. It should be permissible, however, to discuss the music—not the quality of the playing, but the music, itself—which can add a great deal of meaning to the experience.

More helpful, however, is that the discussion center around what each person experiences when he or she is "caught in the act." Physical reactions, ideas, fears and hopes, joys and frustrations and other distractions—as they relate to this performing business—are subjects to which most group members will relate. The person who plays should be encouraged to talk both before and after his or her playing, if that would be helpful—even, perhaps, during, if they have been forced to make an emotional pit stop—with members responding with empathy and like supportive responses when the spirit moves them. I might add that this group experience is not only a fairly surefire way of helping you improve your facility for playing in public—if given enough time, and enough experiences where you both fail and succeed—but a wonderful place to meet people with the same love for music and the same worries about performing the damned stuff.

Here is that sample letter to the music teachers in your area that might help you get your groups going. You might want to skip over this letter as it repeats in substance, albeit in a different form, much of what you have just read.

Dear Ms. Abend:

I'm writing this letter to you to let you know about some groups I am forming which might be of benefit to some of your students. The purpose of the group is to provide a forum for the playing of a musical instrument in front of others on a *regular* basis with the hope and determination that this becomes a more comfortable experience for each player. The actual schedule will be up to the group but I am hoping that it will take place every two weeks or so.

Each participant will have the opportunity to play at each meeting, if there is sufficient time, but each person can opt not to play if they feel they are not ready or sufficiently comfortable.

There are a couple of points on which I am sure we would agree. The first is that playing for others is quite a trying experience for most people. The second is that the only way to get over this hurdle—if it can be accomplished at all—is to do it as often as you can under optimal circumstances. We will try to provide those optimal circumstances.

Before I go on further, I would like to reassure you on several counts. The first is that there is no charge for this experience and there never will be (I am doing it as much for myself as for the others) and, second, and perhaps more importantly, the most sincere attempt will be made to not conflict with your philosophy of teaching in any way. In fact, the experience should be one that complements whatever goals you have in mind for your student. To this end you will be invited to attend the group of which your student is a part, if that would be to your liking. And if you have input, please know that it will be gratefully received.

The groups that I will be forming—I intend to form at least two, possibly three, so I can have a lot of experience and fun doing this—will be constituted to some degree on ability level so that participants will not be unduly intimidated by disparity of achievement.

Group members will be chosen very carefully so that members will be comfortable with each other. Those chosen should agree to attend as often as they can, to simply listen, offer support, and "be there" for the people playing on any particular week. There will be *no critique of any kind of the performer's playing*, the focus being entirely on the emotional impact of playing for others. It should be permissible, however, to discuss the music—not the playing of the music—the music, itself, which might well add meaning to the experience.

The discussion will center around what each person goes through (from his own point of view—it is not a critique or time for feedback) when he or she performs. The player can talk about what it feels like physically, or about his or her ideas and feelings approaching the experience and/or the actually playing, or anything at all that will help the rest of the group know what it was like for him or her on this occasion. All of this discussion, however, will be optional. The player will be given the opportunity to talk about his ideas and feelings, but how much he does this is entirely up to each person with absolutely no pressure to do so. The other members' role at this time is to respond with empathy or other kinds of supportive responses when the spirit moves them.

I might add that this group experience is not only a fairly surefire way of helping your students improve their ability to play in front of others (all of whom will be in the same scary boat) but a wonderful place to meet people who have the same love for music and learning to play the instrument.

To give you some idea of my own level of play and degree of stage fright, I would be glad to come in and play for you. If you can stand it, so can I.

Thanks for your consideration. I will be calling in about a week.

Sincerely hoping that we can get together on this,

(4) You're looking at my soul

Does it please you? This is a fear of letting others see expressions of your unique person. Will they feel good about it (and therefore you) or will they be critical and non-accepting. A variant of this fear, particularly if you are playing for the traditional musician or teacher, is whether your reading of the piece would be considered scholarly, that is, fall within the traditional bandwidth of accepted practice in the music community.

Strangely enough, this is tantamount to a fear of playing something successfully, that is, getting across the musical ideas as you hear them and being criticized for that very success, in other words, for the unique way you go about your musical business (♪ Ain't Nobody's Business If I Do! ♪♪).

To a significant degree, the subtext of this book—lying restlessly beneath the surface—concerns itself with this subject and is given expansive treatment in the chapter on individualism called "Drummer." This element is about standing behind, not being an apologist for, your musical interpretations, however they may depart from the usual. I can think of no better place to work on this than the small group, using it for explorations and acceptance into the uniqueness of your musical being. If you need more help on that score, and most of us do, make sure you have a teacher who gives you the proper Rogerian thrust into musicpersonhood (covered in the chapter on teaching). As noted, so much of this present work speaks to this issue, let us pass, for now, to a related topic.

(5) Fear of not being considered musical or artistic
This one overlaps with number 4, but deserves, nonetheless, its own place in this scheme.

Once you take the steps outlined above for points 3 and 4 this one will take care of itself! However, allow me to emphasize that a careful reading of the text concerning musical fundamentalism in the chapter called "Drummer" might be reinforcing.

(6) General self-consciousness when the spotlight is on you
How you appear to others either in terms of your face and body configuration, your hand and arm movements, your clothes, or in terms of how you respond or move to the music.

For some reason the line from the movie *The Ruling Class*—spoken by Peter O'Toole in that hypnotic way of his—has never left me: "I find myself watching myself watching myself watching myself." The unending circularity and paralyzing properties of self-consciousness are dramatically suggested. Again I refer you to the suggestions in points 3 and 4 above with my best wishes. If you can cut down even one of those O'Tooleian "watching myselves" you will be on the way to musical absolution and the group experience, once again, is a powerful antidote to this looping paralysis.

(7) The weight of responsibility in taking up another's time
Not being sure that someone, or anyone, wants to hear you.

The only thing worse than people wanting to hear you, in terms of evoking nervousness, is people not wanting to hear you—or at least your uncertainty on this point. Are these people who are ostensibly listening to you really wanting to be in that position or have they been trapped by circumstances? And your uncertainty may grow, particularly when there is so little feedback as the process unfolds. "How am I doing?" is not usually a question that will be answered along the way. That is why the Bernard experience was so important. His moment-to-moment response made me know he was with me until "we" had finished the piece.

My playing to browsing customers in the bookstore was a relatively painless way of easing into performing, as the person was not trapped only into listening. He could concentrate on the books, only half tune me in, or go full measure, as the spirit dictated, but the option would always be his. *My* responsibility was minimal.* Thus when a person stopped by to listen—the piano was wrapped by a bar with stools attending—I knew he really wanted to hear me. Of course, this was good and bad, but mostly good.

If you can find a situation where you can play for people who are already involved in another activity, I do think it a reasonable way of putting your toes in the shallow waters of performance. However, it never quite prepares you for total immersion, the cold water shock of Complete Attention focused on your efforts. It is difficult to think of gradations that will lead you there seamlessly. There comes a point when you must actually dive in, avoiding, if at all possible, the stinging rebuke of the belly whopper. (I use this metaphor hoping that the story of Olympic diver Scott Donie, presented in the next chapter, will be read with no more than polite interest and not taken as a model for your entrance into the pianistic natatorium.)

Speaking of this reminds me of a situation, not uncommon in our book store of old, when a person, or, more frequently, two persons, would sit at the piano bar near me and ask me to play something *especially for them*. Assured of their interest, I was always delighted—

* Do no harm!

being an easy mark—and even excited to oblige. But in certain unfortunate instances, hardly a heartfelt measure or two would I essay when I realized that my "audience" had fallen into private conversation. I know this may seem overwrought, but I would become quietly furious at these unintentional slights—sometimes even stopping, to see if they noticed. Most did not. Since you are probably made of healthier stuff, you may not so easily be thrown off key.

An obvious point is to never play for anyone unless you sense genuine interest—in my scheme of things politeness should, but does not, count—and have the staying power to go the distance (short is always better than long, it being much superior for you to stop playing before they stop listening!). The group experience suggested previously is, again, a good place to discuss and work out this plight, although learning to play for yourself, *primarily*, even while playing for others, is unquestionably the best safeguard. Let me explain. If you can get into the habit of enjoying a piece, appreciating the wonder of its composition, listening to it as though through fresh ears, particularly when you are playing for others, it really won't matter if anyone else is listening. And, curiously enough, they will be more likely to...

If only I could take my own advice!

A final tip on combating this difficulty: when you are playing for someone, attempt to play the piece slower than you think necessary. There is an unfortunate tendency to rush this experience. Consciously putting the brakes on should even it out to a more reasonable pace. Have the courage to take your time, to make full use of, even enjoy, silences, rests and long notes. The beginner is often loath to take this time, not wanting to take someone else's in the doing. Getting it over with, unfortunately, seems an important motive at this stage. And although that is a perfectly natural concern, this kind of solution—going too fast without regard to the beauty sacrificed—will bring about disinterest—fulfill the prophecy, if you will—more quickly than anything I can think of.

(8) Nervousness about being nervous (Part 2).
If you have had discombobulating experiences previously when the

spotlight was on you either in playing the piano or doing another activity with similar pressures, you will, undoubtedly, carry this potent memory with you. Even knowing that it happens to others can be highly suggestive.

Of course, having a method for concentrating on the task at hand is a powerful force in the right direction. And, again, the group. I know. It seems a lot to put on the group but I think you will come to agree with the power of that experience. And after you pay your dues (X number of failures) and achieve some hard won success (and you will, I promise), then you can take heart from the observation of Seymour Bernstein, noted teacher, that: "Though remembering these past achievements does not eradicate nervousness, it does tend to lessen its sometimes devastating effects. As every artist knows in his heart of hearts, past triumphs carry the promise of future successes." In other words, these circles, thank goodness, travel in both directions.

But the biggest hurdles are still ahead—placed there knowingly and ignorantly by our kind for the fulfillment of false values. They loom like an indecent obstacle course, one which very few handle with equanimity. Let us face them together.

Performance
The Demons Without

(9) Isolation and separation

The formality of the circumstances and what has come to be the tradition of the concert stage, the non-interaction between those on stage and those listening, the lack of humanity, the fourth wall, the ambiguity of silence before you can receive your performance report card.

These are strong words, I know, and have generated the many pages, driven by hope and vitriol, which follow. Before that, however, a confession. The first eight contributions to stress, most, in some sense, generated from within, were presented for the sake of completeness. (This is, after all, an attempt at being a quasi-scholarly work!) It is not that I think of these eight elements as unimportant and unworthy of thoughtful discussion. They all are real and troubling sources of discomfort to the performer's experience. Further, I hope that the modest suggestions that I make are of some benefit for those who would try them. But in terms of the impact on the performer, they pale when compared to the frightful manner in which classical music is typically presented.

International Terrorism On a Cultural Level

On July 30, 1993, Scott Donie, a world class diver, winner of the silver medal at the Olympic games in Barcelona in 1992, was very much in the lead in a meet at the U. S. Olympic Festival at San Antonio with five dives completed and six remaining. He was poised perfectly atop the platform in a handstand that seemed to last forever. Suddenly, Donie stepped to the back of the diving platform, climbed down the ladder and walked out of the natatorium and out of the competition.

This story actually happened. But if it hadn't, I might have been tempted to make it up, so perfectly does it capture the feeling of a classical solo performer at the beginning of a concert, the almost naked fear of being judged a 3 out of 10, a desperate wishing to be anywhere else.

For those interested in closure, at a subsequent meet Mr. Donie got back up on the board (there being no horse about) and is now back in the competitive swim. He did something that many performers have wanted to do, and feared they might, but were prevented by the specter of a lost career, of losing face and whatever else one can forfeit by this act of courageous cowardice. I don't personally know of any concert musicians who have seated themselves at the Steinway and decided to head for the wings between Schubert and Beethoven, but I'm sure it has happened, or perhaps should have happened. And if the musician didn't get that far before checking out, it is an absolute certainty that concerts, seasons and possibly whole careers have been called off rather than taking that last problematical "dive."

Wouldn't you know? I have been made aware—just prior to the publication of this book—of a case where a prominent pianist/composer/conductor, one Ethel Leginska—once called a female Liszt—did in fact leave the stage just in time for her recital. The story was told to me by Ron McFarland, one of our great contemporary composers who, for some unconscionable reason, the publishing world has not caught up with as yet. Mr. McFarland got this story directly from the legendary performer herself:

She said that she once walked out on the stage of Carnegie Hall, took one look at the audience and walked off the stage and out the back door. No one could find her. She disappeared and was feared to have killed herself. They were even said to have drained some likely lakes. I asked her where she had gone. She said she had joined a traveling theatrical troop, which also, of course, required being on stage. This was, she explained, how she got herself together and continued her musical career later on.

And this by someone who has spent a lifetime preparing to do this thing she loved so dearly. Madame Leginska, and virtually all others of similar accomplishment, have survived the rigors of competition, have played before many audiences, have variously meditated, reflected, been hypnotized, tried drugs—legal and nonaddictive in most cases—and behavioral therapy. And yet that metaphoric moment before the dive—balanced precariously on the platform, the audience waiting expectantly, for the most part humanely—that moment can tear at one as few others in a person's life. Is it appropriate that highly trained musicians feel this way? Are we dealing with a class of people who are seriously neurotic, or is there something wrong with the picture in which they are framed?

In his biography on Glenn Gould, Otto Friedrich describes the contrast between the popular fantasy and the gut-wrenching reality of the solo concert artist:

In the popular imagination, a concert pianist lives a rich and glamorous life. He strides on stage, under the spotlights, with the mysterious authority of a Lohengrin. Outfitted in the most elegant white tie and tails, he sits down at the piano, silences the expectant audience, and begins, with complete ease, to play. Almost by magic, from memory, the Chopin preludes flow forth, or the *Appassionata*. The audience explodes into applause, the men admiring, the women adoring. The pianist bows graciously and disappears into the night.[10]

The reality is quite different...one filled with almost constant anxiety. John Browning the highly regarded American pianist has this story to tell: "On the day of the performance, it begins to build in the morning and reaches a climax by mid-afternoon. That's when it's worst. I don't have bad nerves, but I often wake up with a tight knot in the stomach which gets tighter as the day progresses..." And Paul Badura-Skoda eminent Mozart player: "There are times when you feel that the public is just waiting for your slightest mistake." Glenn Gould saw himself "walking into a gladiatorial arena, where the audience sat ready to give the thumbs-down signal for his death." Gould had acquired a real loathing for the gladiatorial aspects of the concert hall. The audience's eager participation in all

"those awful and degrading and humanly damaging uncertainties,"
Gould felt, made a piano recital one of the "the last blood sports
...To me this is heartless and ruthless and senseless."[10]

Pretty strong reactions from persons who have performed innumerable concerts. Again, I am forced to ask, is it really this bad? Are these
views representative or are we talking about a biased and grousing
sample? After all, we all know about Gould and his rather idiosyncratic
ways.

But from all that I can gather, and a fair amount of gathering it was,
this view *is* representative and may be conservative. From the sampling
of people I have interviewed and have read about, the characterization
of this experience ranges from awful to God-awful. Seymour Bernstein
describes nervousness as *belonging* to performing. "It plagues virtually
everyone who performs and it can in some cases reach appalling dimensions. 'No one suffers as much as I,' is therefore a familiar lament
among performing artists" [and is nearly universal].[2]

In a book called *Stage Fright*, Stephen Aaron likens this reaction to
psychic near-collapse. And, in support, putting vivid imagery on the
bare bones of this psychological razing, the following characterization
is presented by enthno-musicologist* Henry Kingsbury, which seems to
capture for the majority of concert artists what it really feels like when
you enter with the "mysterious authority of Lohengrin."

Although it would be an overstatement to suggest that walking on
stage to perform in a recital hall is comparable to being a prisoner
of war, there can be no questioning the fact that the social distance
that exists during a formal performance separating a recitalist from
his or her audience tends to present the audience in a threatening if
not hostile character. The allusion to the military conditions depicted
in the Bible is corroborated by the words of one medical researcher
who tested a drug for the control of stage fright in musicians: "a
performer, beset by fear, finds his body reacting as it would when
facing...a tiger."[1]

---

* An anthropologist poking around in the dark halls of music conservatories.

Wow! What have we got here? The following is a compilation of the shocking feelings expressed on the previous pages about this experience. You might read the first couple of instances and, when recognition sets in, move quickly on from this chamber of horrors: "facing a hostile mob or a tiger"; "comparable to being a prisoner of war"; "psychic near-collapse"; "plagues virtually everyone who performs"; "reach(es) appalling dimensions"; "heartless and ruthless and senseless"; "those awful and degrading and humanly damaging uncertainties"; "one of the last blood sports"; "public is just waiting for your slightest mistake"; "walking into a gladiatorial arena, where the audience sat ready to give the thumbs-down signal for his death"; "constant anxiety"; "wake up with a tight knot in the stomach which gets tighter as the day progresses."

According to many who have been there, this word collage more or less captures the pressurized milieu of the concert musician. I ask you if there isn't something terribly wrong with a venue devoted to bringing works of great beauty and joy to appreciative audiences that can so terrorize the heart of the messenger?!

To give some focus, let us take a brief look at some of these "messengers," these astonishing carriers of tonal beauty. There are, admittedly, a few who seem to thrive on the problematic conditions of the concert world, described here so darkly. Our generation has its Itzhak Perlman, and Emanuel Ax, the generation before, Arthur Rubinstein. But for every Perlman and Ax, who defy the pressures and seem the better for it, we have a Glenn Gould (or one might say, five Goulds) struck down at much too early an age actually retiring from these "blood sport" wars at age 31. For every Rubinstein, seemingly fearless under the lights, we have had a Horowitz, more vulnerable to the stresses, having to withdraw for agonizingly long periods before taking up the challenge once more in the dreaded and adored concert halls of the world.

One such artist, and a finer musician had not appeared in decades, is Leon Fleisher. Once on his way to becoming Horstein, or, if you prefer, Rubinowitz, in one handsome package, Fleisher played a concert, in Baltimore's Meyerhoff Hall in 1982, remarkably enough, with both hands. In his youth, the prized student of the great Beethoven specialist Artur Schnabel, then protege of both conductors Pierre

Monteux and George Szell, with whom (the latter) he had made legendary recordings of the Beethoven and Brahms piano concertos, and the
darling of pianists everywhere, Fleisher had not had the normal use of
his right hand since 1965, over seventeen years before.

This dramatic 1982 concert, aired nationally over public television,
and celebrated by all who knew this remarkable story, was Fleisher's
gutsy two-fisted return.* He had been trying all these years—bringing
to this heartbreaking, career-dampening, medical mystery the same
ferocious tenacity that he brought to the study of the keyboard—to find
what dreadful thing had caused his fingers to curl spastically, cruelly,
unsparingly into his hand. (Of course there were whispers, there are
always whispers, you know.)

Among the endless attempts to regain his once powerful, yet
delicate, mastery were acupuncture, psychotherapy, witchcraft (a variant
of psychotherapy), surgery, neurological ponderings, rest, exercise, will
power, and the fight goes on, probably to this day. Born of desperation,
having little idea of what had happened to him, he tried anything and
everything reasonable (and some not so) and, although he achieved only
modest gains for his efforts, never gave up hope or preparation for his
next two hander.

Finally, miraculously, after eighteen years of failure upon failure,
modern medicine granted Fleisher some measure of relief, allowing him
to return triumphantly to an emotionally charged audience awaiting the
hero's return. He did a yeoman's job on the Franck *Symphonic Variations,* then, given the supercharged existential moment, a devastatingly
poignant performance of the *Chopin Nocturne in D Flat Major.*

Cut. Fade to black.

If this *were* a movie, the credits would have rolled over that final D
flat receding, then taken over by the roar of the crowd, on their feet, in
tears, applauding as surely no audience ever has, and I would be spared
the telling that it was, in fact, but a brief reprieve. The champagne
hoisted in celebration, the tears that flowed with happiness and relief,

---

* Additionally, Fleisher was given front page treatment by the *N.Y. Times,* the first time
a pianist had been so noticed (with full length pictures, no less) since Van Cliburn's
triumph in Moscow in 1958.

all were to be reserved for this moment only, this luminous but evanescent moment. It was, indeed, a fade to black.

Fleisher had had microsurgery at Mass General. This technique was not available when his hand first "turned" on him. The diagnosis that led to surgery was the now well-known carpal tunnel syndrome. If it was carpal tunnel, it had been too many years in its assault on his finely tuned mechanism.

As with so many things in life, we are left not knowing exactly what happened at that concert—did Fleisher suffer physical pain? was the concert a disappointment to him? would his hand take no more?—only that the rest of the planned comeback died with the echoes of adoration at Meyerhoff. The courageous Fleisher, unbeknownst to the audience that night, had quietly returned to his role of a once great two-handed pianist destined to living out his days as teacher, and as performer of works for the left hand only.

Why so much time spent on telling you about Leon Fleisher? Well, first of all, and least importantly, I am proud to say that I was accepted as the person who would tell this awesome story in book form. I spent many hours interviewing this incredible man, his family, his friends and his colleagues when it was thought that this first concert was just one of many to be played in the years to come. Actually, a tour of thirty-two concerts was in the planning stage, with the final event to be held at Lincoln Center as appropriate capstone to this magnificent achievement.

As it turns out, the comeback concert at Meyerhoff in 1982 was also his last concert as a two-handed pianist, Fleisher deciding that his level of play, particularly with his right hand, just was not up to his expectations. And so, no such book was written or even started. However, as a result of the interviews with Leon and the rest, I became privy to some inside information that I intend to share with you. This may not be cricket but I'm going to do it, all the same.

The primary reason for discussing this heartbreaking story, however, is that what happened to Leon Fleisher has happened to many other fine musicians and is part and parcel of the adverse experience of these brave and talented men and women. His may be one of the more notable examples, but the number of colleagues who share his fate are senselessly high. For example, Fleisher's best friend, pianist Gary Graffman, also an artist of the very first rank, had his career cut short as a result of a hand malady, not the same one, to be sure, but career-ending, in terms of two hands, all the same. In fact, after Fleisher's "comeback" concert, both Graffman and Fleisher were the subjects of a surprisingly expansive article, for a subject so removed from mainstream America, in *Life* magazine, so fascinating were these mysterious ailments which have caused so much torment for these and many other fine pianists.

At this point I'd like to invite Frank Wilson for his observations on many pianists' most dreaded nightmare:

> In the past few years the public has learned of the tragic interruption of the careers of several notable concert artists because of disabling pain, numbness, or weakness in an arm or hand....Two things are abundantly clear: First, physical complaints specifically related to practice technique are widespread among musicians; second the musicians with such complaints rarely bring them to the attention of their teachers or health professionals. Either it does not occur to them that pain is abnormal or they fear the harmful consequences to their careers of a "confession" of such problems.[33]

I, in turn, would like to corroborate Dr. Wilson's remarks. In my interviews with some very well-known pianists, a surprising number had severe hand problems and would talk about their difficulties only in the strictest confidence. The reason given for this need for secrecy was, indeed, that such information in the wrong hands could be career threatening, that a management team or a major orchestra knowing they were having HAND problems would be wary of scheduling them for future events.

While I accept this as a perfectly reasonable concern, I suspect something else is operating that relates to the Fleisher story. (You will recall that I promised you an insider's view.) My suspicion is that these wonderfully accomplished musicians, having risen to the top of their profession, have got their antennae up for accusations of possessing problems of a psychological nature, i.e., being charged with an inability to deal with the severe pressures so manifestly a part of the concert scene. In short, I think they are as worried about being seen as head cases as they are of possessing a physical handicap, that the former would have even more serious consequences for their professional careers than the obvious latter.

The fact that they would be concerned about such a "public" perception does not seem at all surprising. After all, the concert stage is well known as crazy making, and any problem the other fellow has, not clearly linked to physical causality, is subject to this sort of interpretation. Remember I told you there were these whispers about Fleisher. Well, what did you think all the whispering was about?* It really was not a reflection on Leon—although I'm sure that he did not feel wonderful about such suspicions—but harsh commentary on the situation of which he is a part. In fact, he has never been sure himself how much of this problem is of a physical nature and how much a psychological one.**

And now it is time for the inside scoop, something that the world needs to know about Leon Fleisher. I interviewed this astonishing man for almost 60 hours. As noted previously, I interviewed much of his family—ex-wife, his kids, his present wife—many of his friends, his colleagues at Peabody, most of the key members of the orchestras where he had conducted with regularity—the Baltimore Symphony, the Annapolis Symphony—his students including pianists Andre Watts, Lorin Hollander, and many other less known but highly accomplished musicians. And, please remember, like the guy on National Public Radio who announces pontifically, and with tongue in cheek, that he has a Masters Degree in Science, I have a Doctorate in Psychology, and although my cheek is at this moment beginning to resemble Dizzy Gillespie's doing a high C, I *do* have the damned degree, complete with twenty years of shrinkage.

* Everyone else's problems are psychological, a common legacy of Freudian thinking. Don't get me started on this one or we will never find our way back. Fleisher's hand problems were seen by some as psychological, in part, because that is what we do (currently) when it is the other guy, and partially because everyone knows the intense pressure that at-the-top performers are under. It would only "make sense" if they were to buckle under these pressures.

** This in no way provides any information about the problem's etiology. Whatever Fleisher thinks about the situation may be interesting and have an effect on his behavior, but there is not any question in my mind about the source of his problem, at least in general terms, and I intend to prove it to you.

Here then is that trumpeted scoop. Leon Fleisher is a healthy, well-adjusted guy. He is loved and respected by those with whom he has been close and worked, with a trail of adoration and loyalty being the common denominator of his personal wake. His part as mediator, in settling the near disastrous problems in 1981-82 between the Baltimore symphony management and the players, is legendary and has inspired enormous respect and love from all the principles. Fleisher's role as guest conductor for the Baltimore and Annapolis orchestras, and various other orchestras around the country, has placed him repeatedly in a position of vulnerability where his performance, both personal and artistic, is once again up for review. Needless to say, he has been up to the task.

His physical problems are just that—physical problems. He doesn't have the kind of disposition that needs to manufacture artificial protections from stress. Oh, he has the usual assortment of things that assail us all, and he has certainly had his share of problems in living. But down deep, despite some rocky beginnings, and life experiences that would have tested the toughest psyche including, and I guess one must say, especially, the loss of his ability to function as a two-handed performer, he has survived and adjusted to his circumstances remarkably well. This is not a person who makes up pain, who teaches his fingers how to protect him from the critics among us. Leon Fleisher has experienced real physical trauma, a devastating loss, and has responded with surpassing courage and dignity.

What Fleisher has been accused of by some—those with an oversupply of intellectual ammunition from the psychological ethos of our times—is having an hysterical reaction. Freud, when discussing patients with this malady, this experiencing of physical symptoms from psychological conflicts, was confident about its functionalism. The great seer would ask what advantage to the individual did the disease represent which would make sense out of his or her symptoms. Generally I don't like associating myself with Freud's views, but in at least this one instance, they sound right to me. Fleisher's incapacity to play with both hands was clearly not a solution that solved some pressing psychological dilemma.

By the way, almost all hand problems for pianists occur in the right hand. Coincidence? Of course not. Most composers were right-handed or, if they were not, noticed that most of the rest of us are. Also, it is simply much easier to hear difficult passages on the piano north of middle C. That is why the melody tends to be "on top" of the other lines. Thus, upwards of 90 percent of the difficult passages in the piano literature are found in the cool regions of the treble, to be played, naturally enough, by your right hand. (You might wonder where I got this precise information, this 90 percent business. Well, I made it up. However, before you get grumpy, most will agree to something on this order to be true.) This is not, of course, the smoking gun—that rascal is in the next paragraph—but it *is* persuasive.

One would think that such a hand malady would have been sufficient reason for excusing Fleisher from his artistic responsibilities—presumably the function of this affliction—where he would no longer have to deal with comparisons of his own past glorious performances, his own note-perfect and poetic readings captured with Szell and the others who competed for his collaboration. If Fleisher was so disposed to run from the inner demons of performing, how does one explain his tenacity for remaining on the concert stage all these years both as conductor and, more tellingly, as pianist. For Fleisher has been playing the piano literature for the left hand alone almost since the time of his gradual mishap, with fine readings residing in the catalogs, most notably the difficult, even sinister, concerto by Ravel.

There. Let that be the last word on the subject except to reflect that while his story is tragic and more publicized than most, it is not unusual. If the truth were known, this is what has happened to many wonderfully accomplished artists, victims of the relentless demands of the public for a level of play that became more than the hand could endure.

Otto Friedrich, in his book on Glenn Gould, writes about the experiences of a whole generation of pianists of the mid-twentieth century who, as a group, were brought down by the rigors of this experience:

And they were indeed a talented group—Gary Graffman, Leon Fleisher, Van Cliburn, Eugene Istomin, Julius Katchen, Jacob Lateiner, Seymour Lipkin, Lorin Hollander—all young and energetic and ambitious and eager to compete for the rewards of success. Yet the mere recitation of such names today suggests a whole generation devastated by the demands...that Gould rejected. [As you may recall, Gould retired from the stage at age of thirty-one]. Graffman and Fleisher were both stricken by crippling hand injuries, and though they still perform the limited repertoire for left hand, both of these highly gifted artists now devote most of their time to teaching. Cliburn, who once received a ticker-tape parade down Broadway after his spectacular triumph in Moscow, had remained mysteriously absent from the stage for most of the last ten years. Katchen is dead. And the others? Their careers tend to corroborate Gould's judgment.[10]

Well, if Friedrich is correct in his assessment, then we are talking wholesale calamity in the name of high culture. Something is clearly amiss. Not that all of these individuals—and the many others not so named—were downed by the same conditions nor exhibited the same problems. But that so many could suffer for the sake of their art is simply not acceptable nor coincidental. Perhaps if the messenger/artist were bringing bad tidings, you know, off with his hands!, but how is it that these sensitive persons—and you and I—purveyors of some of the most beautiful sounds ever fashioned by humankind, are putting up with this stuff.

What is so wrong with the conditions of the concert artist? Do you suspect that most of these artists are afflicted from birth with more than their share of private demons which come to the fore in these competitive circumstances? On the contrary, most of the artists who make it to the top rung have proven themselves incredible competitors who have had to survive grueling, unbelievably pressure-packed and enervating competitions in which they are stringently judged by the hard-nosed mavens of the musical community. Not only does the physical stamina required rival that of professional sports, but the psychological strain is enough to challenge the most well adjusted of any population. No, this group is responding appropriately to something "out there," something that would bring down any group of stouthearted competitors.

OK. Hopefully I've set the stage. We've seen what some feel about the experience of performing in the concert hall: "resembles a trip to the gallows," "waiting for the thumbs down signal for your death," etc. I've given you a slice of a life brought if not to ruin then to something unimaginably sad for both himself and the followers of Leon Fleisher. We had a brief look at some of Fleisher's colleagues who have their own stories to tell. I've told you what I think of their mental health. Let's look now at what this performing experience is really like, much as an anthropologist would from other walks of life. Let us question seriously, challengingly, the circumstances of the classical music concert in an effort to bring reason and humanity back to this potentially wondrous experience.

Especially for the Performer

It is the performer's comfort, his state of mind before and during the concert that will be our initial focus. If we can improve his lot, all else will fall into place, and audiences will realize the awesome potential of this brilliant and primal form of communication. For in the present circumstances tradition has done us in, not only the musicians but the listening public as well. Of course, the concert experience has been criticized by many before and, in many cases, in ways that this author could not improve on. I will, however, strive to bring these many strands together under one cover and from a rather non-traditional perspective.

This is what the performer of a classical music concert faces, no matter where he or she is playing, or how the audience is composed. It is the same at Carnegie Hall as at Dorothy Chandler Pavilion as at Popejoy Hall in Albuquerque, New Mexico. An artist giving, or a person attending, a concert anywhere in the "civilized" world knows precisely which of his or her behaviors are acceptable and which are simply not done.

Barriers to Musical Humanity

(1) Isolation I — From below
Sensory deprivation — Audience physically and psychologically

restrained from making contact with the artist (and with each other) except within the strictest guidelines. Buddy Hackett revisited.

(2) Isolation II — From above (on high)
4th wall — Performer non-communicative except through instrument. Going to the movies. Where's the words?

(3) Impossibly high standards
It didn't start with LP's.

(4) Traditionalism in carrying out the will of the composer

In reverse order, then:

(4) Traditionalism in carrying out the will of the composer

Typically—and in at least one sense of the word, ideally, composers are dead, and a score is treated, as a matter of reverence and respect, somewhat as one treats a will...Indeed, if you improvise, then you are not "really" playing Beethoven, or doing what the music says to do. Improvising while playing Beethoven, like talking in the audience, would clearly be a violation of a well-defined musical role....Significantly, the notion of "genius" is used almost solely with reference to the composer role.[18]

I must confess that I have included this quote not only for its contribution to the debate but especially for its use of the concept of the will. For Kingsbury the concert "is a sacred event in the sense that it approaches religiosity in its somber adherence to code."[18] In this event the document known as the manuscript of the composer is his "will." And, just as any will of a departed person will be treated with piety and respect on one level and reinforced with legalistic exactitude on another, dying has made any alterations to what should be the marvelous fluidity of a piece of music—a growing organic thing, even, in some cases a blueprint for reasonable growth—as unthinkable as treading on a dead man's grave. And there is at least one corollary: the more honored the composer, the more damning the pronouncements of impropriety when the dailies hit the streets.*

And therein, if you were wondering, lies the source of conflict for the performer. There is a delicate and, for some, maddening balancing act that inheres in every composition, every phrase the performer dutifully recreates for his audience. Again, how much of what you are hearing is properly attributable to Wolfgang and how much a reaction to my self-absorbed prism? And to be clear, I am not plumping for making changes in the "noted" text, the actual sounds that are called for—although secretly, I don't think the heavens would part with an occasional change—but how one brings these notes alive.

For some artists—from here, the less interesting—this conflict is easily resolved in favor of tradition, a fundamentalist's approach to currying favor, a following of the will together with the interpretations of the scholar/apostles. Certainly this is the safer road. But for the more adventurous—or heretical, depending on your view—the torrents of criticism can be overwhelming, the conflicts severe. I shall say no more here on this—what to most of the Great Unwashed is a behind the scenes, stress provoker for the overly sensitive artist—since it has been treated with great love and aggravation in the chapter devoted to the drummer within.

(3) Impossibly high standards
It didn't start with LP's. (But they sure didn't help).

I think the crux of the problem with respect to stage fright is the possibility that failure can inspire real terror because musical performance has become an exhibition of musical skill rather than the event through which music is conveyed to or shared with an audience. Musicians have always been pleased when they play well, and grateful for the applause of an audience. But performers seem to

---

* Due probably to the inexplicable fact that the critics of a classical music performance spend practically no time on the quality of the music written but almost entirely on the performer's interpretation.

work under a nearly obsessive preoccupation with the manner of execution of the music, as a result of which they are extremely vulnerable to worries about mistakes or failure.[33]

"Yes, I think perhaps we were driven more than the previous generation," says Gary Graffman. "I wonder whether recordings had something to do with it. Audiences now expect a note-perfect performance."

While I am quoting other people on the stress of impossible expectations, I have decided to reprint several of my own paragraphs which appeared earlier in the chapter on talent. I could have sent you to hunting for those pages but having the quotes in front of us seemed more neighborly.

The point of including these paragraphs is to underline the increased public hunger and support for the efforts of the musical virtuoso. It may have begun with Franz Liszt—usually given credit for a sea change in terms of showing off the possibilities of the clever solo performer—but there are always predecessors, including in this case the obvious Paganini, but probably going back to Herbie, the captivating cave man, impressively beating a stick on the side of a tree.

(By the way, if your memory is good, or your reading of these recent, please feel free to proceed to the next non-indented section.)

All too often...dazzling displays become the focus of both the player and his audience, eclipsing the intended meanings and aesthetic values of a serious piece of music. This business—and "business" may be right since these displays have undeniable box office appeal—of virtuosity is a seductive phenomenon capable of misdirecting not only concert audiences' minds but the performing musicians themselves. Rousing ovations are more frequently evoked by displays of pianistic fireworks than by the fashioning of poetic statements. In fact, one could say that glitzy technique is to a musical performance as the mechanics of sex is to true love.

Recently I was listening to a radio broadcast of a live performance of the Gershwin *Concerto in F*. At the end of the first movement, vivacious and impressive to be sure, the audience gave the performer a deserved and rousing cheer. At the end of the second movement, played, in my judgment, at an even higher level of artistry but technically unassuming, the audience remained silent. What was being applauded? What effect does this have on the pianist?

What effect, indeed. He not only learns the value of virtuosity for the expression of musical feeling—most certainly the original and still the more respected function of great technique—he learns that virtuosity is a major component of a successful career; that, for good or ill, the audience will often encourage impossible feats of technical wizardry even if such virtuosic obscurantism is at odds with the beauty of a piece.

With an almost overwhelming sense of pathos, then, one can see the young Leon Fleisher, the young Gary Graffman, all those others who would not be named, hands and wrists impacting the unyielding key bed, hour upon hour, mercilessly subjecting vulnerable limbs to incalculable stress. These young men and women, once at the top of their profession, can compete no more. With their need to please and the absolute necessity to maintain their place at the head of the class, these artists attempted to assuage the public's insatiable demands for perfection. One listens in awe to Fleisher's double trills in the first movement of the Brahms' first piano concerto in a legendary recording with director George Szell, and there, suddenly, it dawns on you. Buy the recording, you will need no more argument from me. There's no help being given here by those well-meaning but conspiratorial engineers. I had heard every one of those notes, live in Carnegie Hall, while pacing furiously at the back thinking, nobody can do that. And nobody can. Not without giving up all that is dear.

(2) Isolation II — From above (on high)
4th wall — Performer non-communicative except through instrument. Going to the movies. Where's the words?

Many years ago I attended a concert in Cincinnati in which some fellow—his name long gone from my memory—played a concerto in symphony hall well enough to receive a rousing ovation. We were balconied so high and far away that when the performer turned to announce his choice of an encore, we heard only the uncertain accents of an European tongue. The woman seated behind us turned to her husband and asked what the performer had said. As though ready, the husband's immediate and rather loud reply came: "He said, 'I'm not sure I can play this next piece, but I'm sure going to try.'" How well he tried, I cannot say. The laughter from the three rows surrounding this welcome intrusion completely overwhelmed all efforts from the stage.

Why such a response from those fortunate rows? What, if not context? A classical music audience is simply unprepared for the performer to communicate other than in a serious, non-verbal, and self-important manner. Perhaps more to the point, we do not expect a show of uncertainty over his artistic responsibilities. Would it have hurt the music if he had carried on so? Personally I would have become more attuned to his playing, so taken by the humanity flashing through; and I would not have forgotten the name of one so droll in that high temple of musical art.

But the usual classical musical concert is as far from that kind of reality as we were from the unknown pianist who did not say those words I shall never forget. Recall Kingsbury's description of these events: "The concert is a sacred event in the sense that it approaches religiosity in its somber adherence to code." Kingsbury's "adherence to code" refers not only to the accepted boundaries of recreating the music, but to the restraints on interpersonal communication by participants on either side of the footlights. I would like to suggest that it is not helpful for anybody to be concealed behind this ritual's mask; not the audience hungry to know that person on stage, and most insistently not the performer, isolated by tradition from the distant crowd.

The Fourth Wall

In the room where you are presently sitting, you are surrounded by four walls; in the theatre there is an invisible fourth wall so that the audience can see (and hear) the action. According to one theatrical tradition, you must never break this illusionary membrane.

Well...hardly ever.

Elia Kazan, one of our great directors,* once a bit actor, describes the opening of Clifford Odet's *Waiting For Lefty* in New York City in the thirties.

> Thus far, on opening night, I'd been sitting on the aisle, my cap with the rabbit's foot on my lap, and watching the show like the rest of the Fourteenth Street audience of progressives and left-wingers. I was totally unprepared for the burst of passion from the people out front.
>
> Bobby addressed the meeting, his face wrinkled into a grimace of cunning and deception. The audience found him despicable; they wanted him torn apart. And I did it. I bolted out of my seat, ran up on stage, and exposed Bobby as a deceiver from way back. "He's my own lousy brother!," I cried. The audience exploded. Bobby sneaked off. My appearance was a complete surprise to the audience. I looked like a man off the street outside, and a cabbie for sure. Oh, the balcony, the people in cheap seats, how they cheered!....That night, the audience and the actors were simultaneously exhilarated and exhausted. At first the people out front stood and cheered on and on, as if they themselves were members of that union. Strike! Strike! Strike! they shouted. It was the most overwhelming reception I've ever heard in the theatre. They sat in clumps and talked. Some climbed up on the stage, the place where the miracle had happened, walking, with dazed expressions, here and there, talking to friends, looking out front, then to the side, waiting for the actors to come out.[17]

Two very different events combined to make this an electrifying drama both on and off the stage—the first, the author's timely response to the social unrest of the 1930's, the touching of the communal nerve.

---

* In the movies: *On the Waterfront*, *A Streetcar Named Desire*, *East of Eden*; on stage: *Tea and Sympathy*, *Cat on a Hot Tin Roof* to name just a few of this estimable director's work.

But it is the second element, the imaginary movement of the fourth wall from the proscenium to the back of the theater, that brought this story to mind. Now it was one of us (in the theater seats) who was the hero, and it might just as well been you or me—a seemingly small change leading to an incalculable difference in feeling. Again, Kazan on the staging of *Cat on a Hot Tin Roof* in the theater, with another look at the piercing of this tradition:

> If it was to be done realistically, I would have to contrive stage business to keep the old man, talking those great second-act speeches, turned out front and pretend that it was just another day in the life of the Pollitt family. It didn't seem like just another day in the life of a cotton planter's family to Jo or me; it seemed like the best kind of theatre, the kind we were interested in encouraging, the theatre theatrical, not pretending any longer that an audience wasn't out there to be addressed but having a performer as great as Burl Ives acknowledge their presence at all times and even make eye contact with individuals. Wasn't that the style of Shakespeare's theatre, weren't his long speeches done that way?[17]

If you have ever had the privilege of seeing Bobbie McFerrin in person, you have witnessed this great musician/singer/dancer of jazz/folk/classical/etc. reach out to the audience not only with his infectious personality but his whole person, beating a rhythmic tom tom on an audience member's leather jacket, corralling others—unlikely engineering fellows or corporate types—into scatting* along with him, touching, cajoling, winning completely every one "out there" so that it all becomes one room "in here."

And don't forget Words and Music. Surprisingly, Franz Liszt would have been quite comfortable with the format used in those presentations. He is often characterized as the originator of the concert hall as palace of the virtuoso. He is given much "credit," in the doing, for creating more separation between himself and his audience. Only partly true:

---

* For the few who do not know this word, it is the singing of nonsense syllables with a jazz feel.

But it must not be thought that all pianists immediately fell in line or that recitals soon became the solemn affairs that they are now. It took time for such a new institution to stabilize itself. At the beginning everything was done on an informal basis. At his precedent-breaking "recital" in London, Liszt, after playing a piece or two on the program, "would leave the platform and, descending into the body of the room, where the benches were so arranged as to allow free locomotion, would move about among his auditors and converse with his friends until he felt disposed to return to the piano."[30]

The importance of these stories—the staging of *Waiting for Lefty*, Bobbie McFerrin's forays into the audience, Franz Liszt as one of the crowd—is not the obvious difference in the feel and perception for the audience—which already is a considerable dividend—but *the immediate impact on the performer*. By removing the fourth wall, by making immediate contact with the those who have come to be entertained or moved or changed by the experience, the performer can more nearly know how he or she is coming across and, if well, can provide a centerpiece, even a lightning rod, for great and meaningful things to happen for both "actors" in this dynamic and reciprocal relationship.

Compare the removal of the fourth wall with this description by John Holt as he views a typical classical music performance. It has the feel of an anthropological description—a description that benefits from the observations of one who has spent most of his life outside of the world of music looking in:

What happens at most concerts puts a great distance between the audience and the music. The musicians and conductor come on stage, wearing clothes that no one else wears anymore, and, without saying a word, play the music and then disappear. They might have come from another planet.[15]

Or been part of a motion picture. In Woody Allen's 1985 movie, *The Purple Rose of Cairo*, the hero walks right off the screen and into the heroine's life. This is the ultimate violation of the fourth wall and while we view this with amusement and even secret longing, is it too much to expect that flesh and blood performers would acknowledge, in ways more meaningful than tradition permits, the humanity before them? Again, the giver, the performer, would be the greater beneficiary of this modification of role, as audiences would melt before such generous impulse. Performers at Words and Music, Michael Tilson Thomas, Leonard Bernstein, Bobby McFerrin and all the others who have made this effort know the joy, the comfort, the enhanced acceptance that accrues from exercising this extraordinary option.

I will finish this discussion by once again focusing on the performer/participants of the Words and Music concerts. I have already described for you the joyful state in which audience members typically left our performances, how feeling good was clearly not at odds with the meaningfulness, the emotional depth of the experience. The complement and *major recipients* of this bonanza, of this expression of art in a context of humanism are, of course, the artist/performers, themselves.

Moreover, I am delighted to tell you that musicians using this format were forever transformed. Once they became used to audiences wanting a description of the thought and labor that went into the organization of their presentation, once they found out that people wanted to know them as well as their music, they would never again choose to do otherwise. What was very best about it, to a person, was the absence of formality and those crippling feelings of isolation which I have spent so much time decrying. As proof and bottom line, many of these artists would perform in this environment for little or no remuneration—even though this was in many cases their primary source of living—for the sheer joy of the experience. Having tasted this departure from the usual manner of presentation, having experienced this totally satisfying expression of their art and their feelings, they had become hopelessly addicted—just as I became as audience member, in the sense that I cannot attend a concert now that does not feature this interplay, without missing it in an impatient, even unfairly critical, way.

To return to the model for all of this, Sam Hinton seemed quite different from the other performers, especially in that interval just prior to a concert—typically an unusually tense time for almost every performer—in the sense that he was in tune (present) with everyone and everything around him, not nervously preoccupied with his impending chores. At first I thought it was simply that Sam was put together differently from most of us. But on closer analysis, it had more to do with the way that he structured the event than was it a reflection of his mental health. Oh, he was well prepared, fifty-year years worth, and as far as another person can tell, he was a healthy guy, but, more importantly, he had plans for the audience. They would be with him, giving him programmed strokes, singing along, communication channels turned way up. As the other musicians adopted this model, darned if they didn't become more Sam-like.

Sam was so relaxed on stage that when he would forget the words to a song—he had a repertoire of over 1000 folk songs!—he would ask audience members for help or their patience while he worked it out, *as he went along*. Audience members were smiling most of the time (or crying, like me) with joy and caring, hoping Sam would recover the words but indifferent, really, to these minor lapses.* Contrast that with the horror and intolerance with which many classical music audiences normally receive well-intentioned but imperfectly rendered presentations. Clearly the happiness index in this "folksy" format was perceptively higher, which, again, is not an indictment of classical music but of its presentation.

In terms of an audience member's response, one could sum up the difference between the classical music concert and one put on by Sam as the difference between admiring from afar, and being connected with, the performer. One still respected mightily Sam's art, but he was not so much the object of our experience as he was part of us—a personification of the group mind and spirit. He was a marvelous performer, but for the moment that was forgotten, or, rather, eclipsed by the personal enhancement felt by all in his presence.

In fact, I appear to be having some trouble leaving Sam's presence, but it is time to move on now to the other half of this isolation equation, the separation, by the "rules," of the audience from the performer.

---

* Sam had a number of devices that he occasionally trotted out for just such an exigency. One was a story of two golfers, getting up there in years, who had a hard time following the flight of the ball. Somebody suggested that they get old Bill to help them. Bill was 90 but had eyes like a hawk. So they got old Bill, and one of the pair hit a long drive off the tee and turned to Bill and asked "Bill, did you see where that ball went?" and Bill said "I sure did," and the fellow said "Where'd it go, Bill?" and Bill said "I forget!"

(1) Isolation I — From below

Sensory deprivation — Audience physically and psychologically restrained from making contact with the artist (and with each other) except within the strictest guidelines. Buddy Hackett revisited.

Once again we have Dr. Wilson observing a slice of the musician's life, this time as participant in a piano recital. New to the field of music as an adult, he brings a fresh and perceptive eye to this unique experience. Much like John Holt, he is appalled by its formality and the isolation of the performer from those with whom he would share. Moreover, both Holt and Wilson—originally non-musicians and to some degree still feeling like outsiders looking in—have a better feel for the anthropology of the situation than might those for whom this has been a way of life.

> Contrast this setting with what I found when I walked on stage for my first experience at a student recital. The surroundings were formal, not intimate, and the ceremonial trappings were deliberately arranged to create a feeling or separation between the performer (me, in the spotlight) and the audience (somewhere out there in the dark, on the other side of the border). The single word that best describes the performer's natural feelings in such a context is "isolation"...The separation between performer and audience is not promoted merely by staging, however, at most concerts and recitals there is a rigid protocol which decrees that the audience is to remain motionless and silent until the performance is over, at which time there is to be applause for a few moments, no matter what. In other words, the performer is not supposed to interact with the audience at all during the performance, or to know their true feelings.[33]

Oh! Predictably, Dr. Wilson "lost it" during his recital which makes it unanimous, or nearly so, when just about anyone goes "up against" this experience. If an old pro like Jan Murray was near collapse from Buddy Hackett's sensory deprivation hijinks, you can imagine the trauma on the untested neophyte. It seems important to convey this universality of response. It certainly is not commentary on Dr. Wilson but on these outrageous traditions that we have kept going, this trial by musical fire, this exercise in public isolation and (often) humiliation.

The stark terror of aloneness on stage strikes the most unlikely, the most experienced, veterans of performance. Laurence Olivier, near the end of his career, went through a renewal of stage fright for four years when he returned to the Old Vic troupe. In order to "be released from the terror of delivering a difficult soliloquy 'alone on stage,' Olivier asked a fellow actor to be close by in the wings where he could see him and feel his reassurance."[1]

Almost everyone reports being less stressed when performing as part of an ensemble. Symphony members certainly fall into this category, but even musicians in much smaller groups, e.g., a string quartet, will testify to a lessening of nerves when compared to the solo presentation.

Of course, you say, they can be more anonymous, more "hidden" from view, there being an apparent mystery of who is doing what. While this has the ring of clear logic and is doubtless more true in the largest ensembles, I believe the relaxed feeling to be largely the effects of reassuring togetherness. After all, people in string quartets have extensive segments of time when they are identifiably at risk in their playing, when they can be held accountable for their end of the musical bargain not only by audience members but by other members of their ensemble. In fact, one could make the argument that more, not less, is at stake since the others in the group depend so much on each person's steady competence. Yet members of these groups universally report a greater degree of calm when compared to the unenviable soloist's experience.

How Come Me?

Since many people have a facility for keeping their private demons hidden from view, it is not difficult to conclude that our own case of the shakes must be of some incredibly pathological nature, that we are, in fact, a fundamentally damaged piece of goods. Remember Seymour Bernstein's "No one suffers as much as I."

As a matter of indisputable fact, almost all musicians operating under the traditional rules of the classical music concert are anxious to a distraction. They find themselves wondering why they, in particular, should experience so much tension in the act of doing something they love so dearly and for which they have worked so purposefully.

Listen to Richard Goode, one of the brightest stars currently on tour and hailed by critics and audiences alike:

> But at other times—even now, when, as they say, my career has been taking off—the stage fright comes to me as strongly as ever. Often, it's a horizon of darkness, tension, and anxiety....I've always fantasized that one day I'd quit playing in public. Every three weeks or so, I tell Marcia that there must be a better way to live. After all, why should we always be under the shadow of this experience? We could go to a small town and open a bookstore.[13]

Again, it is clear others don't suffer in this same way. "It simply isn't fair. If only these demons would leave me, people would see what great music I would surely make." (From *The Secret Life of a Musician*—a fictitious book that could have been written by almost any performer.)

Why, of course we/they are nervous. The concert soloist is faced with an ambiguity of appalling proportions from those he would court. There we sit. Row upon row, rigidly quiet, generally unsmiling and often unseen; even, on occasion, slipping into an altered state during your greatest vulnerability. (What else are we to do? We cannot participate. We cannot sing. We cannot dance no matter how rhythmically evocative you become.) Are we your friends? Or are we more critics than you can bear? Of course you are stricken with uncertainties. You are a sensitive human being and anyone not wretched from these uncertainties at a time of heightened personal expression would surely be an anomaly.

The performer in this drama is not unlike the patient in psychoanalytic therapy—Freud's impossibly complex and curiously inappropriate creation—who for long stretches of his treatment will have no idea as to his personal worth in the good doctor's eyes. This purportedly allows the hapless client to project his hopes and fears upon the therapist's blank screen—not unlike the performer upon the respectful but clueless audience above—discover his irrational processes, and in the end, throw away his neuro-crutches. I guess you can become accustomed to this barbarity; people remain in analysis for years having been culturally brainwashed as to its effectiveness. However, except for the general salutary effects of one person attending to another (with some modicum of humanity leaking through), relief is clearly limited, or nonexistent (witness the extraordinary length of time many people will stay in treatment, kept there, more by the promise of the Great and Mighty Oz than the actual relief extended). Since psychoanalysis has lasted all of these years, with a number of hardy souls continuing to swear by its rituals, you could argue that it cannot be all bad. Yes, you might argue that, but you would be wrong.

But it does not have to be this way. The most important difference, between the analytic process promulgated by the Freudians, and the humanistically oriented, client-centered approach devised by Carl Rogers, is that in the latter, you, as the troubled person, have a sense that someone is with you (perhaps it will be Bernard), that for these cherished moments aloneness is not your permanent fate.

Fortunately, many cultural elements are coming together to rid the society of the outmoded tenets of Freud, particularly in the field of psychotherapy. Now if we can just get this same cleansing process started in the halls of the musically disadvantaged.

Kingsbury, an ethnomusicologist, an anthropologist in musical clothing, has described the ritual of the classic music recital.

There is an intensely sacralized distance between the performer and the audience at a recital or concert of classical music. The ritual silence of the audience at such events is in effect the honoring of a taboo against talking, singing, dancing, and eating or drinking. Lest this be taken as unduly trivial, however, it should be pointed out that just such activities, singing, dancing, eating, and drinking, are completely acceptable, and sometimes almost obligatory as accompaniment to music in other contexts. The taboo in classical music against such behavior is, of course, a function of the fact that a recital is a ritual in which individual performers can manifest themselves as specially, perhaps uniquely, gifted interpreters of musical texts; in such contexts, talking, dancing, or eating would of course constitute an utterly unacceptable distraction.

The people once assembled in the auditorium tended to keep virtually silent, speaking only in low whispers. A hush would last not only while the performer was actually playing, but would resume after the applause and for the most part last through the one- or two-minute intervals between pieces when the performer went offstage. Similarly, although people would leave the auditorium to talk during the intermission, within the recital hall a near silence was often effected spontaneously. In this very significant sense, these people were participating in a ritual as much as they were attending a performance.[18]

And it is this ritual surrounding the classical music concert that presents for much of the public *and* the performer, a foreboding, somber, even threatening experience. For the general public, one not acculturated to the accepted mores of the concert hall, it is at least puzzling, and often worse. It is a passive experience with enervating side effects; a passive experience to music which is for most an anathema, a contradiction in terms, an inconsistency difficult to understand.

For most people do not like classical music and will not attend its presentation. But to what are they responding. True, it is usually more complex, often more serious, even profound, but all of these characteristics are to be found in other styles of music, certainly in the best jazz, and most certainly in other forms of art. No, the biggest difference lies not in the music but its cultural milieu.

But this distance, this remoteness, may be one of the things about classical music that puts off many young people. It surely makes it harder for nonmusical people, as I was then, to imagine that they themselves might ever make music.[15]

And for the performer, this ritual of passive non-intervention by the listener, this inkblot across the footlights, fosters, almost nurtures, one's worst fears.

The acclaimed pianist Lorin Hollander says that anxious performers tend to interpret the slightest noise coming from the audience as a sign of disapproval (a critic jotting down notes, or a conservatory student following the piece with a score, recording the missed notes!). Is it really a surprise that this situation should give rise to a sort of primal terror over danger lurking in the dark, and that our brain should respond by ordering up a fast dose of adrenaline just before the house lights go down?[33]

For some years now the classical music concert has been projected as heading into uncertain economic times. The advent of the LP, then tapes, now CD's, all are pointed to as reasons why: the conventional wisdom being that the average concertgoer, content to hear virtually the same sound quality in his home, will attend far fewer concerts. And at home he can be more comfortable, can sing or "conduct," can be moved, and move, in a way that would be distracting to his neighbor in the concert hall.

Actually, it wouldn't matter if music on tape or CD were reproduced with precisely the sound quality created in the concert hall. There is nothing quite like being immersed in live music with the certain knowledge that these sounds, this storytelling, will never be the same again; that all of these brave performers are willing, without a splicing net to fail upon, to risk their personal selves for your personal pleasure.

However, there is a sobering problem, diminishing by far the "credit" given to the awesome CD. The so-called live concert does not measure up. It is in truth, only half so, only fully realized by the precious few sanctioned as players. For the still life below, the audience, it remains an unconscionably static experience.

How much of the manner in which concerts are currently presented is really constructive in nature? Some, of course, or these traditions would not have survived. For example, the formality of the event, the same dimension that I have damned incautiously, can be helpful on a number of levels. The lack of communication between audience and performer is "designed" to facilitate concentration, to cut down the number of extra-musical things that can take the performer's mind off course. Also tradition allows the performer to know how he is "supposed" to act—the mode of dress, the manner of sitting at the keyboard, the traditional way of playing the pieces, even the modest way one accepts the crowd's applause. All of these behaviors, and more, are carefully spelled out, handed down from one generation to the next. All the incurious norm keeper has to deal with, then, is the playing of the music.

But while it may succeed in providing a relatively safe and sane road map for these sacred purposes, it also has been made devoid of a great deal of vitality, at least for the audience and thus, in some reflective sense, for the performer.

How could it be different? Let us consider. As it presently is constituted, my wanting to play for people, as many of you will want to do, puts me, and possibly you, in the horrendous state of devastating stage fright. Rather than having a pleasant and meaningful experience playing the great music of our civilization while expressing an unique part of myself, instead of aesthetically connecting with others on this exquisite communication channel bestowed on us by God knows who or what, I am typically faced with a quivering, unruly organism, once under my control, enormously undermining my straightforward designs.

While a great deal of this difficulty *may* have been caused by my possibly dysfunctional background (which I heatedly disavow), and while some of it is created by the normal self-consciousness that we all seem to have when on public display, I am ready to lay down the gauntlet: I should feel this way; I am responding appropriately to the complex of nerve rattling stimuli and determinants that abound in this situation. In other words, instead of continually blaming myself, as I used to, for this confidence scrambling problem, I have taken to the offense.

This offense will take the form of a concert designed to reorder the actions of all of the players on both sides of the stage into an interactive flow of musically bonding energy. In so doing I immodestly intend to shape the classical music concert into a truly shared experience, one in which every individual makes a difference to the general effect, and to himself, by his or her raised level of participation. Not terribly different from a town meeting: all join in when the spirit moves them, and the spirit moves them when they have all joined in.

And speaking of such, I have left tickets at will call. If you are ready for this new "listening" experience, you know what to do.

Performance
Show Time

The following is a complete, detailed account of a concert that I might give and that you might attend if I were the benevolent despot of the concert world. It suggests, as you can imagine, a severe departure from current practice. Much of what you will read is predictable from the preceding discussion although there are added elements for which I have given no advance warning.

These proposed (by implication) changes are more than unorthodox. They represent, in tone and substance, a radical departure from all that has been held sacred in the high Church of the Concert Classical. I must passionately convey that they are not offered capriciously—there is some danger in your thinking this my motive, so unlikely are some of the changes suggested—but with an insistence that something be done. Something *must* be done to rescue an institution awash in tradition so heavy as to overshadow the glorious compositions they were created to illuminate. Something must be done so that concertgoers may derive the joy and passion that is rightfully theirs from this (potentially) awesome experience. And finally, lest we forget what got us here, something must be done so that the concert artist may be freed from the bonds of crippling tradition, an object of pressures too great to appreciate, a person sacrificed, as surely as the lamb, by the misguided and fundamentalist worshippers of these outmoded traditions.

I know this sounds unlikely. But listen. The unlikely happens an unlikely number of times. At this moment, September of 1993, Arafat and Peres have just clasped hands. Russia—with a close call from its disgruntled and *un*-elected and now deposed parliament, October of 1993—continues toward democracy and the free market. (Reader, it has taken time to write these pages. Now as I report to you {May, 1994}, a new development casts in the shadows the other events: the end of Apartheid in the Union of South Africa.) *Those* were unlikely. All that we need for massive reform of the shared musical experience is for enough of us to want it so. Everything starts with an idea. I invite you to join me in mine.

Our Concert!

I am playing a recital at 8:00 sharp this coming Saturday evening at Involvement Hall, the music auditorium recently constructed with specifications for this new breed of concert. The event will be kicked off by a pre-concert reception in the "green" room at 6:30 and you and I can talk if there is an opportunity and we both have the courage. And if we talk, you can tell me who you are and what you do and why you have come tonight and what your favorite music is or, if you play, a little about what that is like for you, and what you are working on. And if you promise to shake gently, we can shake hands to reassure each other that we are really here this evening, and to begin the process of breaking down that ill-placed and ill-considered fourth wall.

Immediately, of course, a new tone has been set and priorities have been rearranged. In the old (present) setting a premium was on separation and privacy such that the player could "maintain" his or her concentration. Cordiality and togetherness, perhaps even humanity, were sacrificed on this altar. In our concert the important value is bridging the gap between us—I don't even know who most of you are!—*and if this meeting beforehand subtracts a tiny bit from the accuracy and control of my opening notes, it is more than made up for by the relationship we have started, and you will forgive my technical improprieties.*

They are dimming the lights now; it is 7:45. We take our leave of each other and you file down the corridor to the concert hall. This auditorium is reasonably large with a seating capacity of almost one thousand. For this concert, however, there are seats arranged for five hundred, the rest of the space to be kept open behind and surrounding the seated sections. We'll talk about the meaning and use of this part of the room a little later on. The shape of the room is generally circular and the "rows" of seats conform to this circular pattern, surrounding the apex of the stage—jutting into the center of the room much like a slice of pie left in a tin—where I and my pride and joy, a Mason & Hamlin—

favored by those of us who like a big round bass sound—are perched a modest height above you.

The front rows are close to the stage and designed to envelop the player in a pleasant, alert, and reassuring sea of humanity. The chairs are not bolted to the floor and can be moved, within reason, this way or that to accommodate social comfort and to conform to the different-sized groups. In the area behind and surrounding the seats, on a remarkably plush carpet, are cushions spread around the room.

On the stage seated very close to the piano are some family members and friends whom I have asked to be with me on this occasion. We are grinning at each other and chatting in reasonably comfortable anticipation of what is to come. It is all reassuring to my very alert nervous system. Although the lighting over the piano area is brighter, the difference between that portion of the room and the rest of the auditorium is only a matter of degree—an attempt to keep us all in this together. If you like, you may start out the concert in a seat although the option is yours, the other choice being to find an area of the periphery that would allow more freedom of movement.

The seating (and non-seating) arrangement is an attempt to introduce informality and some degree of flexibility and comfort, both physical and psychological, to the concert experience. The large open space is for those who prefer not to be rooted in one place for the term of the concert.

Thousands of people who would never enter a concert hall flock to a classical concert in the park, where they can eat a picnic supper, lie on a blanket under the stars, and allow the music to work its magic on them. The relaxed atmosphere probably helps; it allows them to break through any doubts or fears they might have about their ability to listen and to open themselves to the music. Bringing that relaxed and open attitude into the concert hall can allow us to enjoy listening to music that we might not otherwise feel free to appreciate.[14]

One is not trapped into an either/or seating arrangement. All those who have chosen to sit can move to the open space at any interval be-

tween pieces. Also, those persons who are on the outside of the seating arrangement can slip in and out of the auditorium at any time thus allowing complete freedom to be there, or not, as changing feelings dictate. There are a number of interesting paintings in the hall and plenty of books on shelves along the outside waiting area. The music from the stage is piped out to those areas in a subdued manner so that you know how the program is progressing.

The persons on stage are people who will be with me through this experience rooting me on no matter. (Other audience members will have more latitude!) If the spirit moves them or I look like I am in danger of some psychological untoward, they know to lay a hug on me or a bandaid-like high five.

A man representing the management of this hall comes out just at 8 o'clock and introduces me. He devotes a minute or two to my background and conveys how I came to the particular program being presented on this evening.

With (in)appropriate humility I thank my gracious host and begin to talk about tonight's concert. Much of what I will discuss is printed in the program in outline form. For instance, I will tell you what went into the choice of works for this evening's concert. Additionally, I will talk about the part I will play and the part *you* will play in this new form of musical theater. A hundred years from now, I would not have to tell you about your role, but, since this is new, you may need some encouragement in following the new freedoms being championed.

As you can see by the printed program, this evening's concert consists of a number of piano pieces written as love paeans to people important to each composer, a kind of valentine or tribute to some one the composer cared for deeply. I will tell you first why I have decided to use this topic as centerpiece, and then, before each segment, the story attached to each of the pieces selected.

We will find out, as an example, how Borodin came to compose his insufferably romantic nocturne for Madame Laskaya (Opus 7, number 3), and why he made an abortive suicide attempt when she refused to hear it through. (Author's special note to reader: this story is entirely made up so don't start for the Encyclopedia—I don't even know whether Borodin preferred male or female playmates.) I will describe a particular theme which Borodin thought would serve his romantic purpose, and a few notes of that theme for you to listen for. Finally, I will try to relate these stories to each other so that we are not dealing with isolated anecdotes but an animate theme serving as connective tissue.

Clearly, I have used the Words and Music model for this concert. I cannot think how any concert would not be the better for having the performer share with the audience how his or her current program was put together—and from there into what it is about this music, or this composer, or this time in music history that might be of further interest to them. Letting the audience in on such behind the scenes management gives an immediacy and a context for the proceedings—plus the even more important educational benefits that accrue.

If you have questions that you would like answered, or things that you feel need further discussion concerning this concert, there are note pads next to your seat that you can fill out and submit in between the playing of the pieces. Again, I may not be able to answer all questions but I will do my best. If there are too many to cover during the allotted time, I will pick those that seem of widest interest. In addition, if you like, I will be available at intermission for questions or comments.

Also, you will notice that one of these sheets—labelled Live Classical Juke Box—includes a list of twenty-five relatively modest piano pieces with a place for a check mark in front of each. Two or three of these will be played just after intermission. They will not be a part of the regular program, but an interlude called Listener's Choice. If there are among these pieces a few that you would like included in to-night's program, put a check mark by their names.

These papers will be collected at intermission and tabulated in an effort to include your choice, if possible. Since I won't be able to play all of them—as much as I would like to—the consensus picks will make it to the stage. If you have marked a piece and it did not get played, you might stay over afterwards for the more informal session that will follow.

This giving to the audience a voice in the programming is obviously an attempt to maximize involvement. The hope is that by giving each person some increased participation in what is to happen on stage, he or she will be more likely to stay in a heightened state of eager attentiveness.

And, for the pianist, it insures that his listeners are interested to an unusually high degree—a nice way of relaxing those last few muscles that refused to calm down for this concert. It may appear to be a show off's trick—although most of the pieces are relatively short and simple—but the higher motivation has to do with wanting to please, and wanting to know that my listeners are really with me.

As long as I am still in the italics mode, I would like to tell you a rather lengthy but not unrelated story...One day as I was closing shop at the Words and Music Book Gallery, a fellow came to the door and peered in. He said that he was curious to see the place and particularly to see the grand piano that he had heard was in this unlikely setting, and on a stage at that. Anybody with that kind of interest I roll over for and, as we were walking back to the stage, I asked the obvious question to which I got the obvious reply. Yes, he did play. I asked him what kind of things. He said, everything. Give me a break, thought I; sure, and I can play any instrument. Well, it turned out that he could play anything. As long as he had heard it, he could play it, maybe not flawlessly, but good enough for your author who is a pretty tough sell. A Rachmaninoff concerto, a jingle from the old Burns and Allen show, a folk tune from a children's movie, a Beatle's song, a Chopin nocturne—if he had heard it, he could do a more than passable job of capturing the soul and invoking the structure of the piece. By now, I'm sure you are way ahead of me.

He agreed to give a concert with the entire program in the format of listener's choices. We had people spontaneously asking for music by Duke Ellington, the theme from the Lone Ranger, a partita by Bach, and he played nearly all requests with passing artistry and surpassing joie de vivre. Well, of course there was wonderment, but of much greater importance there was a degree of participation that rivaled any folk concert—and just as many excited and smiling faces. And again the lack of a flawless performance was not even noticed, rather an acceptable degree of beauty—framed by this amazing demonstration—and a great deal of energy flowing back and forth from performer to listeners and back. (If you have ever gone into a bar and asked the piano player to play your favorite pop standard, you know the feeling.) Am I missing something? Why not bring the audience into play at music hall?

And speaking of choice, let us return to the concert as your author-recitalist is just finishing his monologue.

Before the first piece—a song by Schubert, complete with words translated into English and printed on your program—I would like to inform you that I welcome any genuine displays of approval *during* the concert, whatever form they may take, *if you can at the same time balance that with consideration for your neighbors' listening experience.* Waiting until the end of a movement, or any other natural break, to make your sentiments known, will certainly be just as supportive and would risk less the breaking of the mood, but any time at all will be just fine, particularly if you simply cannot hold back.*

The model that I would like to see followed is that of the jazz concert, sophisticated version, where the audience members shout encouraging remarks when the spirit moves them. A kind of traditional moment of encouragement is after individual solos. Since the whole thing in this concert's presentation is in the form of a single soloist, you will have to use your tact and imagination as to appropriate stroking intervals. I would like to stress that you cannot make a mistake no matter what you do. This is a trailblazing kind of experience for all of us, and we shall have to feel our way as to the proper balance! For the first concert, moreover, I shall ask you to limit these displays of support to the first few compositions on the program.

By the way, this already happens at ballet, when a dancer does some amazing or graceful turn of note. The southern, often black, church comes to mind too, the speaker being reinforced by shouts from the congregation approving his way, and letting him know with the force of the people that he is going in the right direction.

Ah, dear reader, I think I see you shaking your head in disbelief. O.K., you say, talk to the audience, put people up on stage if you need that much support, see them beforehand if that will help break the ice, but...have them call out or applaud during a classical music concert? Please! What about your concentration? What about the people trying to be connected with you sitting near a perpetrator of this blasphemy?

---

* Some recommended possibilities: short bursts of rhythmic applause (in sync with the beat, of course); heart felt phrases, e.g., "nice", "lovely", "wow", "I love it (you)"; gasps or sighs; holding up a sign; pushing a button that sends a thrill into my brain. As you can see, we are only limited by our imagination.

Walsh agrees with you:

> *What's wrong with clapping, you wonder? Not a thing. Happens all the time. Time was when folks clapped whenever they felt like it. Composers loved it, because it meant they had a hit on their hands. In the eighteenth and nineteenth centuries, in fact, enough applause and the next thing you knew the piece was being performed again. And now? Now we're much more decorous. It's not a bad idea. Usually, we're listening to a piece we've heard many times before. In one sense, 95 percent of our concert life is an encore. The reason we don't clap between movements in a symphony or a concerto is to maintain the integrity of the piece, to allow our fellow patrons to keep their attention focused on the grand sweep of the composer's argument. It's a form of politeness that is well observed.[31]*

Certainly a case can be made that audience response can get annoying to someone trying to listen. As in all things, such intercessions have to be tastefully done, appropriately done, moderately done, and with consideration for your neighbor. But as anyone who has attended a jazz concert can tell you, it is not only possible, it is generally facilitative both to the musician and to the rest of the crowd! It is the group in its most loving, most supportive, most involved state. It is nothing more than a "Hear, Hear" in a parliamentary proceeding when the listener wants to approve of, or second, the sentiments of the speaker.

Do you think the musician is offended when he or she has crafted 64 bars of ingenious improvisation and hears you applauding his efforts even before the end of his stint? Or the preacher minds who learns from the noisy approbation that his or her flock has joined him lockstep in his mission. Trust me, it is where they live. It is their major form of sustenance, their art not usually one of great financial returns. Does it bother their concentration? On the contrary, it makes them loose, stirs the creative juices, builds confidence for taking the kinds of chances that lead to solid improvisation (either jazzperson or preacher). You're on their side now and they can feel it and ride the wave.

What about the basketball team coming from behind. It's your home team. Your rooting like a crazy person. Do these well-trained athletes need to concentrate in order to call forth their improbable feats of coordination? Of course they do. Will it throw them off if you express your favor? On the contrary, respectful silence will actually interfere with their ability to focus, distraction being in the eyes and ears of the active beholder....But you do the right thing and your team responds. A group effort. You're into the game and so are they.

Remember I told you that the first piece of the evening was to be a Schubert song complete with English translation. Well, I am going to encourage you to sing along for a portion of this presentation—we even have a bouncing ball on the screen for those who need such encouragement. Not in a show-offy way, perhaps hardly more than a soft humming, but enough where you are truly with the music, where there is a subtle but dynamic interplay between each of our efforts. You try to stay with me, and I shall be influenced by your participation. It is a duet of cosmic (comic?) proportions, and it will help to loosen us both.

I am sure that you have noticed how difficult it is to stay focused on a piece of music, especially when you are in the passive orientation (physically) of the typical concertgoer. It sounds like the simplest task imaginable, but the mind clearly, almost perversely, has an agenda all its own. It is self-evident, however, that you can meaningfully improve this facility, this staying with the music, by the degree that you "participate" during its play.

One form of participation, of course, is to sing along—remember all of those happy, active faces at Sam's concerts. In the usual concert setting, of course, this behavior is discouraged with the quickest of rebukes. Since many people have noticed that singing along does help one's focus, you would think a reasonably effective compromise can be reached by singing silently. But, whereas the silent accompaniment is helpful, it falls short of going the vocal distance. I suppose the effort put into the actual making of sound, or the hearing of your own voice, energizes the attention engine far better than the mute version. But however you can manage it, the more time that you spend with the music, the more the evening will be an involving and moving experience.

Which brings up the subject of the "moving" experience just in time. Interesting that this word in this context is used to convey that we have been moved when in fact it refers to some inner state where movement is highly speculative or at the very most, subtle. I propose that we need to have moving concert experiences to which we literally can move, where we can harness our physical apparatus appropriately to the kaleidoscope of body states engendered. But once again I am getting ahead of my story.

George Cukor, the esteemed motion picture director, once said that all poems were too long, as well as operas, books, speeches, movies, symphonies, plays, parades, this list, etc. I am determined, however, that this concert not make George's list. My sincere intention is to stop playing before you stop listening. I have set my sights on being finished by 9:15, plenty of music if you have been listening in this active way. After the formal concert is over, and the hall has "emptied" out, I will be around for a period of free play where I will answer questions and dash off some additional listener's choices, even if that listener is only one person. The length of the concert, then, will depend on the motivation, interest, and time available for each person.

15 minute intermission.

Lights blink.

It's the beginning of the second half now.

Welcome back. I see that many of you have come back to your seats but that others are sprinkled around the periphery in the standing-walking-lying down area ready to do your participation thing. I welcome you all to the second half of the concert—in your various positions, groupings, and modalities—and sincerely hope that what you are about to hear will be pleasing and meaningful. You might be interested to know that during the intermission I had many requests...yet I intend to finish the concert. (After the laughter has subsided): Thank you all very much and now I will play the consensus picks from the list of choices and hope that at least one of your favorites made the short list.

The use of humor in these circumstances—if you will grant me that this sally met some comedic criterion—is one absent from virtually all classical music concerts. The argument that humor has no place in this serious endeavor just does not wash. Great novelists and playwrights know this; poets know it. Shall we alert the impresarios and music managers? Humor provides a nice contrast for anything serious to come, and in no way detracts. Again, it allows the audience to participate in an unbridled way, while revealing some lighter facts of life about the person in the performing chair.

When Victor Borge plays a piece seriously, in his predominantly comic evening, the audience receives the piece on its own terms not even vaguely distracted by the insanity bracketing this music, giving it, if anything, a more tolerant place in their hearts. Borge is probably accorded more, not less, credit for his ability to compete musically in this more formal arena. In fact, the serious playing sets off and elevates the comedic efforts and the reciprocal is most certainly true.

And then there was Harpo, called a divine player by many—the harp having this natural edge—even in the wake of wonderfully outrageous behaviors. Nobody ever questioned, only appreciated, the serious intentions and high level of musicality expressed when he crossed over from his madcap mute.

I am now going to take you on another one of those apparent diversions, this time to think about some facts of animated life; then, I promise, to the conclusion of the concert. There is some chance that without this long way around, you would not be receptive to the argument that follows.

I Got Rhythm (Who Could Ask For Anything More)

Apparently not Ms. Abby Whiteside. We have to say the Gershwins and Abby Whiteside would have much to compare notes on—rhythm serving as insistent leitmotif for her excellent and influential book on the playing of the piano. Indeed, rhythm dominates her program to an unusual degree. Each chapter is ostensibly on a different element of music or performance, but, in essence, each is driven by the importance (insistence) of rhythm. It is for her the real and vital stuff of a composition, the element and life force that makes a composition work, even providing its fundamental character.

Of the elements from the musical tool box—melody, harmony, rhythm and meter—it would be difficult to select *the* one most important to their amalgam, the one upon which all else builds—that is, it would be difficult for many. For Ms. Whiteside plus the likes of Stravinsky, Count Basie and others of their musical bent, it provides no puzzle. For her, rhythm starts the engine; while for Basie, it "takes you home." Moreover, according to Whiteside, rhythmic participation by the body is not only the most important thing to being a performing musician, there seems nothing else really worth spending "time" on. (One is forcibly reminded of Vince Lombardi's "Winning isn't everything, it's the only thing.")

> An exciting rhythm, a unifying, all-encompassing rhythm is the only possible means by which the entire playing mechanism can be brought into full play. A basic rhythm is the only possible over-all coordinator, for it is not merely the instigator of beautiful musical production, but it is the *sole* [emphasis added] factor that can successfully translate the image in the ear and the emotion which must be at the bottom of all beautiful music into a function of the whole body...The problems of the pianist must not be too sharply differentiated from those of the dancer, the singer, the violinist. Indeed, all bodily skills (not only those concerned with music) have this in common: they always involve the whole body if the best results are to be obtained...The body governs the fingers in playing the piano, and no amount of coaching in finger dexterity will ever lead to the easy beauty in playing that must be our objective. Only a basic rhythm can coordinate the body as a whole.[32]

From this monistic point of view, perhaps from Ms. Whiteside herself, must have come the famous jazz shout, otherwise attributed to Duke Ellington, *"It don't mean a thing, if it ain't got that swing!"*

And speaking of jazz, Whiteside has a special place in her heart for the unique persons who do this magical thing:

> It is right here that we need to heed the procedure and results of the talented jazz pianists. They have a tune in their ears and a rhythm in their bodies, and they let these two elements fuse by using noth-

ing else as they learn their instrument. They do not fuss with hand position, fingering, learning to read straight off, learning to count, before they produce a rhythmic tune. Once the rhythmic tune is accomplished, nothing can stop them from having fun with it. They embellish it and in so doing learn to play.[32]

And do you know, she may be right. As you might take the rhythms of your heart for granted, it is easy to slight these lively impulses. But then one day you listen to someone play, someone oblivious to how a piece of music must regularly flow, and you realize that this player cannot *move* you no matter the accuracy of his playing, the thoughtfulness of his ideas, his sensitivity to the tonal palette. Interesting, isn't it? You can modify a melody and get by; you can even rearrange some of the harmonies; but if you do not capture the *motion* intended (if it ain't got that swing!), you will not make your case. And you most certainly will not take your listeners with you. It is the stuff of life and it must suffuse your expression as it beats through your soul.

And, it will! When you have freed yourself of note-bound constraints, when you realize a composition as comfortably yours, the motions of (your) life will come out in your playing. It cannot be helped.

So What!

But in the classical music concert, to what avail? As performer, will your messages in motion have appropriate receivers? When rhythm has taken you over, will others respond to that same insistence? Or are your listeners restrained, overly civilized manikins in thrall? Compare the typical classical concert crowd with the Glenn Miller audience crowded around the bandstand, bodies swaying, then moving off as gravity-defying Lindy Hoppers; recall Lionel Hampton, whose bouncing mallets directed your body into obedient accompaniment, or Elvis gyrating on stage while human tuning forks resonated to his energies. Compared to these, the classical concert is an elegy by Poe.

We will return to this dilemma after a discussion of eurhythmics, the relatively young discipline dealing with expressions of rhythm through our bodies, and the importance of these expressions in the communication of musical ideas.

The Sender (Transmitter)

If you were asked to speculate on the subjects generally offered in a conservatory of music, you would probably suppose such course work as sight reading, the history of music, performance practices, ear training and, perhaps, others. But you probably would not mention the word eurhythmics or, without knowing this technical word, consider that a musician would be taught to "dance" in order to play his instrument. However, in a large number of music schools, that is precisely the case—this encouragement for musicians to express the rhythms of a piece through bodily movement. And in some schools not only does it appear on the curriculum but it is required for the education of the performer and, often, other species of musician, e.g., composers, teachers, even historians and musicologists. Musicians long ago realized the integral place that dance played in the communication of the musical language. Indeed, many (perhaps most) sections of pieces in the early music literature were even given dance names or, minimally, a "stage direction" as to how that section was to be played, i.e., what form of dance this music was to take.

In fact, it is my guess that music evolved from dance, not the oft assumed other way around. This would be very difficult, if not impossible, to nail down, but to me it seems the more likely order. Since dance is something that you do to music, for most it is natural to think of dance as something coming out of music in its genesis. But to my rhythmic brain waves, dance appears the progenitor of music, with music being something that our group fashioned on to certain kinds of movements. This would have happened by the elaboration and transformation of the natural bodily rhythms into sounds, thus "amplifying" that which was already being expressed. Since I cannot prove this any more persuasively than the person who chooses the egg over the chicken, let us be content to agree that dance is at least an integral aspect of the musical experience.

Certainly the following bit of trivia will not untie the two. Laszlo Vikar, Hungarian ethnomusicologist and colleague of Kodaly, says that:

> Instinctive music is always accompanied by movement. He goes on to tell that in collecting folk songs, he has found that the country people, from whom he collects, frequently have to stand to sing because they cannot recall words and turns without the traditional accompanying gestures, dance steps, and turns. He commented that: The two (song and movement) were welded together so much that (the singers) could not abstract one from the other.[4]

Makes sense to me!

And some other sensibleness was derived by the study of Dr. Montessori, who found children between the ages of three and six to be particularly sensitive to both movement and singing; she further discovered that body movement contributed to the acquisition of skill in singing. (Now if they would only construct showers that were large enough to dance in.)

At any rate, eurhythmics became a formalized part of the musician's training in the early part of the 20th century, having been informally so forever. Conservatories, as is natural for places of higher learning, were tending at that time towards the intellectual pursuit of music with emphases on analysis and other head games, leaving the body far behind. Eurhythmics seems to have balanced the scales "just in time."

Perhaps the reader can get some idea how this system relates to the performer by listening to Ristad. She suggests the virtues of dancing to a composition's rhythms for not only understanding the composer's intentions, but, surprisingly enough, for abetting the player's technical facility:

> Book-searching for ideas on interpretation had little of the excitement that we found when we discovered the inner sense of a Brahms

passage by dancing it. Books on technique seemed dull in comparison to solving the technical problems in a Chopin Ballade by freewheeling experimentation [body movement, thus dance].[25]

And, in one of her workshops, Ristad conveys the importance of
dance in the removing of the intellectual functions from musical
interpretation:

> I asked Jane to leave the piano bench and show us her concept of
> the passage in body movement. Back at the piano, she played the
> passage while the rest of us danced. "The way you play it will
> choreograph our movement." The vitality she had experienced in
> her body transferred into the music before she had a chance to put
> her brain to work.[25]

The fact that this formalized dance-like system (Eurhythmics)
became widely utilized in the general conservatory affirms the degree to
which at least some academic musicians embraced the importance of
bodily involvement in the interpretation of music. The paradox is that,
once learned, once inculcated into his fabric, the music maker in performance must eschew full body involvement, relegating his response to a
more subdued, almost internal one. I speak, of course, of the mechanics
of getting the notes played, and equally of the restraints that the classical
concert setting has dictated as proper.

This is a particular difficulty for the pianist. Whereas the players of
many other instruments—violin, voice, clarinet, trumpet, to pick just a
few—can, when removed from the constraints of ensemble play, swing
and sway with some abandon, the pianist is confined to staying where
the piano is planted and must limit his own "dance" to the restricted
possibilities left to the upper portions of his body.

Some players are more inhibited at the piano than others, not by the
physical limitations dictated by the instrument, but by their own
emotional restraint. This reserve is reinforced by fear of criticism by
others, especially critics, who will often label such movements, manner-
isms, i.e., movement inappropriate to performance. Doubtless this
tendency to be critical of such movement arose from watching individ-

uals, more showpersons than artists, who used affected movement as a way to sell what otherwise might be a limited talent. However, it does not seem appropriate to then limit the natural beauty of the sincere, involved pianist, moved by the natural tendency to express with his entire being the "driving" mechanism he is bringing to tonal life.

As you might recall, the criticism of Glenn Gould was not usually about his playing, although he received his share of that, but for his manner of play. And it was the hounding of this expression of his good musical will, of his being with the music as few are, that ultimately drove him from the concert stage. Whiteside, who so hopes the artist will accommodate and accept one's bodily rhythms into the performance, feels that...

> It is most unfortunate that the movements which express emotion are labeled mannerisms, for we think of mannerisms as unnecessary. If they are always present with a great performance, can they be unnecessary? Rather, isn't it safer to believe that they are necessary for the expression of the emotion which must be a part of any great performance?[32]

In the pop world, particularly that of the jazz artist, movement by the musician is not only accepted, it is embraced as an integral part of the scene. It is expressive of "what's happening," and it certainly helps to convey the message visually. And, of course, there were the big bands, a once-upon-a-too-short-a-time affair, where the movements of sections (trombones, reeds, etc.) were often choreographed to the music. A relatively subdued patterning of rhythmic movement, for example, in the Glenn Miller band, brought great response from the crowd who seemed to crave for, and were energized by, its expression.

For the jazz artist, whose body movements tend to move overtly in sync with his expressed musical feelings, the involvement of his or her body serves him well: it allows for utmost concentration, invoking his creative process to the maximum; and it is contagious, particularly when it is clearly an extension of, or basis for, the sounds he is making.

But what about the critical other half of this process. Without the receiver, we have in an important sense, no sender—something about a tree in the forest falling. Let us now explore the other side of the equation, the complement in this exquisitely two-sided process. Let us look at how well the receiver is prepared for all that has gone into these timely messages.

Remember, the performer has been schooled in the importance of rhythm to his musical art. He or she has processed his message through his instrument with the energy of rhythmic drives that you, in the usual concert setting, are receiving in a most unrhythmic manner. It is hardly your fault. Those are the rules. Should you tap your foot, you will receive a great deal of attention. Stand up and move to the music, you will be escorted from view. No, to get a modicum of gratification you must invite your mind to stay with the rhythms of the music while instructing your body to ignore such outrageous temptations.

You have listened to classical music in your home. Have you "conducted" it? Have you moved, even danced to its rhythms? Wasn't it exciting, and did it not contribute a great deal to the *listening* experience? When the body is moving to the music, or singing along, you have had to stay in focus. You cannot sing or dance to patterns to which you pay no attention.

Do an experiment. See how long you can stay completely involved with a piece of music while quietly listening as you would in a concert hall. Now compare the average time of undistracted, pure focus in that mode with your ability to concentrate while either singing along, conducting or whirling about the room to its time. You will note a startling difference. And not only can you stay with the music substantially longer while practicing some form of sympathetic activity, but it is a whole new experience, a whole new feeling about the "listening" to music.

The following description by Ristad I find wonderfully creative and ineffably sad. The creativity does not need commenting on. The sadness has to do with the plight of the listener in the concert hall—having to be resourceful, battling upstream, so to speak, when with changed circumstances, one could involve the listener in a profoundly more satisfying manner.

How about the listener? When we listen, does it change our perceptions if we are tuned in to movement? Sometimes we blame the performer wrongly, for at times we go to a concert and become inert lumps of flesh, challenging a performer to move us out of our sophisticated lethargy. I sometimes enhance my enjoyment by giving free rein to the intuitive side of my nature, allowing imagery to develop, characters to emerge, and invisible dancers within to respond to the choreography of the music. My muscles come to life in response, yet to an onlooker's eye I am sitting as sedately as can be. When I listen this way I know I've hit a real loser if the music only lulls me into a state of indifference. If I play recorded music at home I...can turn the dancer loose whenever I wish.[25]

Well, you see where I am going with all of this. With my keen eye for the obvious, nothing I have said can come as a surprise. Yet it needed to be said, since despite agreement across the board on how music and dance are more closely related than drawing and color—one brought to life by the other—we provide the concert hall setting with only enough room for the drawing (room), and a still life at that.

And now that you have been rhythmically prepped for what is to come, it is time to return to the concert.

♪ Gotta Dance, Gotta Dance ♪ (choreography by Gene Kelly)

Now that you have had a chance to sing with Schubert, to hear about the Brahms piece written for Clara Schumann hastening Robert Schumann's decline* and madness, to listen to me play a lovely piece by Chopin on my own, then to have your three favorite pieces played, it is time for an even more active involvement on your part; one which may feel a trifle daring and a little scary.

It will not be for everyone, but for those of you who would like to move about during the playing of the next few pieces, even, if you can summon the nerve, something approaching dance, then this is that time. You will achieve a sense for what this music is about in a way only hitherto suspected, to feel what the musician feels as he transmits these impulses, to be fully under the spell of its rhythmic contagion.

* Before you get on your trivial-pursuit-high-hat, remember, I'm sort of making this up.

For those of you who have remained seated, the peripheral space is designated for these moving purposes. If you are one, however, who prefers to let the energy of the evening come to you, and subscribe to never standing when you can sit, never sitting when you can lie, you are most cordially invited to perform that inactivity with all the passion you can muster. Of course, I hope you will at least bob and weave. But whatever you decide, I will play my best for you. And, you will have plenty of company since tradition is your ally. Moreover, I have a certain place in my heart for the sedentary and the frightened. Finally, I would like to assure you that those dancing in the rear will do so with utmost consideration for your relaxed manner of participation.

But for those who want to try this thing, it is time now to migrate back into the dance/humming/free-fall area. Please note that the usual rules of civilization have not been suspended. Perhaps some attempt to stake out your own territory would be a reasonable guiding principle. Other than that, let 'er go. Anything that you can allow your body to do that expresses the rhythmic impulses you are feeling will be appreciated by yourself, those around you, and especially, by me. In fact, if good vibes do travel, I shall be picking up on yours while you are being with mine.

> If you are lucky enough to have a dancing friend available, the music can also move the dancer while you play. I mean "dancer" only in the sense of someone who enjoys responding to music. I may think I have discovered all I can about Chopin, Scarlatti, or Brahms in a particular piece. Yet the instant someone starts dancing to the music I am playing, I feel it change beneath my fingers. The phrases find a more beautiful shape. I discover fresh nuances. I give myself more time for unself-conscious drama or tenderness. It is as though someone else's movement makes the drama, tenderness, or passion legitimate and more authentic. The dancer responds to my sense of the music, I respond to that person's sense of my sense of the music, and as we toss the energy back and forth, the music intensifies and finds a new freshness, a new magic.[25]

If you prefer, however, to a more sedate swing and sway, then that is what you must do. Every way of being is equally and wonderfully valid as long as it is true to your self, the rule being—that which maximizes the pleasure most exquisitely for you! (If that sounds sexual, well, that is why projective tests were created.) We shall do this for just the eight minutes that these two pieces take: the first by Beethoven followed by a short composition by his soul brother, Thelonious Monk.

Now you see why I took so long to fashion this case. Otherwise, it is conceivable that you would have questioned the wisdom of having something so obviously distracting as dance forms wheeling about. But by the time we got to that point in our sequence, you were well prepared and were one of those on your feet moving gracefully to Beethoven, then doing your best to stay with Monk's unexpectedly playful rhythms. The evening may have left you breathless. It seemed to fly by on the wings of these shared rhythms. You got some much needed exercise that brought you closer to both composer and performer. You moved when you wanted to, you sang when you felt so inclined, you had a say in the program. When the performer was on, he sometimes talked, he sometimes played, he sometimes listened. It was always different. But, it was always with the same end in mind. *We are in this joyful experience together. Without all of us, it would not have been the same.*

Obviously this proposed concert is not going to appeal to all, or possibly any, but perhaps it suggests a way to bring in the people, give them a part in the program, have them leave with a spring in their voice and a lilt in their step (perhaps that is not quite right), while providing a setting for the artist that comforts, rewards and excites, rather than reduce his ability to digest food, destroy his hands and quash his spirit.

It is the difference between the formal Catholic Mass or high Episcopal service in the hands of (the once) staid New Englanders compared to the (once) primarily black Baptist congregation in the South. Encouragement, participation, rhythm, mind and body, energy, alertness, all in the Baptist church abound where no one could possibly be uninvolved.

And now that the concert is over and you are on your way home— smiling and humming and feeling the good feelings—you have a chance to think about the possibilities for the next time you turn to the role of performer. You return to your Tuesday evening group eager to tell the others that the model which they have been witnessing in the concert halls all these years is not the only possibility. Classical music can, after all, take place in a communal context.

Your friends and family can put the spotlight on you but with a glare reduced by their own participation. Let people, no, *encourage* people to move a little bit while you are playing. Perhaps just standing and swaying accompanied by a sympathetic blend of their voices. Ask them not to be so quiet if something moves them—that it will do worlds of good for you and will, when they get accustomed to it, even feel good to them. Tell them that your playing is really all about groupness and that you need their help and they will feel the better for lending a hand. This will be going directly into the face of tradition and habits long since accepted and banked, so you will need patience and a few episodes before this will take. And then how much easier to ascend center stage.

Instead of a monologue for your friends to endure, it is now a shared activity in which you are merely a leader. But one who can play shamelessly for a much longer time.

And speaking of time, we haven't much left. We have one more chapter where a surprising turn is made. I would tell you more, but you are so close to it. Why not all the way? After all, surprising turns are not everywhere to be had.

Sculpture

Recently at a dinner party, I told one of the guests that I was almost through with my book and she said, "How will you know?"

Take Care

Regretfully, we are now but a short distance from where you and I will be parting company.* It has been, at least for your guide, a deeply gratifying and surprisingly eventful experience. Indeed, if you have received even a fraction of my own pleasure, I shall be the happiest of men. Having assembled and shaped the ideas vying for space on these pages; having felt the project stretch, flex, then come to life; having come closer and closer to expressing the values of my heart, and then having you join and be with me in that once secret place, all of these have made it a once-in-a-life-time experience.

Which we *must* do again!

But that question at the dinner party; it lingers in the air. How *will* I know when I am finished? Should I have stopped before? This moment? Frankly, I'm not sure I will ever know, but perhaps this is that time—the time to embark on a brief summary, the time to make sure I have not left any inspirational stones unturned, and, finally and reluctantly, the time to bid you a heartfelt farewell.

Before that, however, and at the risk of overstaying my welcome, I must share something with you that has been bothering me since the very beginning. I am troubled by the choice of vehicle upon which this book's message has been carried, thus those who will likely make the journey. Do you remember my saying that:

This book is for *anyone* who wants to express themselves musically, but thinks that they do not have the right stuff—the talent, for God's

---

* However, in the not too distant future I do hope to have the pleasure of meeting you. For more details on this exciting prospect, see the last page of this chapter.

sake—to make it happen; that even if they might have at one time, that time has long since passed them by....The vehicle for this journey to artistic fulfillment will be learning to play the piano but the choice is arbitrary....And although this may be reaching for an audience not mine for the taking, I propose that much of what is discussed has direct application for anyone seeking artistic expression whether through tap dancing, an artist's canvas, decorating houses or the tops of cakes.

Honest expressions of our selves are not easily come by. So much of our inner life is lived in secrecy and benign neglect that we spend most of our time not expressing (thank God) our real feelings, our most profound responses to the world around us. Although this risks losing vital connections to those we would be close to, it does allow the delicate clockwork of society to self-wind, our neighbors to carry on with a minimum of fuss.

But for this very reason, it is critical that we have some artistic outlet, some way to mine and articulate our special contribution to the social fabric. There is no shortage of media ores for this mining operation. You can find a wonderful release for your unique qualities through the exploration and manipulation of color, of sound, of forms, of movement.

But though my intended audience is broad indeed (everyone!), my execution has been resoundingly particular. On stage, slightly off center, has been the piano. Making an occasional reference to the study of other musical instruments, or to other forms of artistic expression, my sincere wish to address and encourage *any* form of artistry may have been lost in an overly myopic attentiveness to this grand instrument of the soloist.

Even had I the literary imagination to captivate the full spectrum of music makers, I would be aware of my failure to include the potter, the architect and all the others striving for fulfillment through the magic of fine art. And then (you see, it is not so easy to know when you are finished), what about those artists of everyday life, the person who would start a business, be a mother, or practice counseling in ways that are artistically expressive of that individual.

Yet, though I did not have the imagination to address all who would follow their dreams of self-expression, that was at bottom my quest. I chose the piano, and the strategy for playing that instrument, because it was something I knew more about, and because, in putting forth my arguments, it was easier to address this more familiar audience.

This, then, is my apology to all who would find themselves through some means of artistic expression which does not happen to have 88 keys. I root for you with the *same* energy, the *same* interest, the *same* passion, as I do the player of Beethoven's *Moonlight Sonata*.

For what it is worth, my favorite musical instrument is not the piano but the acoustic guitar. My favorite musician, outdistancing such luminaries as Leon Fleisher, Murray Perahia, Jascha Heifetz, Thelonious Monk, Paul Desmond, Johnny Mercer (as singer) and all the rest, was the incredibly sensitive jazz drummer, Shelly Manne, who mysteriously raised everyone's playing to new levels by his loving musical insistence and timely support. My favorite form of art is architecture, and whenever I have a choice of listening to music and reading a book, I generally pick up a book. I sincerely hope I have not slighted (or more importantly, lost) anyone due to my inability to broaden the "playing field."

And now, as evidence that my heart is in the right place for all you non-piano players (and non-musicians) alike seeking artistic fulfillment in other directions, I shall use this final chapter to show how the principles developed in the practice of music making can be applied to the mysteries of writing—and even turn into a book, this book, for example. This self-conscious exercise has several goals: (1) To show a degree of generalization of the principles presented here to at least one other art form and, by implication, to others; (2) To summarize those things that I think most likely to help you on your excellent adventure, whatever the direction; (3) For the sake of variety, to help us get from here to the end of the journey aboard a different mode of travel.

In a paragraph following is a list of those elements utilized in this writing, drawn from learning how to play the piano. To begin with, if it isn't altogether clear, I simply don't know the "proper" way to write—never having written so much as a report on my summer vacation—and, if I hadn't taken a lesson from Neil Simon on his own approach (from watching a televised interview), I wouldn't even have made it to the starting line. I *still* don't know how to do this thing; yet somehow I was able to get, at the beginning of things, from staring into the infinite space of the deep blue monitor to where we are now. With such a short way to go, I most likely will make it to the close. Whether

I would have been better served by formal training and a more organized approach I cannot say. Doing it "my way," however, was largely responsible for the inordinate gratification derived from this invigorating, even life-nourishing process.

I am recapitulating these principles, then, useful for at least these two modes of expression (words and music), for those persons like myself, intimidated by their own perceived shortcomings—lack of talent, training, experience, etc., etc.—who I feel will be helped by an approach possessing self-help tools for every one!

- **Platespinning**: the widening of one's attention span
- **Just a little bit**: making modest demands on yourself
- **Happiness scheduler**: playing with time
- **Razing of the fourth wall**: accessibility for audience
- **Being with those you love**: working close to your heart
- **Drummer**: listening to your own voice
- **Teacher**: the importance of meaningful support

In a short while I shall take each of these principles and demonstrate how they can be applied with little modification to the expression of who you are through words. Before I do, I want to share with you how I got the nerve to do this thing, this absolutely alien thing, of committing my point of view onto these pages for others to see. It is done with the sincere hope that it will help to start you on a project of your own that you, too, thought unlikely.

Earlier I mentioned Neil Simon and the advice that he gave me (along with millions of others rudely trying to horn in on our special relationship) as I watched the *Larry King Live* show. Let us listen in at the point where he was asked to talk about his approach to writing.

Simon says......

that he simply starts writing. He doesn't know where he is "coming from" or where he is headed. He has gathered a few ideas, but does not impose a structure before the facts of his fiction. In fact, his description reminded me—albeit with somewhat more control of the material—of an approach used by another author, named White (first name unknown, source of information unknown),* who, as a solution to writer's block, devised a strategy for the writing of fiction. His method was to write whatever came to his mind for 40 days (presumably while waiting out some other great flood), spending most of his waking hours at this rudderless event. He censored nothing, carried forward by the ideational currents of his unchecked imagination, capturing his ideas as quickly as his furiously scribbling pen would allow (for this was long ago). There were, of course, many seeming digressions, blind channels, irrelevancies, but he followed them all without complaint, barely using an oar. When at last he came to the end—signalled only by the calendar—he retraced his journey, searching for connections in his verbal wanderings. This then was the raw material that spoke to him, ouija-like, on the themes and characters his story would tell.

Neither White nor Simon behaved in a way that teachers of writing in my experience (English 101) would judge acceptable. I hear them still: It is of the highest importance to prepare an outline. You have to have a blueprint. You cannot write with coherence or a sense of purpose unless you organize your materials in advance.

It sounded all scientific and reasonable and terminally daunting. Creating an outline implies a mind functioning as an information processor, when clearly it is more nearly—at least for this recorder of internal events—a cauldron of swirling ideas all struggling to be heard one before the other. In the case of the project before you, I hadn't a notion of how I was going to put things, where I was going to put things, even what was to be included, only that something was important to me that I needed to get down.

Moreover, starting with an organized structure suggests symptoms of advanced analysitis. Usually such non-functional probing occurs after art has "taken place" and the viewer or appreciator or, more likely, an academic attempts to understand (explain!) the meaning of a piece (what, ugh, makes it work). Recall the discussion on analysis earlier:

---

* I read of White long ago and remember only that he was, through his approach to writing, of seminal influence on Freud.

Analyzing an object of art to better capture its essence is not only rubbish, it is aesthetically dangerous. Putting a musical composition through the paces of a detailed examination brings us no closer to illuminating its heartbeat or its power to move, uplift, or change us. ....Far better the sheer joy of wide-eyed wonder to carry us deliciously among life's unexpected treasures.

Making too much of a fuss over structure in the initiation of the expressive process will influence not only its form but *its content*. I'll not argue against the ultimate value of structure—only a fool would admit to such a position—but its timing in the process. A balancing of the passions with the rigors of form is all well and good and even critical for the worthy transmission of your message. The structure, however, should not be the starting place, rather a way of making the feelings or passion more accessible—and...more persuasive.

Whew! I started out by telling you that too much consorting with structure can interfere with the creative process and concluded with its importance in the regulation of its moving parts. Interesting where the mind can take you, particularly if you are not paying attention.

In a microcosm it is illustrative of what can happen when the author relinquishes tight rein of his material. In fact, this book, as originally conceived, was designed to relate the *adventures* of a platespinner, that is, the wondrous things that can happen to a person (this person) who finds himself finding himself through artistic exploration.

But it didn't turn out that way. At least not entirely. If I had run a tighter ship, if I had kept a steadier course, this would have been a very different work, perhaps a more entertaining one. But, it would not have captured the same feelings, the same primitive character as the one that has emerged. I didn't realize just how important it was to me that you, out there somewhere, discover some manner of expression that would reveal your incredible potential. Only when it began to appear on these pages, in theme and variation, was it clearly revealed. I could see *by what I was writing* that I was more intent on your ultimate participation than a telling of my tale. And because I gave in to this mysterious process, this book became the most important adventure of them all.

The words once written also made it abundantly clear how anti-establishment I have become towards the "practice" of an art form, or, at least, the practice of the music art form. I would have thought this tilting with windmills more appropriate for younger folks. At the proper age, however, I was much too intimidated by my musical betters (virtually everyone) to even consider such an outrage.

The list of things that I have variously questioned and damned is long indeed: talent, scales, fundamentalism, performance practices, structural and other kinds of analyses. Makes you wonder. Could your author have developed an attitude born of old age and cynicism, or are a lot of things in the world of traditional music making simply in need of the big overhaul? I leave that for you to decide. But at least know that I am a clean shaven, tax paying, short-haired kind of guy who follows most of society's rules and even more of its laws. My own view, for what it is worth, is that when I rebel, it is because rebelling needs doing, not from some unrequited slay-your-authority-figure urge deep within.

Oh yes. Simon said—and so, of course, I played along—that once he had written a draft, he would forthwith begin the editing process, making it, on each pass through the material, more and more his own, removing all false impressions and impersonations. In an apparent contradiction he characterized the manuscript as having a life of its own, taking him to unknown destinations and personal destinies.

He said the wonderful thing about writing is that you always get this second chance (and third and fourth and on) until you have got it "right." Even when you have "finished" the play and have the actors go through their lines, said Simon, you hear it differently, with yet more chances for grateful reshaping. It is the againness that Simon characterized as the joy, perhaps saving grace, of writing—and I would add sculpture, the composition of music, poetry, architecture and, well, maybe any art form where you do not have to show anybody your first draft—unlike the incredible gutsiness, and great swings of quality, of the jazz artist, calypso rhymer, or improv comic.

Well, this was an incredible revelation, this description of Simon's "strategy" for writing, for someone like myself, who thought such cavalier treatment of the language was not "allowed." Here was one of the most successful playwrights of our time confessing, at least on an initial and private level, to winging it. Suddenly, I knew that I could do this thing; I could be a writer.

Except for those damned questions.

What questions? Well, for example, did I have the skill to edit the raw material once I brought it to the surface? It is one thing to say that all I needed to do was to return the unused portion, but would I know which was which? And even if I did, would I know how to build a structure that helped make my case? What if I couldn't learn to refine, polish, tighten, choose vocabulary, be interesting and do all the other things required to sustain a reader's full participation?

At about that time, as luck would have it, I was working on a questionnaire which matched couples or families with other couples or families for the purpose of extending social networks (no, it was not for swingers; however, you're not the only person who has wondered), and I thought of a terrific guy, who is also a more than terrific poet, to ask his general reactions to the text of this questionnaire. His name is Steve Kowit and his reactions, it turned out, were wonderfully wise, his editing help invaluable. I asked if there was anything I could do in return. He said he was working on a book on the writing of poetry and wondered if I would want to give my frank reactions to his efforts. He said that my ignorance of poetry, even my disinterest in its place among the arts, made me a good choice for his purposes.

I was delighted to help. To my surprise, I enjoyed his efforts, but found myself wanting to make changes—a choice of words, a reducing of the verbiage, even the order of things. *Having* to react probably encouraged the omnipresent critic in me. I called and asked him how he would feel about a nervy display of this sort. He was delighted and, presto, I was an editor. After all, Steve is an established poet, who has been *published* for God's sake, and has a wonderful reputation. Well, I thought, the worst that can happen is he will ignore my efforts.

But, of course, that was not the worst that could happen. I let the ignorant, aggressive part of me come bitingly to the surface and whacked away at that chapter without governor or conscience. I don't know that it was better when I finished with it. I know *I* liked it better. I sent it back and waited for an annoyed poet to call me.

A rare surprise! He said I had done a good job and that he would use some of my changes. Wow, said I. Would you like me to do more? Yes, said he, possibly cursing his good manners, and off we went. I had a new calling. I was now confirmed as editor. OK. So, nobody was going to pay me, but in my own mind I had been elevated onto a superior literary station.

I have not yet had a chance to see my impact into the world of letters, but I wanted to believe Steve, and even if he hasn't used any of my blue pencil efforts, changing words until they pleased me was such a fascinating and gratifying act I was permanently hooked into the process. When put together with Neil Simon's way of working with a continuous loop of his own fashioning, I thought myself ready to do this thing always out of reach. It seemed that all I had to do was write something about which I felt strongly; then invoke the revision process until the voices coming off the pages began to agree with my own.

A mathematically minded philosopher once suggested that if you had an infinite number of monkeys plunking an infinite number of typewriters in infinite time, they would ultimately produce the complete works of Shakespeare. As a statistical model, that was good enough for me (I was in no hurry and I *did* plan to live forever). If you could read my first whack at this chapter and the iterations that followed, you would see instantly that I start out far behind most people (and some monkeys) in the production of chaffless wheat and unadulterated signal.

And...no one can edit your writing—or your music making, or your cake decorating—like you can. Nobody knows how close you are coming to saying precisely what you want, or knows what pleases you more. Nobody!

Now that we see what helped me get to the point of feeling like writing was not only possible for me, but even probable, I was ready to apply the principles that I had tested so vigorously over my years of associating with the likes of Brahms and Chopin. Let me put them before you again.

- **Platespinning**: the widening of one's attention span
- **Just a little bit**: making modest demands on yourself
- **Happiness scheduler**: playing with time
- **Razing of the fourth wall**: accessibility for audience
- **Being with those you love**: working close to your heart
- **Drummer**: listening to your own voice
- **Teacher**: the importance of meaningful support

Platespinning: the widening of one's attention span, and the maintenance of a high degree of interest and alertness, by working with a number of challenges "all at once."

It should be noted that there exists an inherent difference in the writing of a book from the learning of music repertoire. If one is ever to complete a single literary work, there needs to be restraint exercised on the number of plates set in motion. In this instance, for example, I had to quell my need to discuss every aspect of music in which I had the slightest interest. The musical version of this juggling act, you will remember, aimed to get as many plates going as time would allow, but a book must fit between a reasonable cover. The following quote comes from the chapter on platespinning, parenthetically updated for writing application.

We all share a need for change, an almost insatiable hunger for variety. In order to stay alert and alive to the possibilities, in order to maintain proper focus, it is essential that the pieces (chapters) we are studying (working on), and spend so much time with, must not lose their sense of romance, their ability to engage and beguile us. Once that is gone we do not approach them with the same alertness, sense of dedication, or passion.

Instead of working on a chapter until its final form (whatever that could possibly mean), the immediate goal was to get each of a number of these to some semblance of stability, a kind of holding pattern, leaving it then to address another of its kin, then another, restlessly darting here and there, keeping the writing experience ever changing, always new. Ten or eleven of these were brought along at nearly the same "speed," always returning to the unattended in time to bring their respective movements up with the others. This kept each chapter alive, novel, evocative to my roaming inquiry. More importantly, when I criticized (edited) a chapter for its 4th or 11th time, I did not take it personally. It actually had been written by another, less experienced than I.

Just a Little Bit: making modest demands on yourself

Just as in the musical plate environment, I would gladly settle on modest improvement each time I came back to a chapter taking particular care not to overstay my visit. A little polish here, a nudge there, just enough to let each animate object know the spin doctor had made his visit. Always making progress made me a happy guy, ever wanting to keep at this activity—which forcibly seques us to the principle of The Happiness Scheduler.

Happiness Scheduler: playing with time

From this element, of course, came the book's subtitle and the stratagem most likely to offer relief to the most overwrought type A personality. To remind you of its formal definition, it is the arrangement of activities in a given interval such that the time allotted is more than enough, even preposterously so, to accomplish the assigned activities. The more accurate subtitle, of course, would be "Playing with Your Mind," since it is a benign delusional process leaving you with a constant supply of timely dividends.

My description of how this works in the writing turn is the same—albeit with appropriate substitutions—as the active pursuit of one's well being during the practice of music. If I thought I could write four pages in a day, I defined momentary happiness as the completion of two, with every page written above that as well-earned gravy. If I guessed it would take me two hours to edit a chapter, I would allow four and be inappropriately pleased, even "surprised," when I finished in three.

Razing of the fourth wall: accessibility for the audience

You'll recall in the chapter on performance the strident suggestions that we should do something, perhaps many things, to enliven, enrich, and make more meaningful the presentation of classical music, with particular emphasis on the reduction of the real and psychological distance between the performer and those he would court. In the present writing I have tried to do the same by talking directly to you and by trying to imagine what it is like for you to "hear" my words. I wanted this exchange to be as interactive as this soundless, frozen medium would allow, and kept you in my mind's eye as I went along.

Being with those you love: working close to your heart

In the case of playing music and choosing repertoire, I suggested the obvious: play only those pieces that touch your soul, or, at least, are enormously interesting, since these may be a part of your life style for some time to come. I suspect the key to finishing this book—as opposed to the many false starts before—was that it concerned so much which touches me even as I bring it closer to you. The first, of course, is music, but just as motivating is the desire to help you get started on your personal quest (as I continue on mine). If you can write about something that means a great deal to you, the chances of your getting to the finish line are much more likely.

For example, if they would have the good sense to give me the job, my next book would be on Tom and Ray Magliozzi, that exhilarating pair on their nationally aired radio show, *Car Talk*. Unquestionably the best offhand conversationalists since Bob and Ray (on their old radio show in New York City), these affectionate brothers may well have passed even that estimable pair. They are by turn outrageous, loving, creative, risk-taking, unaffected, consistently brilliant and brilliantly consistent. I am not sure where the engine in my car is, but I am certain that I am just one of millions who would listen if those guys discussed the glories of Latin, or even (my God, am I really saying this?) the wisdom of Freud, on a weekly basis. By the way, I'm mentioning it here just in case this subtle bid will help my chances of getting the gig.

Drummer: listening to your own voice

This is a tough one. I have sermonized at length on the importance of staying in touch with your own way of doing things, particularly in an endeavor as profoundly personal as the expression of your self. Frankly (and off the record), I've never been sure whether I'm one of those immature child-adults working against the never-ending dictates of society, wanting others to take me *exactly* as I am; or whether I am one of those psychological healthies—an actualized type getting ready to happen. I just know you feel so much better when you can do it your way and still be accepted (get away with it!). It is pretty tricky stuff, this being true to yourself, with most of us slowly inching out into that territory, then running for cover when it doesn't work out. This book is still another foray for me into that forbidden land. Moreover, should I succeed, I shall be quite unbearable. If I can speak my truths and have it work at the market place, I am more than capable of passing myself off as an expert.

But, getting back to you (not always an easy thing for me), remember, to express yourself in a way that reflects your inner voices, it is necessary to invoke the patient self-editor, the fellow who doesn't mind going over the raw material many times over, to sift and shake, stitch and sew, until what appears on the outside reflects what's going on inside.

Somehow, you must get to the editing process. That's where the games really begin. Waiting for a finished product to emerge in the early going will make one humble, and quite a bit older. Someone recently asked me if I was going to use the services of an editor for this book. I have an editor (remember who did Steve Kowit's book of poetry lessons!), said I. It is the writer that is most sorely lacking. If only I can produce generous amounts of raw material, enough of it, with enough time to mold into shapes that seem familiar, only then will it finally resemble the uniqueness that is mine and that is all that I can ask..... which, to a substantial degree is why I have decided not to submit this manuscript to a publishing house. You will either be attracted or not by what you read here, but you will always be sure whose voice you are hearing. It is the "auteur" process of movie-making in the writing of a book. That this is not the usual case seems odd, indeed. I suppose it is a function of the way books are usually published which is to indenture the author to a publisher—who buys the rights to the product. Since they own the property (and you!), they want, and usually receive, control of editorial rights. This is especially true, alas, for the new writers on the block—those who are unsure whether they will be published unless they make a pact with the publisher-devil.

But in this effort, for good and ill, no one stands between us. No Max Perkins type made this his own. No long list of credits for editing/criticism/proofing efforts adorn the early pages. If you love these words, you and I would probably get on famously. And if you do not, well, I figure you can't win 'em all.

To give you an experiential idea of what I am talking about, let us take a so-called "now" break, signalled by the indented material, and consider the following which unquestionably would not have survived the blue pencil efforts of your average, keep-on-a-straight-line, well-meaning editor:

By this time, I was hoping to have the kind of impact that would have you charging from the locker room through closed doors. Instead I grow uneasy. What I have seen so far of this last chapter does not reflect my hopes and aspirations for you. And I just can't tolerate the thought of letting you (myself?) down.

Yet I know, having been through this before, watching with apprehension the other chapters evolve, that this one, too, will be serviceable. What I must do, with *mindless* abandon, is to keep loading characters into the bottomless word processor. And that is just for starters. It will take many times working through the same material, so many times I would be embarrassed to tell you. If you knew what it takes for me to get it "right," perhaps you would try it yourself. I'm not sure I would like making a fool of myself, even for your edification and reassurance, but if I were so inclined, I would save for you a batch of iterations getting me from inception to final draft, letting you see what happens from one to the next. When you viewed that progress, the babbling beginnings, the shapeless speech forms spewed with little purpose onto the mystifying electronic table, you would be aghast and encouraged together. How could someone so slow of wit, illogical, wordy, and egocentric arrive—even with endless revisions—seemingly socialized, coherent, and on occasion, not uninteresting. You would see from this perspective that I am not different from you in talent bestowed, certainly not better. Yet I intend to call myself a writer. I already call myself a musician. Anything I can do, you...

It's as though familiarity breeds some kind of aesthetic contempt until, and unless, near perfection—in the eyes of the author/beholder—is achieved. I have found the editing process to be amazing. Scraps of writing that once seemed perfectly agreeable, even exceptional, virtually *demanded* modification the next time around. Apparently, one's editing mind, restless for novelty, becomes an eternal honing instrument.

Anyone can be this editor. An editor is someone who changes things for the better (hopefully), revising expressive materials within some medium to preconceived standards or biases. When you see a work of art—a building, a painting, a dance—you know, in fairly rapid order, whether this expression of the artist pleases you or not. And if you had to, and had the time and determination, you could change the thing that you didn't like into something that pleased you more. You may not know anything about art, as the saying goes, but you know what you like. Exactly. With this affirmation you know all that you need to know. *You know what you like.* Further, what you like will be different from all other carriers of these preferential patterns.

Without much trouble I am the critic. Whether it is an artistic expression, a political position, a social interaction, I often "know" a better way. It is not a trait of which I am particularly proud, but it won't soon go away. If you, too, have this propensity for criticism, please know that you, too, can turn it to good use. You can be a tough but fair-minded editor of your own efforts.

However, you must be judicious. It can be difficult to turn the critic's scalpel on yourself. This is particularly true if the effort is current. If you have just written a passage, you may be too close to your work and too vulnerable to endure the savaging of relentless criticism—even if your own. But perhaps tomorrow, or the next day. Now the one that you are criticizing is someone that you've outgrown by all that has transpired since that distant time. You forgive him his limitations and go for the jugular.

The writing of this book was not unlike the storied sculptor's chipping away the unwanted matter from the rock mass until the figure, in residence from the beginning, stands clear. If the sculptor is worth his rock salt, he or she knows that figure is in there; he even "sees" it. His task is to remove the material that obscures the general view.

In this light, you probably remember the story of two boys visiting a psychologist. The first boy was taken to a room filled with wonderful toys; the second left in a room overflowing with mounds of manure. On the psychologist's return, the first boy was found on the floor sobbing away. When asked what the matter was, he cried that he was sure that someone was coming to take back his new toys.

The second boy was found, happy as a lark, shoveling excitedly through the piles of manure. When asked how he could possibly be having such a rollicking good time, he explained, breathlessly, that with all this shit, there had to be a pony in there somewhere.

What this less than holy parable seems to suggest is that whatever hand you are dealt, your attitude will certainly effect your search for self-expression, and whether you even feel like digging.

What has kept me digging—the uncovering of these words from the awesome mounds accumulated from the indiscriminate exploration of my soul—was Annie's faith that there was a book in there somewhere. Even after incessant talk over the years about the latest project (a kind of unwritten book of the year tradition), she was, somehow, always ready for more. Among the lowlights was *The Miracle of Psychotherapy*, then one on the courageous Fleisher, then a book to be called *The Art and Craft of Lying: A User's Guide*, all of which she made major contributions to, all of which were deserted by me when some other project or adventure (any project, any adventure) vied for our time. She was always ready to start with the next book, never chiding or reminding me of past unfinished (read failed) efforts. She always believed, without foundation, that the next book would make it to term.

My approach on past and fruitless efforts was to embark on a program of exhaustive research. Despite these honorable beginnings (or, indeed, because of them), the effort would die in utero. The coroner's report: researchitis, a sickness rampant in academic circles in which the victim, overcome with the imbalance of his intellectual purity, loses his bearing in mazes of stacks, and bears his losses in stacks of references.

But this time it'll be different, she urged (eyeing uneasily the final sentence of the last paragraph). *Keep at it, this time it's going to happen.* Would she never learn? Did she not recognize the failed booka-holic reeling in front of her?

And miracle of miracles—perhaps I sensed this was my last go— this time it *was* different. The research came *after* the book was well on its way, with the direction of the various chapters already in mind, and, more importantly, bytes and pieces already entered into the safekeeping of Word Perfect. The words, sentences, paragraphs, chapters were piled horse manure-like into the electronic working area and shoveled through a number of times before checking for accuracy or support by the literature and whatever other lofty aims one pursues by these activities. This time I was not to be denied or Annie (secretly) disappointed.

But I had first to get the material onto the table, all of the ideas under mounds of debris, all of the signal with its covering noise, before the editing could finally begin; and certainly before getting involved in that special kind of holding action that takes place so (im)perfectly in the mysterious labyrinths of the library. My hope—actually it amounted to much more—was that when the excess was removed, the message would have been worth both your time and mine. And finally, for my dear Annie, loyal and true, I will have become a writer, I will have given her a gift—these words—for her labor, her steadfastness, her love.

It has been said that everyone has a story to tell, a book within. I have spent a life not writing, wanting to write, but not writing. My God, if I can write this book, if I have something to say, and even more importantly, if I could find a way to say it, so could anyone. What you are reading is an edited down version of epic proportions. For every word on this page there are 25(!) that have been made invisible by the variously merciful and ruthless delete function of Word Perfect. And what often started in one direction went in three of four others before being shown to you. And if it is readable, it is because I (or more likely, Annie) knew that something was in there; and I kept hacking away until what was left was the story I could claim as my own.

I tell you this so that you will know that the same or better is waiting for you on canvas, reed instrument, or word processor. I tell you this so that you will put down this book, and all else keeping you in the spectator role, and take your rightful place in the famed Doers Club, membership of which is limited to those with a quest for finding themselves through artistic expression.

Let them go, those words or sounds or movements you've been holding back. Put them out there where they will beckon you on, tugging on you for refinement and polish. You must have something to work on, something that allows the process of successive approximations to come closer and closer to who you *already are*.

The daring to take such chances, while still envisioning a happy ending, comes from the last element for making both music and words: the support of significant others. You'll recall that I have some mixture of feelings about the roll of a teacher in the expression of your art, since I worry that you will fall in the hands of one of the bad guys—one who would mold you to his precepts, rather than finding out and supporting the uniqueness that is yours. But the fact that you need someone to bolster your own unmitigated acceptance of your self and its expression is undeniable. Let's look once more at this dimension.

Teacher - the importance of meaningful support

In order to find your own voice, your unmistakably unique manner of expression, I think it necessary to believe in your personal worth (or, is it the other way around?). And in order to possess these valued feelings, it is generally required that others have helped along the way. I have had, during the long stretch of my turn at bat, the good fortune of having several of these good and generous people, especially and most convincingly, Ann.

And on the fifth day Annie created Victor, not from her rib but his own. He wasn't altogether formless but had no real definition, no confidence, no direction. She engendered confidence into his bones and though she completely made him up, convinced him of his reality.

It is my observation that all of us have two polar types in residence tussling over home rule. One insists I am special—possibly at the head of the table—very different from the rest; the other that I risk being found out when you seat me as your equal. You can forget about Simon and Kowit. They were important and recent and catalytic, but the critical stuff needs to come from much further in, that hidden place of certainty/uncertainty. If only Annie had lived on the same side of the street when I was a child, I could have competed for that pony. Oh, if you haven't figured it out, I was the boy in the room with the toys.

This is critical stuff, this acceptance from out there, since without it, occurring at least somewhere in your history, you are consigned to psychological bootstrapping. For most of us, this is an unlikely scenario, it being necessary to find *some* social support for just getting through the day, and especially for having confidence in one's profound expressions of self. If you have not been lucky on this score and are having trouble finding someone to celebrate your efforts towards artistic self-expression, it might help to get a teacher in the mold of an angel (Rita variety). And, if you do not succeed in finding such a teacher—unfortunately,they are *not* in abundance—all is not lost. You still have me!

Yes, that is right. I am steadfastly in your corner. A more avid second you cannot imagine. I believe you are special and I mean to prove it to you. (I know we are very close to the end, but we're not finished yet! I am very determined!!) This book, finally, is about every person's potential, right, capacity and need to experience this coming out. I am one who believes that every last one of us has something wonderfully special to say, that every last one of us is as unique, full of untapped marvels and as magic-filled as every other last one of us.

I believe in your potential and I would have you write me and tell me about yourself. I pledge to read anything that you write as you are making a dedicated effort to find yourself through honest, true to your inner voices, artistic expression. And I will support you in your efforts. That is a guarantee I make to back up my belief in you and my sincere intention to help you on your way.

Down the Stretch

Well, we have made it to the end together. I'm exhausted but happy. Happy because I'm sure, now, that you are going to do this thing for yourself else why would you have come this far. You could have gotten off a lot earlier, even in the first chapter when I asked if:

Isn't this something that you've always wanted? What about those ways of expressing yourself that come in your package only? Wouldn't it be wonderful to share these qualities freely and be accepted and loved in the doing? It is probably presumptuous of me to want this for you, yet I do. But then, I know what it is like; I know what can happen...For many, it can take far too long for this journey to begin—this quest for your own inner voice. But finally, driven by personal victories won, a stroke of good fortune, or, as sometimes happens, by events of a more desperate nature, playing a musical instrument and shaping notes and phrases to your personal vision can reveal that part of you that no one else shares or even knows about—an inner space which defines the person like none other.

And how about our social order? Can you imagine everyone doing this? Why people would be so caught up with these incredibly involving activities that social ills would fail from disuse. It could be the answer to crime, war, even Rush Limbaugh.

My life now has meaning for me and possibly for others. Let me hear from you, lets talk about all of this, where you have got to and where you must go. Or perhaps you have questions. Remember, I've got all the answers. They might not be the right answers but, as you have seen, that doesn't stop me. I've got time and, now that you will be practicing platespinning, so will you. It is a matter of playing with this time we have, and winning. None of this gloomy Bergmanesque chess playing with death. You are playing art(fully) with life!

And now...

I am taking my "show" on the road. I'll be starting in San Francisco, where they are used to unusual sights, and make my way into as many cities as I am able, hoping to find you, and be found by you. Look for me in the parks with my trusty Clavinova attempting to keep too many plates aloft. If you want to sing along, you know the rules. If you are into dancing, see if you can stay with me.

Hey, we'll play with time together.

Bibliography

1. Aaron, Stephen. *Stage Fright: Its Role in Acting*. Chicago: University of Chicago Press, 1988.

2. Bernstein, Seymour. *With Your Own Two Hands: Self-Discovery Through Music*. Milwaukee: H. Leonard, 1986.

3. Bloom, Benjamin S. *Developing Talent in Young People*. New York: Ballantine Books, 1985.

4. Choksy, Lois. *The Kodaly Context: Creating an Environment for Musical Learning*. New Jersey: Prentice-Hall, 1981.

5. Colman, Carol. *Late Bloomers: How to Achieve Your Potential at Any Age*. New York: Macmillan, 1985.

6. Cooke, Charles. *Playing the Piano for Pleasure*. New York: Simon and Schuster, 1941.

7. Dahl, Roald. Willie Wonka and the Chocolate Factory (movie) from *Charlie and the Chocolate Factory*. New York: Knopf, 1964.

8. Dart, Thurston. *The Interpretation of Music*. London: 1954.

9. Dorian, Frederick. *The History of Music in Performance*. New York: W.W. Norton, 1942.

10. Friedrich, Otto. *Glenn Gould, A Life and Variations*. New York: Vintage Books, 1989.

11. Gallwey, Timothy. *The Inner Game of Tennis*. New York: Random House, 1974

12. Gerig, Reginald. *Famous Pianists and Their Technique*. Manchester, New Hampshire: Robert Luce, 1975.

13. Goode, Richard. Article about him in *New Yorker*, June 29, 1992.

14. Green, Barry. *The Inner Game of Music* with Timothy Gallwey. New York: Doubleday, 1986.

15. Holt, John. *Never Too Late*. New York: Delacorte, 1978.

16. James, William. *The Principles of Psychology*. Chicago: Great Books of the Western World, 1952.

17. Kazan, Elia. *Kazan, A Life*. New York: Knopf, 1988.

18. Kingsbury, Henry. *Music, Talent, and Performance: A Conservatory Cultural System*. Philadelphia: Temple University Press, 1988.

19. Lloyd, Norman. *The Golden Encyclopedia of Music*. New York: Golden Press, 1968.

20. Lorge, Irving. *Adult Education: Theory and Method*. Washington: Adult Education Association, 1963.

21. Marler, Peter. A sensitive period for song acquisition in the song sparrow. *Ethology*: 1987, Oct. Vol. 76(2), 89-100.

22. McLeish, John. *The Ulyssean Adult: Creativity in the Middle and Later Years*. Toronto: McGraw-Hill Ryerson Limited, 1976.

23. Newman, William S. *The Pianist's Problems: A Modern Approach to Efficient Practice and Musicianly Performance.* New York Harper and Row 1974

24. Prakesh, P. Second language acquisition and critical period hypothesis. *Psycho-Lingua*: 1984, Jan. Vol. 14(1), 13-17.

25. Ristad, Eloise. *Soprano on Her Head: Right-Side-Up Reflections on Life and Other Performances.* Moab, Utah: Real People, 1982.

26. Rogers, Carl. *On Becoming a Person.* Boston: Houghton Mifflin, 1961.

27. Rothstein, Stephen. Brown-headed Cowbirds learn flight whistles after the juvenile period. *Auk.* 1987, Jul. Vol. 104(3), 512-516.

28. Schonberg, Harold. *The Glorious Ones, Classical Music's Legendary Performers.* New York: Times Books, 1985.

29. Schonberg, Harold. *The Lives of the Great Composers.* New York: W.W. Norton and Co, 1971.

30. Schonberg, Harold. *The Great Pianists.* New York: Simon and Schuster, 1963, 1987.

31. Walsh, Michael. *Who's Afraid of Classical Music?* New York: Simon and Schuster, 1989.

32. Whiteside, Abby. *Indispensables of Piano Playing.* New York: Macmillan, 1983.

33. Wilson, Frank R. *Tone Deaf and All Thumbs? An Invitation to Music Making.* New York: Vintage Books, 1986.

Index

Index

Index

Index

Still more about the author

The author, as a result of yet another wrong turn in the vocational maze, labored as a psychologist in private practice for far too many years. In a failed attempt to recover his balance, he escaped unnoticed to create a glorious book store called Words and Music in San Diego featuring live and informative musical entertainment. Despite an astonishing lack of talent, he took up the piano relatively late in life, as these things go, and has been amazed by its benefits. He feels (as does his alter ego, the spinner of tales and plates) that if he could do this thing, so could anyone. Since few books have been written on the subject which give the reader credit for even a modicum of sophistication or wit—with the notable exception of Charles Cooke's *Playing the Piano for Pleasure*— he threw himself furiously into this activity. If he could encourage even one person to find his or her way through self-expression, he reasoned, he will have found his own.

The Hard Sell

If you found reading this book a rewarding experience, perhaps you would be kind enough to tell your friends. Or better still, you might buy a copy for them (all of them). A recent study conducted at the Stanford Center for Inquiring Minds has shown that those who give books as presents (and give up smoking) add, on average, 2.7 years to their life expectancy.

The more copies that sell, remember, the more time I will have for practicing the piano, writing books and, generally, leading the good life. After all we have been through together, it seems the right thing to do.

☐ Single Copy — $14.95 (plus $3.00 shipping and messing with — If you really loved the book, you can deduct a dollar.)

☐ Six copies for the price of five. You figure it out! Plus one dollar for postage per book and the ostensible handling that goes on.

☐ Ten copies for the price of eleven. Watch out on this one. You might be better off ordering multiples of six.

Ship all the cash you can afford, or respectable checks to:

Victor Margolis
337 Ridgeway Ave.
Cincinnati, Ohio 45215